T0165394

# THE INFINITE GIFT

### How Children Learn and Unlearn the Languages of the World

## Charles Yang

SCRIBNER

New York London Toronto Sydney

SCRIBNER
1230 Avenue of the Americas
New York, NY 10020

For information about special discounts for bulk purchases, please contact Simon & Schuster Special Sales: 1-800-456-6798 or business@simonandschuster.com

DESIGNED BY ERICH HOBBING

Set in Sabon

Manufactured in the United States of America

1   3   5   7   9   10   8   6   4   2

Library of Congress Cataloging-in-Publication Data

Yang, Charles D.
The infinite gift : how children learn and unlearn the languages of the world / Charles Yang.
p. cm.
Includes bibliographical references and index.
1. Language acquisition. I. Title.
P118.Y359 2006
401'.93—dc22
2006044307

ISBN-13: 978-1-4516-1299-8

For Russell Cheng Legate-Yang

# Contents

# THE
# INFINITE
# GIFT

CHAPTER 1

# The Greatest Intellectual Feat

Chromosomes. Sex. Grasshoppers. "Pick me up, Mommy."

This is an odd list, except in the eye of evolution. For in the major developments in the history of life, the ability to say, "Pick me up, Mommy" features prominently along with the emergence of genes, sexual reproduction, and multicellular organisms.[1] On a smaller but no less wondrous scale, the ability to speak opens one mind to another. Babies announce their arrival with a loud cry, but it is their first words that launch the journey of a lifetime:

"Kitty."
"Big drum."
"Drink tea."

This is the miracle of language, the ability to arrange sounds into infinitely many ways to convey infinitely varied meanings. Language is what we use to tell stories, transmit knowledge, and build social bonds. It comforts, tickles, excites, and destroys. Every society has language, and somehow we all learn a language in the first few years of our lives, a process that has been repeated for as long as humans have been around. Unlike swimming, using Microsoft Windows, or making the perfect lemon soufflé—which some of us never manage to do—learning a language is a task we can all take for granted.

Although every form of life is a testament to the power of evolution, language is an achievement of humans, and humans alone. The talents for cooperative hunting, tool making, and having sex for fun, once thought to be unique to us, have all been found in other species.[2]

However, as far as we know, there is nothing like language in the vastly varied systems of communication in other animals,[3] which makes it a lasting—and perhaps the last—grip for our anthropocentric arrogance. The centrality of language to human nature is what prompted the great French thinker René Descartes to separate men from beasts:

> It is a very remarkable fact that there are none so depraved and stupid, without even excepting idiots, that they cannot arrange different words together, forming of them a statement by which they make known their thoughts; while, on the other hand, there is no other animal, however perfect and fortunately circumstanced it may be, which can do the same.[4]

Just how do we do this?

My son, Russell, had just turned three when I started writing this book. A medium-sized newborn, he soon shot off the growth charts that now populate parenting books. At three, he was wearing size five. However, Russell was rarely mistaken for a five-year-old. When he ran, he still waddled. Although he could throw, he couldn't catch. And he still couldn't tie his shoes. Children develop along a fairly consistent schedule, which leaves landmarks of physiological attributes and abilities. If you watched Russell in the playground, you would see just an unusually large specimen among three-year-olds.

But you didn't need to see him at the playground to know Russell was just three. Every waiter or waitress who greeted us was successful at guessing his age. As soon as Russell started insisting on pizza over anything else on the menu, his language betrayed his age. What his words sounded like and how they were put together are familiar to anyone who has been around kids.

Much like motor skills and head-to-body ratio, language also develops along a fairly consistent schedule. Out of the cries, coos, and laughs, all infants start babbling around the eighth month. Deaf babies babble too—with their hands. For children learning to speak English, the first words more or less coincide with the first birthday, and sentences—the arrangement of words—start appearing when the child is a year and a half. By age three, most children know over a thou-

sand words. They have command of many complex sentence structures, and can carry out fully independent and undeniably cute conver-
sations with adults. And similar successive stages show up not only in
English-speaking children, but also in those learning to talk in French,
German, Chinese, and Swahili.

All children learn a language and they do so in similar ways. This,
coupled with the fact that language learning occurs only in *human*
youngsters, suggests that the root of language is in our biology. There
is something in our genes that other species don't have, which is why
a child's puppy, which grows up in the same household and hears the
same sounds, never learns the language that the child learns.

Claiming language to be uniquely human may sound like a desperate
attempt to assert our special place in nature: the latest count shows
that chimpanzees share 96 percent of our genes.[5] But every species is a
unique product of biological evolution. Bats can find their way in the
dark. Squirrels can hide and find thousands of nuts to pass the winter.
Frogs are far better than us at catching mosquitoes. Biologically speaking, language is no more special than any of these abilities; what *is* special is the things that humans have done with language, including
writing and reading books on how language is learned. Thus, Charles
Darwin, the ultimate destroyer of our self-importance, didn't hesitate
to remark that "Man has an instinctive tendency to speak, as we see in
the babble of young children, whilst no child has an instinctive tendency to bake, brew, or write." Furthermore, humans' specialty for
language is not at odds with biological evolution. As Darwin notes,
"the faculty of articulated speech does not in itself offer any insupera-
ble objection to the belief that man has developed from some lower
form."

But a biological basis cannot be all there is to language. Learning a
language is not like walking, which is simply (and automatically) a
matter of neuromuscular maturation, occurring around a child's first
birthday. Again, in Darwin's words, language "is not a true instinct,
for every language has to be learnt." After all, English children grow
up speaking English, and Chinese children, Chinese. And for a lot of
people, the most impressive thing about languages is how different
they seem. This means that the neural hardware for language must be

*plastic*; it must leave space and possibilities to respond to the particular environment a child is born into, and to result in different organizations of the brain for different speakers. To put it simply, language learning requires both nature and nurture.

This book explains how nature and nurture work together to give children language. To develop such an explanation, one necessarily faces many obstacles that are not present in other disciplines; there can be no poking around in a child's brain, for instance. An indirect route of research must be sought when direct tampering with a child's nature or nurture is not possible. And a useful clue may be found just outside your bedroom window. [6]

Songbirds constitute the largest order of birds in the world, and their songs vary considerably across species and even by geographical location. Think of these as English vs. Chinese, Harvard accent vs. Texas twang.

Chicks do not start singing at birth: songs have to be learned. The onset of learning is a period of listening to adult songs and memorizing them for later use. This is followed by a stage of unstructured chirps: the chick experiments with its vocal organs.

But then song learning takes off. The youngsters quickly become specialized in their native songs and dialects; by then, avid birders can identify their species and origin by their songs alone. For some birds, a period of creativity follows. The bird may thump out a few variations, all of which are potentially songs native to the species, but only those unique to the geographical region are eventually retained.

Birdsong learning is the work of both nature and nurture. Of all the acoustic events in its environment, a young songbird can somehow pick out the songs of its own kind: songbirds don't learn from ducks or hawks, for instance. In an experiment, chicks were hatched in a laboratory so that they had no experience with adult songs whatsoever. They were then exposed to the recorded songs of their own species as well as others. Remarkably, a strong preference for the native tunes was discovered; this affinity must then have come from the genome.

At the same time, songs that are unique to a species must be learned from experience. A songbird that grows up without ever hearing adult birds of its own species never sings. In addition, songs can be learned only if the experience comes within a *sensitive period* as the bird matures; this window of opportunity then shuts permanently. The chaffinch, for instance, cannot learn new songs after the tenth month.

Birdsong learning and language learning have unmistakable parallels. Human infants aren't born talking either, but they come fully prepared. Somehow babies can tune out radios, telephones, and their sibling's tantrums and zero in on the sounds of speech. Just as songbirds listen and store up their adult songs, babies quietly register many specific features of their language in the beginning of language learning. Babbling is babies' experimentation with their vocal organs. While young children's speech may sound imperfect to adults, there is no doubt that the children are working on the language that they will eventually attain. After all, children generally understand us (though sometimes it does seem that they pretend not to). And when Russell says:

"Tickles me"
"The sun is sweating you"
"Super Grover flied away"

he is not just mimicking adults, who would never talk that way. Children, like some songbirds, are innovators, not just imitators.

No scientist has reared a child in a laboratory in isolation, but the necessity of experience for language learning cannot be doubted. The ultimate experiment, so the legend goes, was carried out by Psamtik I, who ruled Egypt in the seventh century BC. As told by the Greek historian Herodotus, the king wanted to know which people were the most ancient in the world, a distinction he thought could be identified by seeing who used the most ancient language. He gave two newborn babies to a shepherd, who was responsible for their survival but forbidden to utter any word in their presence. The king reasoned that the "original" tongue would come out if the child was not polluted by inferior languages.

The first word that came out, the legend continues, was *becos:* it meant "bread" in Phrygian, which was the language, now extinct, spoken in what is modern-day Turkey. Psamtik thus conceded that the Phrygians, speakers of the original tongue, were an older people than the Egyptians. No one is sure whether these events actually happened, and of course, if they did, the king's conclusion would not pass a scientific journal's review board. He failed to establish the premise of his cruel experiment: the king apparently assumed that language could be learned without experience.

A wild boy was found in 1798 who had somehow survived after having been abandoned in the woods. He was believed to be eleven. Jean-Marc Gaspard Itard, a French physician and pioneer of special education, did everything to guide him back to a normal life, including "to lead him to use of speech by inducing the exercise of imitation." He never spoke, but always responded "Oh" when Itard said "Victor," so the boy became known as Victor. Itard eventually gave up:

> Finally, however, seeing that the continuation of my efforts and the passing of time brought about no change, I resigned myself to the necessity of giving up any attempt to produce speech, and abandoned my pupil to incurable dumbness.[7]

In 1920, two children were captured in India by a hunting party fearful of ghostly figures roving in the woods. Later christened Amala and Kamala, they had been reared by wolves (some say leopards). Amala, one and a half when discovered, died soon afterward; Kamala, eight, lived until the age of seventeen. In five years, Kamala learned about thirty words; normal children learn that many in three days. Her vocabulary improved a little in later years, and she could respond to simple commands, but there was no spontaneous or novel use of sentences.[8]

Each story of wild children is a tragedy of deprivation; some are almost too painful to describe. Each reaches the same somber conclusion: no experience, no language. And the experience has to come early enough. Indeed, wild children were given their own place, a subdivision within *Homo sapiens* by Carl Linnaeus, the great classifier of life: *Homo ferus* (*feral*, or "wild man"), whose defining characteristics include "mute."

There are obviously differences between song learning and language learning. Birds don't speak, and we don't chirp. Nevertheless, the characteristics of song learning and language learning are strik-

ingly similar, suggesting that neurological growth during learning may
involve mechanisms common to humans and birds. Indeed, that's the
theme of this book: language learning takes something old and something new.

Nature doesn't build things from scratch.The gift of language is the
latest step that led to the rise of *Homo sapiens,* but this great leap forward must have been preceded by many other strange turns in the history of life. Evolution is a thrifty tinkerer, recycling and reusing old
parts, and when a new piece of equipment arrives, it has to work
together with existing structures.[9] The gift for language, therefore, must
build upon and interact with other cognitive and perceptual systems
that existed before language and are partially shared with other
species. Without the auditory system, we could not hear; without the
vocal tract, we could not talk; without the capacity to understand the
world and ourselves, we'd have little to talk about; without complex
social structures and networks, we'd have no one to talk to. And to
such a list of prerequisites, we can add this: ancient neural mechanisms
that helped numerous species to survive in a constantly changing
environment. The gift of language is the foundation for arts, science,
and other crowning achievements of human civilization, but as we shall
learn in this book, the process by which children master the gift is the
decidedly lowbrow biology that guides birds to seeds in the woods and
rodents through mazes in psychology laboratories.

This book is about the science of how children learn language. Curios-
ity about language learning didn't start with modern linguistics. In all
likelihood, it started out with parents who paused to think about their
children's achievements. We have always wondered what language is
and what it comes from, much the same as we are concerned with our
nature and origin; with the Tower of Babel, the Bible offers an account
for both. The raw materials for the study of child language initially
came from diaries of linguists who kept track of children's speech. One
of the earliest was published in the 1880 *Transactions of the American
Philological Association,* fittingly entitled "A contribution to infantile
linguistics." My wife and I—we are both linguists—often jot down
fabulous sentences when Russell talks.

The science of language learning took off only when linguistics was revolutionized by Noam Chomsky. Chomsky became the first in modern times to give children the credit they deserve in learning a language. He writes:

> The child who learns a language has in some sense constructed the grammar for himself on the basis of his observation of sentences and nonsentences (i.e. corrections by the verbal community). Study of the actual observed ability of a speaker to distinguish sentences from non-sentences, detect ambiguities, etc., apparently forces us to the conclusion that this grammar is of an extremely complex and abstract character, and that the young child has succeeded in carrying out what from the formal point of view, at least, seems to be a remarkable type of theory construction. Furthermore, this task is accomplished in an astonishingly short time, to a large extent independently of intelligence, and in a comparable way by all children. Any theory of learning must cope with these facts.[10]

The only way for children to learn something as complex as language, Chomsky contends, is to have known a lot about how language works beforehand, so that a child knows what to expect when immersed in the sea of speech. In other words, the ability to learn a language is innate, hidden somewhere in our genes. Leonard Bloomfield, who ruled the academy of linguistics before Chomsky took it by storm, was in perfect agreement with his successor on one critical point. As a scholar who was intimately familiar with the complexity of the world's languages, Bloomfield once remarked that learning a language "is doubtless the greatest intellectual feat any one of us is ever required to perform." One of the consequences is that we need a whole book to explain "Kitty," "Big drum," and "Drink tea."

One more note before we begin: this is not a parenting book. As a young father, I understand parents' anxiety about their children's development, but this book will not tell you how to help your child learn a language. As far as language is concerned, your child doesn't need help. You do not need to make a special effort for your child's language development; all you need to do is talk to him or her as loving parents. You will see that children are infinitely better at learning languages than we are, and why. And you will see that the "errors" in their speech are inevitable and will go away in due time.

Now, let's see why language "is of an extremely complex and abstract character," and why learning a language, as effortless as it looks, is indeed our greatest intellectual feat.

CHAPTER 2

# Mission Improbable

It ought to be impossible to learn a language.

Imagine yourself suddenly plunged into a distant land, surrounded by strange sights and sounds and other novelties, one of which is the language you're about to discover. This famous thought experiment was proposed by the American philosopher W. V. O. Quine to contemplate the nature of human knowledge and experience.[1] For many linguists, though, such a challenge is just another day in the office: the first contact with a previously unknown language starts just like this.

A rabbit scurries by and a native says: "Gavagai!" The linguist, Quine points out, would be ill-advised to conclude that Gavagai means "rabbit"; for Gavagai could well mean "running," "furry thing," "animal," or "supper tonight." Moreover, the native might have been saying something completely unrelated to rabbits, and it was a pure accident that the rabbit hopped out of the bush at the same time—in which case Gavagai might mean "Nice day, mate!" Even if the linguist does manage to penetrate the language and figures out that Gavagai has something to do with rabbits, she would still be uncertain whether the native was talking about the rabbit's swift legs, characteristically large ears, or what a good fur hat it makes. After all this, Gavagai might indeed mean "rabbit." Faced with this infinite range of uncertainties, the linguist in the field would be at a loss, unable to get past the first word.

The dilemma at hand illustrates what the English philosopher David Hume calls "the Scandal of Induction." It highlights the fallibility of experience when we set out to explore the world—and by extension, language. A plain example: suppose that every emerald I have seen so far is green; am I entitled to believe that *all* emeralds are green as well? Evidently, no. It is possible that most emeralds are in fact blue and I've seen only a very partial (and green) sample; it is also possible that emeralds were sprinkled on the Earth by space aliens and were programmed to turn red on April Fool's day, 2034. Philosophers are justifiably worried about the foundation of knowledge, because for every dose of experience, infinitely many conclusions can be reached, and there is no guarantee that we'll ever know which one is correct. Closer to life (or fantasy), the entire *Matrix* entertainment franchise based on the 1999 blockbuster movie rests on precisely this dilemma of experience: what we see, hear, and touch may be real, but it may also be part of a giant illusion created by a network of computers.

Yet for all its philosophical intrigue, the Gavagai dilemma just doesn't ring true. We don't pause to contemplate whether our loved ones or last night's dinner were a virtual reality. More pertinent, the outlook of my profession is decidedly brighter than Quine predicted. Of the approximately six thousand languages spoken in the world, many of them have been deciphered by linguists; in some cases, formerly extinct languages are being revived with linguists' help.[2] And missionaries have been translating the Bible into indigenous languages for centuries. The study of these languages has contributed enormously to the understanding of how language works and, as we shall see, how language is learned. Evidently, linguists do not get stalled, pondering on the infinite range of possible meanings for the first word they hear.

Children also steer free of the Scandal of Induction. The linguist goes to the field already knowing a native language, possibly carrying notepads, pencils, and a tape recorder as well; the child, on the other hand, starts out with no language, and no technological aids, facing a job that is immensely more difficult.

But before we talk of language learning we, or rather, the baby, must be clear just what counts as language. Language doesn't come in neat packets, ready for the child to digest and absorb. Every moment of a baby's life is a wild cocktail party, where the sound of language is embedded within the ambient acoustics that constantly bombard her eardrums. The first step in learning a language is to find it, and to find it, the baby must block out the noise.

Second, unlike the words on this page, which are separable by spaces and punctuation, we—do—not—pause—between—words—in—speech. When we study the acoustic details of speech we see that most words bump into one another, without any delineable boundaries in between. We can't honestly blame non-English-speakers—so a joke goes—for mistaking a restaurant server as the distinguished play-wright Edward Albee: "My name is Ed ALBEE your waiter." Similarly, "Gavagai" may be a sentence that consists of "ga," "va," and "gai." To learn words, children have to find them in the continuous stream of speech.

And then, a word always sounds different spoken by different speakers, and on different occasions. There is tremendous variation in human speech. In fact, voice quality can be as good a signature of an individual as a fingerprint. Scrutiny over speech, as we now all know, plays a critical role in determining whether the latest Osama bin Laden tape is genuine or fake. Closer to our own lives, we can instantly recognize our friends and family members as soon as we hear their voices. But this useful trick for social bonding poses a big prob-lem for a child learning language: how does she know that "dog" spo-ken in Mom's mezzo-soprano and in Dad's baritone are the same word? Even for the same speaker, a word may sound very different when pronounced on different occasions: "hot" comes out with differ-ent grades of urgency—and thus different acoustic properties—depending on whether it's an unusually warm day or you spill scalding tea on your hand. The variability in speech is a main reason why talk-ing (and listening) machines exist only on *Star Trek*. For all the advances in computer technology, speech recognition software still doesn't work straight out of the box; it needs a training stage to adapt to one's unique way of talking. Bear in mind that the software already "knows" hundreds of thousands of English words, which the programmers have built in; the baby, however, starts with none.

To compound the issue further, speech, under close inspection, turns out to be a remarkably messy means of communication. What comes out of our mouths is rarely the crisply articulated and neatly arranged words sanctioned by our high school English teachers. By contrast, about 10 percent of the sentences we speak contain speech errors: false starts, slips of the tongue, "ughs" and "arghs."[3] (It's remarkable that we manage to understand each other.) Everyone's speech is messy though politicians make easy targets: as a widely circulated Bushism goes, "If the terriers and bariffs are torn down, this economy will grow."

All this mess has to be sorted out before the child starts to learn a single word. But understanding the sound of a word is only one part of word learning. The quandaries of word meanings in the Gavagai dilemma haven't started. Despite all these challenges, children are astonishingly good at learning words:[4] from the first year on, children learn on average at least ten words a day.[5]

Why doesn't the philosopher's worry translate into a child's misery in real life? The answer is simple: humans just do not live up to philosophical standards. Philosophers are interested in absolute truth: every logical possibility must be considered, and no rock is left unturned. But evolution didn't make us logicians; it couldn't have, because we would be confused by the infinite possibilities presented by every Gavagai-like problem and never get anything done. A word may mean many things, but we can afford to contemplate only a very small portion of them— and we do just that. To avoid the Gavagai dilemma is to stay tuned to and act on only a very narrow selection of the information that the environment presents, and to consider only a limited number of possibilities out of a potentially infinite array. For instance, we know now that when learning words, children generally assume the name refers to the whole object, rather than its components or properties.[6] For a lot of children, "hot" can become the name of the oven, rather than a property of the oven. When a child hears "rabbit," she automatically assumes it is what we call the whole rabbit, rather than its color, ears, or body parts. And by attributing the same assumption to the natives, the linguist could reliably decipher the meaning of "Gavagai."

So, for learning words, it sometimes pays to be narrow-minded. In fact, it pays *all the time,* and not just in the case of language, because that's the only way we can make it in this chaotic world overloaded with information. Think—I mean *really* think—about what the environment is inflicting on your brain at this very moment: the temperature of the room, the humming of the air conditioner, the smell of the coffee, the color of the page in front of you, the size of the print, . . . The list goes on and on. Yet the vast majority of these are filtered out, automatically, as if they didn't exist. In other words, not all stimuli are created equal: the mind has built-in biases, and here, "bias" is a very good word.

The biases in the mind are what might usefully be called *hidden assumptions,* because we are generally unaware of what they are but nevertheless take them for granted—without proper logical scrutiny— and apply them automatically. It's fun to think of some examples. We know that body parts don't fly off on their own, that the sun always rises in the morning, that $2 + 2 = 4$ whether we are counting apples or oranges, and that a sock however wrinkled or soiled is still the same sock. These hidden assumptions are the essential guide to the world: they tell us where to look, what to expect and to believe, and how things (and other humans) generally work. Though very little is known about how these hidden assumptions are implemented by our neural hardware, their existence is established by logic. Without them, we would be soaked in sensory overload, never sure of anything, and never learn a language (or a single word). Since we get on just fine, hidden assumptions must reside somewhere in the brain.

Unfortunately, for many aspects of human cognition, we have come to know the necessity of hidden assumptions, but precisely what these are and how they are integrated in the brain remain a mystery. This is not helped by the tendency to underestimate the complexity that lies beneath these "easy" things such as seeing, walking, and talking. In the 1960s, a legendary pioneer of artificial intelligence infamously assigned the problem of replicating human vision as an undergraduate summer project; robotic vacuum cleaners notwithstanding, computers still don't "see," much less make sense of, the visual world. But we do know a good deal about the hidden assumptions of a particular component of the mind, and an essentially human and incredibly complex component at that: for language, we have Noam Chomsky's celebrated theory of universal grammar. Like any successful scientific theory, this theory makes several major claims—in this case about the nature of language, and how language works. But for now, let's get a Big One out of the way.

\*        \*        \*

The most fundamental claim, and also the best known, is that universal grammar is innate. Here, the term "grammar" refers to how language works in general, and is not restricted to the narrow sense of how to make sentences. According to Chomsky, the child is born knowing what language is made of and how it is put together; she is well prepared for the task of language learning and knows exactly where to look for the relevant evidence, and before you know it, she starts making up complex sentences and fancy stories.

An innate universal grammar is not news. Not these days. Almost every week there is a news report that babies are smarter than you think, which presumably means that they are smart innately rather than through learning and experience, for smart physicists are just not that newsworthy. It doesn't take a leap of faith to conclude that the uniquely human ability for language must ultimately reside in some uniquely human genes. How times have changed! Merely fifty years ago, in an age when behaviorism reigned supreme in American humanities and social sciences, ideas about innate abilities were utter heresies: conditioning, associations, stimulus and response were the lingua franca of the day. Ivan Pavlov's famous demonstration of salivating dogs had been extended to mice and pigeons, on more and more complex tasks; anything and everything seemed possible as long as the conditioning was set up right. Just as a blank canvas offers infinite possibilities, the supposed infinite malleability of the mind relies on the assumption that there is nothing in the mind to begin with. Moreover—and hence the namesake—a behaviorist theory of how an organism works focuses exclusively on its behaviors: the observable, the measurable, and hence the scientific. Any "inside the box" notions, such as feelings, thoughts, and mental states, are deemed mysterious and unscientific.

The behaviorist doctrines did seem to carry the cool-headed allure of dispassionate science. We are animals after all, so models of human behavior ought to be extrapolated from models of animal behavior. If a pigeon can associate pecking the lever with food, surely a child could associate the sound "kitten" with a furry feline. Conditioning would extend to language, which, as B. F. Skinner, the dean of American behaviorism put it, is just "verbal behavior." This view of language learning, by making just the right kind of associations, actually goes far back in the history of thought. The English philosopher John Locke (1632–1704) once remarked:

> If we will observe how children learn languages, we shall find that, to make them understand what the names of simple ideas or substances stand for, people ordinarily show them the thing whereof they would have them have the idea; and then repeat to them the name that stands for it, as "white," "sweet," "milk," "sugar," "cat," "dog."[7]

The behaviorists merely dressed up this notion in a lab coat.

In 1959, Chomsky published an enormously influential and devastating review of Skinner's book *Verbal Behavior,* where the bankruptcy of behaviorist psychology was fully exposed:

> A typical example of stimulus control for Skinner would be the response to a piece of music with the utterance "Mozart" or to a painting with the response "Dutch." These responses are asserted to be "under the control of extremely subtle properties" of the physical object or event. Suppose instead of saying Dutch we had said "Clashes with the wallpaper," "I thought you liked abstract work," "Never saw it before," "Tilted," "Hanging too low," "Beautiful," "Hideous," "Remember our camping trip last summer?" or whatever else might come into our minds when looking at a picture. . . . We cannot predict verbal behavior in terms of the stimuli in the speaker's environment, since we do not know what the current stimuli are until he responds. Furthermore, since we cannot control the property of a physical object to which an individual will respond, except in highly artificial cases, Skinner's claim that his system, as opposed to the traditional one, permits the practical control of verbal behavior is quite false.[8]

Missing in Skinner's verbal behavior is what Chomsky calls the "creative aspect of language." The creativity here has to do not with literary genius, but with the plain fact that language use is unpredictable, as demonstrated by the numerous possible sentences that a

Dutch painting—or a rabbit scurrying by—could elicit. And this creativity is ultimately rooted in the boundless creativity of human thought, imagination, and free will, coming out through the infinite combinatorial power of language. Skinner's learner requires matching stimulus and response, or things and words, to establish associations; the problem is, however, things and words rarely match in the real world. As the psychologist Lila Gleitman put it succinctly: a picture is worth a thousand words, and *that's the problem.* Many "things" have corresponding words in language, but it is difficult to envision what kind of stimulus would be necessary to learn them. How do we point to an "idea"? What is "water"? The thing in the glass, or in the river, or the absolute purity of $H_2O$? When we are talking about "writing a letter to grandma," the letter is only imaginary, and the grandma might well be tending her garden in Canada.

Nature vs. nurture, PCs vs. Macs, Red Sox vs. Yankees. The world would be a far more pleasant place without these interminable debates. Although you *must* choose a side for computers and baseball—I have chosen mine—nature and nurture can, and often must, work together. In hindsight, the behaviorist denial of nature was an inexplicable period of irrationality: really, if conditioning were the universal gadget for retooling behavior, why couldn't dogs be conditioned to do dishes? By the late 1950s, behaviorism was crumbling under its own weight, failing to deliver on its grand promises.[9] Even some of Skinner's followers found that animals had instinctive behaviors that were often difficult or impossible to modify, and rebelled with academic papers with titles like "The misbehavior of organisms."[10] It is probably an exaggeration to say that Chomsky's critique single-handedly killed behaviorism, but it is safe to say that Chomsky put the nail on behaviorism's coffin, and helped usher the study of language and mind into the modern era.[11]

Half a century later, as every psychology undergraduate knows, behaviorism is dead, finished, passé. We now know that the mind of a newborn infant is vastly different from the "one great blooming, buzzing confusion" supposed by the early twentieth century American psychologist William James.[12] In contemporary cognitive science, the baby's mental power is routinely assessed and measured thanks to technological advancements, but when Chomsky first proposed an innate universal grammar, his demonstration was decidedly low-tech.

Let's see how Chomsky made his argument, not for the first time, but most dramatically.[13] In October 1975, at the magnificent Royaumont Abbey near Paris, philosophers, biologists, and psychologists convened to witness a "dialogue" between Chomsky and Jean Piaget, the renowned Swiss psychologist. (In the academy, this was the closest thing to the World Series.) Piaget was the chief architect of a highly influential theory of child development that holds that a child passes through several stages of mental evolution. The child approaches the world like a little scientist; she first touches objects, observes and manipulates them, and then discovers their properties. Language learning, according to Piaget, follows pretty much the same motor-sensory routine, except in this case, the child is observing, manipulating, and producing symbols: sounds, words, and other units of language. Both Chomsky and Piaget were staunchly against behaviorism, and both attributed the marvelous achievements of a human child primarily to the child, rather than Skinner's stimuli. In short, they were both strongly "for nature"; Piaget and his colleagues were in the mood for a compromise, sure that there would be an inevitable convergence of their respective views.

But Chomsky's debate team from MIT would have none of it. Chomsky and Piaget diverged sharply on the conception of language in two critical ways. For Piaget, language is a manifestation of a general process that also encompasses the perception and understanding of objects in physical space. The knowledge of language is a product of the child's construction, and occurs by tweaking the existing mental system to accommodate and adapt to new experiences. For Chomsky, language, to use a term championed by the philosopher Jerry Fodor, is a *module* of the mind.[14] The organization of a language system has its specific principles and functions that are not used in other cognitive systems. If the mind is a big computer, then language is a special program sitting on the hard drive along with many other special programs designed for distinct tasks; a word processor is not a web browser. This is not to say language has nothing to do with the rest of the mind—it clearly does. For instance, language encodes and expresses our thoughts and conception of the world. The claim is that there are unique properties that show up in language but will not help you hit a baseball or achieve emotional stability. Moreover, Chomsky believes that the foundation for language, universal grammar, is available through the child's genetic endowment; the child plays no active role in its creation.

To make a compelling case for a universal grammar requires some careful thought. First, we need an articulated theory of just what universal grammar is before we set out looking for evidence of its innateness. Second, the case must be made in the face of the plain fact that humans are powerful learners, and there are plenty of things that are undeniably learned. We learn, for instance, that leaves turn colors in the fall, that fall is the season that the Red Sox will falter (until very recently): all of these bits of knowledge are picked up through experience with the world.

Chomsky's approach employed a technique with ancient roots. In Plato's *Meno,* Socrates, in a truly Socratic dialog, pulled off a stunning demonstration that an uneducated servant boy nevertheless actually had, buried in his mind, the knowledge of geometry, the crowning achievement of Greek science. Socrates's conclusion was that this knowledge came from past life; in contemporary terms, it comes from the human brain and ultimately the human genes. The only way to prove the innateness of universal grammar, then, is to find some nugget of linguistic knowledge that children doubtless possess in the absence of experience.

Here is how Chomsky presented his case at the Royaumont Abbey. Take a most basic type of English sentence: simple questions. Continuing the rabbit example in this chapter, consider the declarative statement and its associated question:

Rabbits **are** nimble.
**Are** rabbits nimble?

How is the question derived from the declarative? The simplest hypothesis, obviously, is to take the second word and drag it to the beginning of the sentence. But this turns sentences into garbage:

Brown **rabbits** are nimble.
**Rabbits** brown are nimble?

A **purple** mushroom is growing near the rabbit hole.
**Purple** a mushroom is growing near the rabbit hole?

The Scandal of Induction shows its ugly face again: How does the child stay clear of all the logically possible, though grammatically impossible, ways of asking a question? Evidently, as these examples illustrate, not just any word can move; to form a question in English, we need to move *auxiliary* verbs such as "am," "is," "are," "do," and "does." But even knowing that only auxiliaries move is still inadequate. Consider a perfectly simple and sensible strategy: the child has decided to move the *first* auxiliary to the beginning of the sentence.

Simple ideas are not always the right ones: in this case, however, it would be quite difficult to find out. The hypothesis "Move the first auxiliary" works virtually perfectly, and the loopholes are revealed only when a sentence contains *two* auxiliaries. Below is the exception that disproves the rule:

The rabbit that **was** chasing the tortoise was losing the race.
**Was** the rabbit that chasing the tortoise was losing the race?

But there is almost no chance for a child to hear questions like this. English sentences that children hear are generally short: each, on average, contains about four words, and it is difficult to pack two auxiliaries into short questions. It has been estimated that an average three-year-old has heard about 2.5 million sentences. While it is impossible to go through a database of that magnitude, the linguist Julie Anne Legate and I did painstakingly comb through a transcript of about one hundred thousand sentences directed to children, and we came up with zero instances of double-auxiliary questions.[15]

Why do these perfectly sensible rules fail? Because when it comes to the specific properties of universal grammar, common sense just doesn't apply. Notions such as first, second, last, or next are sensible because they describe *linear* relations: how things are ordered, listed, and lined up. Linear relations are pervasive in the physical world and are permanent fixtures in our thinking: "take the first left after the gas station," "the second suspect to the right," "the last person in line."

When we see a sentence, where words apparently line up like beads on a string, common sense tells us to look for these linear relations. Piaget's doctrine of child development would fit right in: children figure out how language works by extending their perception of the physical world.

But sentences are not like beads on a string at all; by implication, Piaget's theory, for whatever merit it deserves, does not extend to language. Sentences are actually processed in chunks called phrases. When we hear "Rabbits are nimble" as words arriving one after another, the language processor in our brain actually "hears" a first chunk, the subject phrase "Rabbits," followed by a second chunk, the verb phrase "are nimble." The correct rule for asking questions is to move the auxiliary verb that follows the subject *phrase*. In "the rabbit that was chasing the tortoise was losing the race," the subject phrase is actually the long seven-word chunk "the rabbit that was chasing the tortoise." And that's precisely where no linear relation can possibly work, because the subject phrase of a sentence can take all kinds of forms, and can be arbitrarily long; this can be seen in cases below, where the subject is delineated by brackets for your convenience (and with apologies to Lewis Carroll):

[The rabbit] was late.
[The white rabbit with pink eyes] was late.
[The rabbit who took a watch out of its waistcoat pocket] was late.
[The rabbit that Alice followed down the hole—"Down, down,
    down. Would the fall ever come to an end"—] was late.

It turns out that linear relations, so simple, natural, and pervasive, are not used in the sentence structure of any language. Universal grammar includes a principle called *structure dependence,* which states that sentence formation operates around linear relations not among words but among chunkier units of phrases. While some of us eventually learn about phrases and perhaps even the much-dreaded sentence diagrams in elementary school, the principle of structure dependence is innately available to all of us, children and adults alike. The plausibility of an innate universal grammar is built on the implausibility of learning a language without it, and this implausibility in turn is built on the realization that language is extraordinarily complex. Just figuring out the rule for question formation takes a good deal of thought, as we have seen.

And yet, question formation comes naturally to even very young children, as the linguist Stephen Crain and his colleagues demonstrated in a cleverly crafted experiment.[16] Instead of giving children a quiz about the correct rule for forming questions, Crain followed the first principle of child psychology research: kids would much rather talk to puppets than to strange scientists. A group of children were brought into the lab, with the youngest just past their third birthday (any younger would result in serious attention span problems). The researchers set up a puppet show that cued children to spontaneously ask questions involving exactly two auxiliaries. Jabba the Hutt, of *Star Wars* fame, was visiting from another planet and saw pictures of, say, a smiley dog sitting on a bench. The children were then prompted to "ask Jabba if the dog that is happy is sitting on the bench." Jabba would get to eat a frog—another puppet—if he got the answer right. Remarkably, no child used the "sensible" strategy of moving the first auxiliary verb. Even the youngest child never constructed the question like this:

**Is** the dog that happy **is** sitting on the bench?

That would have been a linear rule and a blatant violation of the principle of structure dependence.

Adults are equally bound by universal grammar. In a delightful but mischievous experiment,[17] the linguists Neil Smith and Ianthi-Maria Tsimpli designed an artificial language they called Epun that makes sense but violates universal grammar. ("Epun" is rumored to be a play on Nupe, a language of northern Nigeria, on which Smith is an authority). For instance, Epun has a special word "nog" that is used for emphatic expressions, kind of like "did" in "I did finish my homework." However, unlike "did," which typically goes after the subject phrase, "nog" always attaches to the third word in a sentence:

| Lodon | habolu | guv-**nog**. |
| Lodon | yesterday | go-**did**. |

"Lodon did go yesterday."

Now it was up to a group of undergraduate students, the favorite guinea pigs for linguists and psychologists, to figure out how this rule works. Piece of cake, isn't it? Surprisingly—that is, if language were designed and learned by logical reasoning—the students were utterly baffled by the placement of "nog." But Smith and Tsimpli were not surprised: the principle of structure dependence preemptively struck out linear relations such as "the third word" as not within the realm of linguistic possibilities. When it comes to language, common sense shuts off and universal grammar takes over.

The theory of universal grammar has turned the traditional conception of language upside down. For many among us, language is something "out there,"[18] an idealized form of behavior that we are trying to imitate—only not doing so well, as the language mavens remind us daily. The French, who apparently take the integrity of their language more seriously than we take ours, established the Académie française (in 1635!), whose primary function is to regulate French grammar, pronunciation, and other matters pertaining to the purity of the language. So French is one set of conventions, and English another; children will pick up those conventions in due time, much like picking up table manners or fashion trends. Language is, in this view, like any other social convention that dictates what we do.

The investigation of universal grammar, by contrast, reveals what we do not do and can not do. True, part of language is indeed negotiated by community consensus. Unlike Humpty Dumpty, we can't go around making up words at will; the warm fuzzball at my feet is a "dog," and both you and I know it. But a community can get together and make conventions of whatever form: just look at hand signs in baseball, which can change on a daily basis as long as they are agreed upon. The principles that govern the form of human language, however, are not arbitrary: perfectly sensible rules, such as those making use of linear relations, are actually impossible. This is a telltale sign that language is not a social convention—something that is "out there"—but is rooted in our biology.

Fast-forward from Chomsky versus Piaget to October 2001, when newspapers around the world heralded "Language Gene Found." Similar headlines had appeared somewhat prematurely over a decade earlier in 1990, when the linguist Myrna Gopnik at McGill University published her study of a British family known as the KE family (to protect their privacy) in which half its members spanning four generations suffered severe speech and language disorders of a unique kind.[19]

To understand the KE family's disorder, it's important to note that English, and indeed all languages of the world, make use of grammatical features that do not always convey additional information but nevertheless cannot be omitted. Notice the past-tense -ed and the plural -s in "Bart smashed up two cars yesterday" and the third person singular -s in "Lisa practices the sax every day." Their meanings are adequately covered by "yesterday," "two," and "Lisa," respectively, yet omitting them, which native speakers of English never do, would make the sentence ungrammatical. Such frequently redundant but necessary grammatical features, however, were frequently missing in the speech of the affected members of the KE family:

Yesterday he walk.
The boy eat four cookie.

But interestingly, the symptom in the KE family does not run across the board: not all redundant linguistic information is eliminated. For example, in many cases, omissions of pronouns do not affect the understandability of sentences; for normal speakers of English, it sometimes sounds unnatural to leave pronouns in, precisely because they are redundant:

Homer went to Moe's, (he) had a beer, and (he) went home.

The affected members of the KE family, by contrast, often couldn't resist pronouns (but note the inconsistent use of past tense):

On Saturday I watch TV and I watch plastic man and I watch football.
On Sunday I had pork and potato and cabbage.

The inheritance patterns in Gopnik's findings strongly suggested that
the genetic basis of some aspect of language learning and use was dis-
rupted in the KE family. Yet it would take another decade, and quite
a scientific detective story, to find the culprit.

First, language disorders are often the joint deficit of several sources.
To conclude the KE family's problem was linguistic, some extra work
was needed to eliminate alternative explanations. When a computer
breaks down, one shouldn't rush to replace the hard drive; it could be
that the monitor is dead. In the case of language, there is indeed
such an output device: the vocal tract that makes speech. Indeed, the
KE family also had significant problems with coordinated face and
mouth movements. But the problem ran deeper: later studies revealed
that the disorder was not limited to language production but affected
language comprehension as well.[20] Another complication came out
when it was found that language was not the only problematic cognitive task: for some of the affected members, difficulties extended to
other learning and memory problems, as shown by low IQ scores.[21]
This was less of a worry, however. It has been long established that
"intelligence" measurements like IQ tests have little to do with the success of language learning. (The most dramatic illustration is the com-
parably normal development of language for children with Williams
syndrome, a congenital disorder characterized by limited spatial and
motor control and moderate to severe mental retardation.[22]) Therefore,
language disorders in the KE family were not limited to the input/out-
put device: the core language engine was somehow out of sync.

Second, the KE family's disorder could be traced to a single gene,
and this was pure luck. The Human Genome Project has revealed that
humans have only about 20,000 to 25,000 genes (or about the same
number as mustard weeds): this number pales in comparison to the
number of traits that are genetically determined. Every behavioral
deficit, then, is highly likely to be the joint product of multiple genes.
Fortunately, the KE family language disorder can be traced to a single
gene with dominant effect.

By 1998, a team of researchers studying the KE family was able to trace the suspect gene to a small segment on chromosome 7.[23] Still, any one of the approximately one hundred genes in that location could have turned out to be the elusive "language gene." Again, the gene hunters had a lucky break: a boy unrelated to the KE family was found to exhibit similar language deficits. This boy carried a chromosomal abnormality in which the segments at the ends of two chromosomes were swapped: one of them was in fact chromosome 7, and the swap site was very close to the region identified through the KE family. Following this lead, and putting together all the pieces scattered over ten years of research, scientists finally located the gene responsible for the language deficits; it was subsequently named FOXP2. A simple mutation is all it takes to disrupt speech and language.

The story doesn't end here; in fact, it only begins. The big news is not quite "Language Gene Found": since humans and humans alone have language, *some* language gene is bound to be found sooner or later. Rather, the big news is how unremarkable the FOXP2 gene actually is, and thus how distant the mystery of language still lies ahead of us. While the FOXP2 gene is responsible for the KE family disorders, its function is not limited to language. The gene turns out to be a multitalented player that affects the expressions of many other genes in the making of the human body, including the lungs, the gut, and the heart. Although the modern human form of FOXP2 appeared in the last 200,000 years, the gene actually goes way back in evolutionary time and is present in many animals.[24] In fact, a recent study that links FOXP2 to brain development was carried out on mice, who carry a version of FOXP2 that is evolutionarily and functionally related to ours.[25] And finally, FOXP2 is not *the* language gene; obviously, the affected KE family members still have language, albeit in a somewhat anomalous form. FOXP2 is only one of what are bound to be many genes that interact in extremely complex ways to give us language, and much of this process remains a mystery.

It has become common to call universal grammar an instinct for language. But that term is not entirely accurate, for it misses the most important and revolutionary aspect of universal grammar. Surely, to speak is human, but language is an altogether different kind of instinct from the homing of pigeons, the waggle dances of bees, or other human instincts like walking, crying, and seeing—and that's why language is so fascinating. As Darwin pointed out, language is not a true instinct because it has to be learned. Adam growing up in Boston will learn English, and Gianni growing up in Milan will learn Italian. But this is purely an accident of the environment, not a result of their genetic makeup. If they switched places at birth, Adam would learn Italian, and Gianni would learn English. Likewise, my Chinese and my wife's Irish heritage will not give our son the slightest advantage in learning Mandarin or Celtic languages over, say, a Navajo baby. So if the universal grammar is in the genetic code of every child, as linguists claim, then it cannot be about the sounds, words, grammar, or any other properties of any specific language. Now this is a *very* radical idea: the adjective "universal" in universal grammar has to be taken seriously, and literally. For most people, what's striking about the world's languages is how different they look; by claiming the innateness of universal grammar, we are saying all languages must be pretty much the same! That, I think, is the most significant and exciting result of modern linguistics.

This is where things stand today. Linguists now believe that all human languages are variations on a basic theme, which consists of a set of universal *principles*. To give a few examples: all languages have consonants and vowels; all languages have pitches, contours, and intonations; all languages have nouns and verbs; all languages have operations that move words and phrases from one place to another; and all such operations are governed by the same laws, including the principle of structure dependence. The points of variation, on the other hand, are called *parameters,* which can be thought of as power switches on a complex circuit: turning one on here and another off there can lead to radical changes in the circuit's behavior. Different languages have switched the parameters one way or the other, and those switches control how sentences are constructed. For example, there is a parameter that controls the ordering of the verb and the object: in English, the verb comes before the object, but in Japanese, the verb comes after it. There is a parameter that controls the ordering of the subject and the verb: here, English and Japanese are in agreement; in both languages, the subject comes before the verb phrase. These two parameters then give the basic word order of English (subject-verb-object) and Japanese (subject-object-verb), as well as that of Tagalog (verb-object-subject), a language of the Philippines. The construction of a sentence in every language follows the same assembly line: the universal principles specify what kind of linguistic information can be put together, and the parameter values—specific to individual languages—instruct where all the pieces go.

This refined theory of universal grammar, dubbed *principles and parameters*, was a speculative but spectacular hypothesis. To test it, linguists have gone to every corner of the world and returned with remarkable success. Yet confirmation for this radical theory of language can also be found in every toddler around us.

Baby Thomas Babington Macaulay was said to be a genius. According to the legend, his first words came out when his hostess spilled hot tea on him. After a good round of bawling, Thomas eased the hostess's worries: "Thank you Madam, the agony is sensibly abated."

Little Thomas *was* a genius, at least as judged by his later achievements: Thomas became one of the greatest historians of all time (and Lord Macaulay). But even his astonishing linguistic precocity paled in comparison to a certain Christian Heinecken. Mr. Heinecken was "one of the most remarkable beings recorded in the history of mankind," stated the 1891 edition of *Chambers Book of Days,* a popular almanac of its time. "He spoke, we are told, spoke sensibly too, within a few hours after his birth; when ten months old, he could converse on most subjects; when a year old he was perfect in the Old Testament and in another short month he mastered the New. . . . He next acquired Latin and French, both of which he spoke with great facility at the court of Denmark, to which he was taken in his fourth year. His feeble constitution prevented him from being weaned until he was five years old, when he died in consequence of this necessary change of diet."[26]

Legends are almost never true; these two are clearly false. Babies cannot possibly speak, not to mention "sensibly," "within a few hours after birth." A newborn's vocal tract is more like that found in nonhuman primates than it is like adult human's: its larynx is positioned high in the throat, and the tongue fills the entire mouth, making it physiologically impossible to speak. Important anatomical changes will take place in the next few months. But more personally, legends of baby language geniuses, if true, would put me—and thousands of child language researchers in the world—out of commission.

We delight in children's language; "Is she talking yet?" is on the lips of every visiting friend and relative. And children do not disappoint: by the age of four, all major pieces of language are in place. For the rest of their lives they only learn more words and fine-tune language use for social and cultural functions. But I, for one, am glad that children are not *too* good at language. Imagine what would happen if every child were like Mr. Heinecken, speaking languages perfectly at birth. Parents would surely miss the "darnedest things" coming out of those pudgy cheeks; and scientists of child language would never be able to observe language learning at work.

In fact, children's language often looks quite different from adults', and this gives us a unique opportunity to study what lies under their remarkable feat of language learning. Child language has a smaller vocabulary and shorter sentences, and is often full of errors:

A my pencil.
Tickles me.
I don't want no milk.
I weared my jacket.
Eve jump self.
Who do you think who is in the box?

The errors in their language are neither random, as if they were scrambling words at will, nor all alike, as if they result from some developmental bottleneck that puts complex sentences or big words out of children's reach. When I was a graduate student at the MIT Artificial Intelligence Laboratory, I suddenly realized that the errors are in fact entirely grammatical—in languages from different places or even times.[27]

"A my pencil" would be fine in Greek; "Tickles me," with the subject missing, is spoken by Chinese adults. "I don't want no milk," where the child expresses milk agitation twice, is the norm in Spanish. "I weared my jacket" walked straight out of Chaucer's *Canterbury Tales* ("And forty years a wifeless man was he, A girdle she weared").

And "Who do you think who is in the box?"—with two "whos" rather than one—works perfectly in German.

Surely no one would suggest that the child has traveled to these foreign places and times. But we can make sense of these oddities thanks to the principles and parameters theory, which solves the problem of language learning with a one-two punch.

First, there is a set of universal principles, like the principle of structure dependence, that all languages obey. These principles lay out the bounds on how words are put together into phrases, phrases into sentences, and how phrases can (and cannot) move around in sentences. The principles are innate and don't have to be learned: they explain the absence of the impossible errors like the linear rules that all children steer clear of, even when talking to Jabba the Hutt.

Second, the differences among languages can be very compactly described by about a few dozen parameters. Learning a language becomes a problem of "twenty questions": the child needs only to fix the values of the parameters, and that's it. Now the main thesis, and the subtitle of the book, will make sense. The process of picking parameter values for grammar learning can be given a familiar name: *natural selection*. The child tries out various options in the parameter system, which turn up as "errors" in her speech: these imperfections actually belong to perfect languages in universal grammar, just not the one she eventually learns. These wrong options, however, cannot last forever; a Bostonian child trying out the parameter values for Japanese will not generally understand English or be understood. Only the grammar actually used in the child's linguistic environment will not be contradicted, and only the fittest survives. In other words, children learn a language by unlearning all other possible languages.

This is a preview of how children, with the help of universal grammar, complete the improbable mission of learning a language. Now we need to start from the very beginning, with the acoustic mess that conceals consonants, vowels, and words. To learn a language, the child first needs to find it.

CHAPTER 3

# Silent Rehearsals

Babies are helpless when they come into this world. They can't crawl, sit, smile, or do much else. They can see, but only about eight to ten inches away; farther or closer, things turn into a haze. They can't see colors—this ability kicks in only at the second month—so, as parenting books tell you, stick with black-and-white pictures. Depth perception doesn't develop until the third month; only then can they get a consistent fix to grab a toy (or your glasses). And of course, babies can't talk.

But they can listen, and that's tremendously useful for someone just setting out to discover language. Although holding her newborn baby right away is every mother's sacred right, scientists have rushed to the birth scene pretty quickly. And the findings are, without exaggeration, shocking. At the very tender age of a few days, newborns can pick out their native language from foreign languages. Unlike their parents, who usually have a terrible time with a new language, infants have no trouble recognizing consonants and vowels in speech—not only of their native language, but for *all* the languages in the world. Not bad for someone whose umbilical cord hasn't fallen off.

You have every reason to be skeptical about these assertions. We have just described the challenges of fishing language out of the acoustic chaos before language learning can begin (and hence why talking computers exist only in science fiction). And now we are asserting that newborns have got the problem solved. But how do we *know* if the baby can recognize language, not to mention the specific consonants and vowels that make up speech? A newborn infant doesn't talk or even nod, so how do we know if she knows *anything*? To put those doubts to rest, we turn to the science of language in the crib.[1]

*       *       *

It was long thought that the baby's first words mark the onset of language learning; after all, what's language good for without words? But stories from French maternity wards cast some doubt on such conventional wisdom; the babies of foreign-born mothers got fussy when their mothers switched from their native language to French. In the late 1980s, a team of researchers led by the cognitive scientist Jacques Mehler took notice.[2] With some technical wizardry that will be explained in a moment, the anecdotes were thoroughly confirmed: newborns of French-speaking parents, for example, readily distinguish their native language from Russian. Of course, this is not accomplished by having the knowledge of French vocabulary, which is simply nonexistent for a three-day-old. But maybe the babies had picked up the sounds of the language despite a *very* short immersion in the French-speaking environment? This possibility was quickly rejected: the French newborns could also distinguish English from Italian, neither of which they had been exposed to, before or after birth. As they say, if the impossible has been eliminated, whatever remains, however improbable, must be the truth. So the truth must be that the journey to language starts in the womb.

The human auditory system begins its development around the sixth month of gestation; soon afterward, pregnant mothers can feel the fetus kick if it is startled by a loud noise. The womb, however, is not the best place for learning speech. Dunk your head in a warm Jacuzzi tub and try to listen to the radio; what you hear is a good approximation of prenatal acoustics. Liquid is not a good medium for transmitting sound, and the womb is full of amniotic fluid. In fact, while the human auditory system is sensitive to sounds in the frequency range between 20 Hz and 20 kHz, only those below about 800 Hz manage to pass through the womb; that generally filters out the sounds of language. So the fetus hears the mother's blood flow and heart beat, though her words are muffled. Not all is lost, however; the little bit of language that does survive fetal filtering is the rhythm and contours of speech, or what linguists call *prosody*.

Prosody is a set of complex properties of speech such as volume, pitch, and intonation. Much of prosody's function is to add color to language: as the primary means of human communication, monotonic speech not only bores but also fails to convey the richness of our thoughts and emotions. A firm and polite "No" may be appropriate when answering a police officer but did not do at all when my book manuscript vanished following a Microsoft Windows crash. Not surprisingly, universalities in human emotions lead to some universal features in the prosodies of the world's languages. All languages seem to make use of falling and rising pitch patterns, typically associated with statements and questions—and as a result identical sentences pick up different meanings:

Lisa gave Bart
            a worm
                        to eat.
                        to eat?
            a worm
Lisa gave Bart

But languages, and even dialects, do vary in their prosody; this is obvious because deviations from the "norm" are often perceived through social, cultural, and aesthetic lenses. The so-called uptalk, which raises the intonation even in statements, also managed to raise some eyebrows in the early 1990s when it became popular among teenagers and, supposedly, Californians. Talking about California—if you think Governor Arnold Schwarzenegger sounds wooden even when he's not playing a cyborg, you'd be absolutely right. Because he is a native of Austria, Arnold's first language is German, which does have less varied intonation and sounds less lively than English,[3] and this pattern apparently spills over to his second language. (True, his overly formal English grammar doesn't help either.)

The harshest treatment of German came from Charles V of Spain, who remarked, "To God I speak Spanish, to women Italian, to men French, and to my horse, German"—though English deserved a similar degradation. Value judgment aside, there are objective differences in the prosody of these languages. Italian, French, and Spanish belong to the *syllable-timed* class of languages, in which each syllable takes approximately the same amount of time to produce. This leads to a particularly rhythmic speech, which many have maintained—and I tend to agree—is inherently suited to opera. Indeed, recent research has uncovered some correlation between the prosody of a spoken language and the melody of music in that culture.[4] German, Dutch, and English belong to the group of *stress-timed* languages, in which the rhythm of speech is determined by stress on words, i.e., the syllable in a word that is pronounced more heavily than the rest, as in "*baby lan*guage." Since words can be of various length, the rhythm of the stress-timed languages is less regular or fluid than the syllable-based languages and, in King Charles's assessment, suitable only for the horse. On the other hand, a singsong Italian-accented Terminator would be incredibly funny.

Back to the maternity ward and French babies listening to Russian. It is notable that Russian, like German and English, is a stress-timed language, and therefore has very different prosody from French, a syllable-based language. While the womb has rendered words inaudible, prosody does come through. (To get an idea of what it sounds like, try humming a sentence, the same way you hum a song.) This, Mehler and his colleagues conjecture, is how the native language, stripped down to only its prosody, comes to a baby. This hypothesis would immediately explain the finding that French newborns can distinguish English from Italian: if they are already familiar with the prosody of French, which is not all that different from Italian as both are syllable-based languages, the prosody of English would sound alien in comparison.

How can this hypothesis be proved? After an intensive workout through the birth canal, babies are as tired as mothers. And the world feels like an utterly alien place after the dark, warm, and cozy womb. The smart strategy in such a crisis situation is to eat and sleep, and that's what newborn babies do—nursing frequently and sleeping up to sixteen hours a day. Such an indifferent state makes it difficult to do science with babies, whose communicative ability is already limited to say the least. So Mehler and his colleagues turned to an ingenious technique called *high amplitude sucking*, or HAS. HAS has been as instrumental to the study of infant development as DNA sequencing to modern genetics.

In a landmark 1971 experiment, the psychologist Peter Eimas and colleagues propelled the science of language straight into the infant age.[5] Their clever design banks on two things babies are best known for: sucking and short attention spans. Propped up in a basket in a sound booth, the baby gets a pacifier with a pressure-sensitive device hidden inside, which in turn is connected to a polygraph machine— nowadays a computer—that monitors the rate of sucking. The original experiment was to see whether babies could hear consonants used in languages (they can, and spectacularly; a lot more on that later). But the technique can be used to test if any two sounds can be distinguished. First, sound A is played through a loudspeaker; the baby gets interested and starts sucking vigorously. Soon, the novelty wears off, and the rate of sucking drops off to a stable plateau; now the baby is sufficiently *habituated* (the psychologist's way of saying "bored"). We can then switch to sound B. If the baby recognizes the difference, rigorous sucking will resume; something new has captured her attention.

French babies do distinguish French from Russian. When one language is switched for the other after the baby is habituated, the sucking pace picks up significantly. But for Mehler and his colleagues, this demonstration alone was not quite enough. Their hypothesis was that the first step to language is taken in the womb, through prosody. They needed to do a "control" experiment, that is, to rule out the reasonable doubt that the baby *might* be using other sources of acoustic information to tell the languages apart. In other words, babies should be tested on prosody alone, with everything else in spoken language wiped out. Thanks to digital signal processing technology, the same kind that goes into cell phones, it is possible to extract prosody, and only prosody, from speech. This is accomplished by filtering out all the sounds above a certain frequency, which strips away the sounds of words but leaves the prosody intact, and hence gives a good approximation of what speech sounds like when heard in the womb. As predicted, babies can still distinguish "French" and "Russian," this time around on the basis of prosody alone.

So the specialization to the native language starts far before a baby hears, much less says, its first word. This is only a small step toward language, to be sure: newborns cannot yet distinguish languages *within* the same prosodic group. French newborns can tell stress-based English from syllable-based French but cannot tell English from Dutch, which is also stress-based, as refinement within prosodic groups will come later. But this small step goes a long way. Amid the acoustic chaos, the melody and rhythm familiar ever since the womb days will continue to guide the baby on the journey to language; all she has to do is to follow the beat.

Knowing what to listen to is, of course, just the beginning. Words in different languages make use of arbitrarily different sounds: there is no reason why a canine is called "dog" in English, with two consonants and a vowel, but "gou" in Mandarin Chinese, with completely different consonants and vowels. For the baby, the discovery of these building blocks of speech is the next task at hand.

This doesn't seem too hard. When we hear a word, say, "bat," we hear three distinct sounds: *b–a–t*. For the language learner, this seems like good news. The acoustic signal of "bat," it seems to follow, can be spliced into three corresponding regions, representing the sounds of *b* (consonant), *a* (vowel), and *t* (consonant), respectively. All the baby has to do, then, is to pluck these out of speech. Unfortunately, that's where the bad news begins.

In the 1950s, Franklin Cooper, Alvin Liberman, and their colleagues at the Haskins Laboratories, housed at my home institution of Yale, set out to solve the problem of splicing speech but with a different purpose: to build a reading machine for the blind. The original plan was to extract from speech acoustics what individual consonants and vowels sound like. The rest would be easy: translate a text into a sequence of consonants and vowels, for which a dictionary would suffice, and then glue them together—a predecessor to "rip, mix, and burn," familiar to every fan of digital music.

The task, however, turned out to be impossible. Words, as we have seen in Chapter 2, don't have pauses between them, but this was not the main problem. Although stopping after every word in a speech synthesizer may sound stiff, no intelligibility is lost. The challenge turns out to be more fundamental; even consonants and vowels cannot be ripped out of speech (not to mention mixed or burned).

To understand how we perceive speech, it is useful to understand how we produce speech in the first place. The physics of talking isn't so different from playing the saxophone. In both cases, sound is created by a stream of air, for which the lungs are the source, rushing and resonating through a tunnel. The tunnel for the sax is the tube and the keys, and the tunnel for speech is our vocal tract: the throat, tongue, teeth, lips, and for some sounds, the nose. As the tunnel changes its shape—by the pressing of the keys on the sax, for instance—the traveling of the airstream alters speed, changes course, and consequently produces various sounds. X-ray movies of the vocal tract during speech production reveal hundreds of muscles twisting and turning in all directions but with precision and in perfect coordination; the human voice remains the most versatile musical instrument.

Let's see—or rather, feel—how we speak. All consonants are formed with some constriction in the vocal tract as the air flows out. For example, the constriction in *b* is formed by the lips, which initially remain closed and then abruptly release with a small explosion of air, which is unmistakable if you hold a candle right in front of your mouth. Some consonants such as *b, d,* and *g* involve the vibration of the vocal cords; these are called *voiced* consonants. Others, such as *p, t,* and *k,* do not use the vocal cords, and are therefore *voiceless.* The contrasts between the two groups won't be missed if you put a finger on your throat as these consonants are made. Vowels, on the other hand, never involve any air constriction (and always use the vocal cords). Molding the vocal tract into different shapes and positions leads to different sounds. For *ee* (as in "bee"), as you can feel, the tongue is at the front of the mouth, while for *oo* (as in "boo"), it is at the back. Recent work in neuroscience has confirmed our low-tech division of labor between consonants and vowels: the brain handles them with different processing mechanisms.[6]

Funny things happen when consonants and vowels are put together. Although "bee" sounds like *b* followed by *ee,* and "boo" sounds like the same consonant followed by a different vowel, words are not formed by simply gluing a chain of consonants and vowels. Acoustic analysis shows that the *b* in "bee" and the *b* in "boo" are actually as different as the vowels that follow. To see this, get ready to say "bee," but *don't say it*! You will notice that the tongue already shifts to the front of the mouth, in anticipation of the *ee* that follows. Now get ready to say "boo" and again don't say it. This time around, the tongue is already at the back in preparation for *oo,* well before anything is uttered.[7] In the complex dance of speech articulation, the next move is always planned ahead.

Every speaker of English knows this dance routine, albeit uncon-
sciously. To play the game the other way around, researchers synthe-
sized a short burst of air—a fake consonant—just in front of the
vowels *ee* and *ah*. The listeners, however, swore they heard two different sounds—"*pee*" and "*kah*," respectively. In other words, they
heard—more precisely, they *thought* they heard—two different consonants for the very same burst of air.[8] Consonants and vowels in speech
aren't like the combinations of letters neatly lined up on this page. They
are mixed up and mumbled out together, a process that speech scientists call *coarticulation*: there is a little bit of Bob Dylan in all of us.

Coarticulation makes it impossible to rip consonants and vowels out
of speech, which is a major reason why computers still can't understand human language. The sounds of consonants and vowels are not
fixed, but always depend on the neighborhood—how they are arranged
within a word, with further complication when words are put together
in sentences. Hence speech recognition software generally asks you to
speak slowly, often word by word, because it has stored only the
acoustics of whole words in advance. Efforts to find reliable acoustic
cues for consonants and vowels—to combine for words on the fly—
have never made much progress. But from the perspective of *Homo
sapiens*, coarticulation is a very good thing, for it makes speech fast and
rapid communication possible.[9] English averages five sounds per
word, and we typically speak at a rate of 150 words per minute; this
comes to 12.5 sounds per second. However, fast speech is a good thing
only if the listener can keep up with it, reliably; how do we pull out a
sequence of consonants and vowels when there are no acoustic boundaries in between?

The answer may be found in the rainbow. When we look at a rainbow,
we see the familiar six bands of color: red, orange, yellow, green, blue,
and purple. That, however, is an illusion. The rainbow really is one
large band of color, varying over the smooth range of light frequency;
the visual system, however, breaks this continuum into a few blocks of
color categories. Moving along the rainbow, it is very easy to pick out,
say, the yellow-green transition, but it is very hard to distinguish different hues within the green region, even though the rate of change in
wavelength within and across categories is the same. We are capable

of discerning those within-category differences; it just takes a lot of effort, and hence many trips to Kmart before we find the perfect orange-ish yellow for the sunroom. In fact, our visual system is designed to respond rapidly to only a few main color categories, so Martha Stewart has had to invent utterly uninformative labels— "morning moon," "downy duckling," or "dandelion"—for her infinite supply of paints.

Understanding speech works much the same way: by illusion. The sounds of speech are like colors on the rainbow, falling along a continuum of acoustic properties. Take, for instances, the distinction between the sounds *bah* and *pah,* which consist of different consonants and the same vowel. Recall that both *b* and *p* are produced with the lips initially closed, followed by an eruption of air when the lips open, but they differ in terms of voicing, that is, whether the vocal cord vibrates. Since *p* is voiceless, the vocal cord vibration (from the vowel *ah* in *pah*) has a tiny delay—about 80 milliseconds, or 0.08 second. On the other hand, since *b* is itself voiced, the vocal cords start vibrating right away in *bah.*

What happens if the delay is somewhere in between 0 ms and 80 ms—say, 50 ms? Does it sound more like a hybrid between *pah* and *bah,* perhaps a bit heavy on the *pah* side? With modern speech synthesizers, it is possible to generate a whole spectrum of sounds that vary only in the timing of vocal cord vibration.[10] Yet strikingly, we don't hear the many different sounds in the spectrum: instead, we hear only *two.* For the range between 80 ms to approximately 25 ms, all sounds feel like *pah;* after the 25 ms break, and all of a sudden, *bah* leaps out.

Yellow vs. green, *bah* vs. *pah:* these stem from the ability to distill a continuous range of signals into discrete units; scientists call this *categorical perception.*[11] At first glance, categorical perception seems a poor representation of reality. Well, it *is,* because so many details of what the eyes see and the ears hear are simply tossed aside in favor of relatively few points of interest. But as we have seen in the Gavagai puzzle in Chapter 2, to make it in this world, it often pays to ignore details. To understand speech, we need to recognize the sounds that make words; for "bat" and "pat," a sharp cut between the acoustics of *b* and *p* gets the job done (and quickly).

While both speech and color perception involve breaking up a continuous spectrum into discrete categories, speech has a unique complication, the variation across individual speakers. Red is red, and it doesn't matter—on a purely perceptual basis, that is—whether I, or Picasso, splashed it on the canvas; speech, however, is always different coming from different speakers, as we noted in Chapter 2. This is not surprising; at the very least, no two people's vocal tracts are exactly the same. Again, if we choose to, we are capable of picking out these differences; we can tell that women's voices are pitched higher than men's, and that certain voices in *Toy Story* belong to Tom Hanks and Tim Allen. The variations among individuals can be truly enormous.[12] But at the same time—and more important for the sake of speech communication, and for the baby trying to learn a language—many aspects of these variations are neutralized into the abstract categories of consonants and vowels. Although a particular four-letter word comes out quite differently from a three-year-old boy than from his thirty-year-old father, the mother knows that it is the same word, and is to be discouraged.

The production and the perception of speech add up to a perfect system. Just when the vocal tract poses the challenge of coarticulation and individual variation, which scatter consonants and vowels all over the place, our auditory system comes up with the trick of categorical perception, which breaks the continuous acoustic range into a few discrete categories. Two systems working in tandem seemed too much of a coincidence. Indeed, Alvin Liberman and colleagues at the Haskins Laboratory, who discovered the phenomena of coarticulation and categorical perception, proposed a radical theory:[13] we can hear *because* we can speak. We can extract speech categories even when they are mushed up because we know how to make the mush in the first place.[14] The coarticulation and categorical perception of speech are, therefore, parts of the same codebook delivered to the human species by evolution.

Liberman's theory gained popularity as Chomsky's universal grammar became prominent: both postulated innate and specialized systems for linguistic structure and knowledge. It is worth emphasizing, though, that the *knowledge* of speech is something more abstract and fundamental than the *ability* for speech. Suppose I broke my ankle, thus losing the ability to ride my bike; this would still leave my knowledge of bike riding intact. That is, certain neurological wiring was formed when I was five and was refined during the next twenty-five years. And this knowledge would readily kick in again when my ankle healed. Similarly, Liberman's theory holds that the abstract knowledge of speech is available innately, and coarticulation and categorical perception are the necessary consequences that will unfold in due time. Although babies do not have the ability to produce speech categories—that has to wait for the physiological maturation and fine-tuning of the vocal tract's dance—Liberman's theory does predict that categorical perception is available at birth: children must arrive with the codebook of speech in hand.

And indeed, they do. The HAS technique, which Mehler used to test newborns on French and Russian prosody in the 1980s, was in fact invented for the express purpose of testing Liberman's theory. Babies, some only one month old, were first habituated to the sound of *pah,* as their rate of sucking stabilized to a plateau. Peter Eimas and colleagues then started rolling the tape from *pah* to *bah* with nine intermediate sounds in between. Babies stayed bored until the boundary of 25 ms was crossed; the sucking rate then picked up and they were now in *pah* territory.

The *bah-pah* experiment was quickly replicated all over the world, on a much wider range of sounds—with unequivocal success. It was found, for instance, that babies are never going to confuse "mama" with "baba."[15] The consonants *b* and *m* differ in how the air travels through the vocal tract: out of the lips for *b* but through the nose for *m*. With a speech synthesizer, the amount of air passing through the two channels can be varied along a continuum, but babies again pick out two discrete categories.

Then came a striking revelation, which in turns offered striking support for Liberman's theory. Newborns are in fact *universal* listeners, equipped to grasp the sound patterns of all languages. For instance, Kikuyu, a language spoken in Kenya, doesn't have the *pah* vs. *bah* contrast used in English; Kikuyu newborns, however, distinguish the two sounds as easily as English babies.[16] Canadian (English-learning) babies can recognize utterly foreign consonants that are used in Polish and Czech.[17]

The little globetrotters' abilities can be most appreciated when contrasted with those of their feeble parents. A big challenge that Japanese and Korean adults face when learning English is the distinction of the consonants *r* and *l* as in "right" and "light." Both consonants are produced by the tongue curled up but in slightly different positions and therefore sound acoustically similar. Japanese and Korean speakers often can't detect the difference and, moreover, get the two sounds confused in speech.[18] As the stereotype goes, "ridiculous" becomes "ridicurous," and "fried rice" comes out as "flied lice," and as you can imagine, more embarrassing examples may surface during "*el*ection" years. Yet Japanese newborns have no problem telling *r* and *l* apart.[19] When it comes to the art of listening, babies aren't just smarter than you think, they are smarter than you.

A good detective story usually has a few twists and turns. Recent decades have brought out a more refined understanding of babies and speech, with more surprises along the way. Yes, babies are smarter than you think, but so are monkeys, chinchillas, and quails.[20]

For most categorical perception tests, we can count on some animals to do just as well as humans. Naturally, experiments have had to be modified. Novelty can be measured in a bird not by pacifier sucking, but by head turning, pecking, or other means more suitable to the animal's natural abilities. Categorical perception of consonants, measured with the same audio materials used in human infant experiments, can be found in many species, and often (but not always) around the same acoustic boundaries as humans. Evidently, the ability to recognize speech categories doesn't necessarily need a special codebook of speech. Categorical perception, once held to be evolution's gift to humans that came along with speech production, is unique neither to speech nor to humans. As we discussed earlier, categories pop out of the color continuum as well: it is just easier to see things as black and white rather than attempt to discern shades of gray.[21] Other species have their own favorite categories as well. Crickets, for examples, are sensitive to sounds in two frequency regions: around 4–5 kHz lies the call from other crickets, while in the 25–80 kHz range—ultrasound, and thus inaudible to us—are the signals produced by predator bats. Sounds in the intermediate range, however, do not cause any indecision. Researchers can continuously jack up the frequency from 4 to 5 kHz all the way to 10 to 20 kHz without causing any alarm. But after the threshold is crossed, make way for the cricket![22]

These findings appear to have put a dent in the exciting discovery of babies' talents for speech. To be sure, merely replicating human behaviors does not make animals human. Elephants and horses, for example, can be trained to walk on their hind legs but that doesn't make them bipedal like us. Conversely, doing bunny hops doesn't make me a kangaroo. Indeed, one of the criticisms of the animal studies is that while human babies are capable of categorical perception immediately after birth, animals often have to be trained extensively; perhaps qualitatively different mechanisms are at work. Nevertheless, categorical perception in other species does create some mystery and, in the academic world, debates and controversies over the nature of speech. Just how special is speech?

Make no mistake, language *is* uniquely human; here everyone is on the same page. But in what sense is it unique, now that monkeys and quails pick out the sounds of language much like human babies? To complicate matters further, we don't know enough about how a monkey's brain processes the sounds of speech, and for obvious reasons we know still less how a baby's brain does it. Therefore, we don't yet know whether or not comparable behavior across species is due to comparable neural mechanisms. However, we have every reason to welcome the discovery of impressive auditory abilities in other species—if only because it makes us less weird in the biological world, and our language less like an anomaly. The advent of molecular genetics has placed our departure from the rest of the animal kingdom at approximately 5 or 6 million years ago, when we took a separate path from the chimpanzees. On the grand scale of life, however, a few million years are merely a blink of the eye. Evolution didn't, and didn't have the time to, design us from scratch; old parts were recycled, so we find overwhelming similarities between humans and everything else in the biological world. One of these old parts—apparently shared to varying extents by crickets, quails, and monkeys—is the ability to roughly cut up the perceptual world, be it sight or sound, into discrete categories: the perception of human speech consonants may be the latest beneficiary. And it is easy to imagine potential advantages in the evolution of this ability. Who cares if that red spot in the jungle is pinkish, orange-ish, or cherry-ish: if it's red enough, run away!

Ultimately, human speech is special not because of the perception of categories; that is not even about speech per se. The fact that we can produce and recognize sound categories obscures what we *do* with these categories.[23] It is possible that a monkey can be trained to distinguish the pitch A-flat from C-sharp, but it is absolutely certain that he would never put those notes together like Brahms (or Eminem, for that matter). The same goes for language. We must remember that language is a complex package of abilities, only one of which is speech, and only one aspect of speech has to do with categories. And speech may not even be the prerequisite for the emergence of language. To wit, sign language users have categorical perception of manual gestures as well.[24] Deaf children learn sign languages. And where there isn't one already, they get together and invent one. A group of deaf children in Nicaragua created a brand-new sign language in the few short years after the Sandinista government's new education program brought them together.[25] Language doesn't have to be exclusively about the mouth or ears; speech may be a highly efficient physical medium of language, but it is not the only one, just as typing on a keyboard is only a (nonessential) physical means of writing. A 2003 BBC news report confirmed that, as long suspected, monkeys do seem to enjoy banging on a keyboard; but that doesn't turn them into Shakespeare.[26]

Distinguishing sound categories is where monkeys, chinchillas, and quails stop; the human baby, on the other hand, is just getting started. The uniqueness of human language lies in its *symbolic combinatorial* power. Only a human child will go on to treat *b* and *p* as linguistic units and combine (and recombine) them into syllables and words. Without this ability, *b* and *p* are just acoustic oddities that the auditory system can pick out; with it, their acoustic differences take on a new mission: their contrast is crucial to represent meanings, for "*b*at" and "*p*at" represent very different things. The uniqueness of speech lies not so much in the categories of sounds we can hear or produce, but in the ability to combine categories into messages in our native language. And perhaps the sounds in the world's languages are exactly those that fall into the sensitive regions of the auditory systems, which allows categorical perception (and fast speech) to take place.

We can push this thinking even further. What if other species did talk? Imagine a monkey that can talk—do bear with the gruesome thought—if we replace its vocal tract with a human's, which can produce speech categories such as *bah* and *pah*. Such a transplant, however, won't give the monkey language: the symbolic combinatorial system, which resides in our heads, would still be missing. Parrots, for instance, while good at imitating human sounds, show no sign of any combinatorial use of the sounds whatever.[27] Ultimately, it is the symbolic combinatorial system that separates human language from other communication systems. And it is this very system that turns universalist babies into native-tongue-tied adults.

Languages use different consonants and vowels. For native speakers, these peculiarities become a permanent fixture of the brain, which is obvious when we struggle to master the sounds of a foreign tongue as adults. A less obvious, but equally permanent, effect of learning a native language comes from *how* sounds are used. Recall the *r-l* challenge that Japanese and Korean adults face when learning English. Interestingly, these languages *do* make use of *r* and *l*: "Seou*l*" and "Ko*r*ea" are (naturally enough) words in Korean, where acoustic analysis reveals a measurable difference between the consonants—to which Korean speakers nevertheless remain oblivious. On the other hand, Korean babies would pass the *r-l* test with ease. And hence the puzzle: how come a Korean adult, who is an expert on her native language, does *worse* than a baby, who is still a novice?

This paradox is an excellent example of how the symbolic system of language makes use of sound categories in ways above and beyond acoustics. Why do English speakers readily recognize *r* and *l*? Because in English, these two consonants *compete*. They often occupy the same position in the syllable, and substituting one for the other turns a word into a totally different one. Below is a list of words that linguists call "minimal pairs":

| | |
|---|---|
| *r*ight | *l*ight |
| *r*ide | *l*ied |
| *r*eek | *l*eek |
| *r*ed | *l*ed |

English speakers, then, must take notice of the subtle acoustic differences between *r* and *l*, for they'd be confused otherwise. The very same two consonants, despite their presence in the Korean language, do not compete: *r* always appears before vowels, and *l* always appears after vowels. The fine contrast between them pays nothing, and Korean speakers are happy to ignore the distinction—just like one needn't remember which way to turn on a one-way street. The different roles that the *r-l* contrast plays in these two languages—in the case of Korean, none—leads to a curious phenomenon: English speakers actually hear *more* acoustic details in Korean than Korean speakers do. The contrast just leaps out; to wit, "Ko*r*ea" and "Seou*l*" end up in the English spelling system with two distinct letters.[28]

As Korean babies grow into Korean adults, a perfectly distinguishable acoustic contrast gets lost; only those sounds that are important to the words in the Korean language are retained. But exactly when does it occur? We all have friends who moved to another country at a young age and ended up learning the new language perfectly. However, what sounds like native command of a second language conceals the profound (and perhaps irreversible) specialization to the native language that has taken place very early.[29] In a series of important studies, the psychologists Janet Werker and Richard Tees tested English-speaking Canadian children on categorical perception of consonant pairs from Hindi and Salish (a Native American language still spoken in British Columbia, Canada), both of which were utterly foreign. They started with eight-year-olds and twelve-year-olds, with the expectation that the younger group, who generally could acquire a new language without perceptible accents, would pass the test, and the older group would not. Surprisingly, all these children failed just as badly as English-speaking adults. The researchers then tried four-year-olds; still no success. As the bar had to be pushed lower and lower, younger and younger children were brought into the lab. It turned out that as early as the eighth to tenth month, only half of the babies succeeded. By a baby's first birthday, the nonnative contrasts are gone.[30]

The specialization to the native tongue, then, sounds like an example of "use it or lose it," which would lend good support to our main thesis that language is learned by unlearning all other languages. Indeed, many parenting books have popularized this interpretation, which, coupled with the legend of baby Mozart, has caused endless worries among parents who fear that their toddlers may have "lost" their intellectual potential already. But I would urge caution.[31] We need to be careful about exactly *what* is lost in the specialization process. It was once thought that the native language permanently dulls out the universal auditory system available at birth, but the reality turns out to be more complicated.

First, it remains true that (sufficiently) young children can move to a new country and speak the language very well; this would not be possible if the auditory system lost the sensitivity to nonnative contrasts altogether.

Second, even adults can sometimes be *tricked* into being universal listeners again, but "tricked" is the key word. In one experiment,[32] a group of English speakers were told that they were listening to the sound of a dripping faucet. The sounds were in fact Hindi and Salish consonants, those nonnative contrasts "lost" before the first birthday. Yet differentiation remained possible. The auditory system remains perfectly sharp well into adulthood—that is, before old age gets to us—but that shows only for nonlinguistic sounds. When it comes to the perception of language, the fully specialized *mind* overrules the ears, guiding us to the native sounds.

Finally, Korean and Japanese speakers shouldn't give up either.[33] The contrast between *r* and *l* is still largely salvageable with diligent training if the drill mimics or amplifies the English-speaking children's experience—in other words, if the listener hears a lot of minimal pairs with *r* and *l* jostling for positions:

| | |
|---|---|
| *l*ash | *r*ash |
| b*l*ue | b*r*ew |
| e*l*ect | e*r*ect |
| ma*l*t | ma*r*t |

After a few intensive sessions of bombardment with such pairs, Japanese adults showed vast improvement on these two notorious consonants.[34] The unlearning of nonnative sounds, then, has little to do with auditory dulling, but rather reflects the growing stature of the native sounds as they are turned into linguistic symbols: the nonnative sounds have to make way.

There is no evidence that the unlearning of speech categories ever takes place in nonhuman species. It's inconceivable that a pet monkey raised in Boston would retain the consonant contrast between *r* and *l*, while its cousin raised in Seoul would lose it—though this should be verified by primate biologists. Speech still is, and will always be, a special gift for humans. Ultimately, though, the uniqueness of speech resides in our heads, rather than in our ears or on our lips. The power of speech lies in the cognitive ability to turn sounds (or signs) into symbols, and to combine them into meaningful messages.

Zeroing in on the native sound categories paves the road to words.[35] Between the sixth and the twelfth month, the baby doesn't have much of a vocabulary, but she has extracted the sounds that will be combined into words. She probably doesn't know what "bat" or "pat" means, but she's seen plenty of examples with *b* and *p* in competing positions: "bee," "pee," "bad," "pad," "buy," "pie," "bit," "pit," . . . Whatever these words are, they clearly mean different things; better pay attention.[36]

To get better at languages, the child seems to get worse first. But why? Why do we become narrow specialists of one language at the expense of universal potentials? A lifelong universalist capacity would be a useful thing to have around, if only for foreign language learning and thus a better traveling experience. But from a child's perspective— now we are speculating—there are good reasons to specialize. Life is already confusing enough and there is so much to learn. Specialization to the native language makes things simpler; if it doesn't fit in, throw it out.[37] Like in that old Simon and Garfunkel song, "A man hears what he wants to hear, and disregards the rest."

In the long journey to the native language, the first year is largely a silent rehearsal. The baby has been following the score, so to speak, but has not sung a single note. Not that she could: after all, the word "infant" comes from Latin, meaning "not able to speak." But it's almost time to put the sounds together, for the parents are getting anxious for the debut.

# CHAPTER 4

# Wuckoo

Massachusetts Avenue in Cambridge, not far from our old apartment, was under perpetual construction. It was there, on a noisy afternoon shortly after Russell's first birthday, that the long-awaited first word finally arrived.

"Wuckoo."

My wife and I never quite figured out what it meant, but something in the arena of civil engineering was a good guess: backhoes, excavators, cement mixers, and many construction vehicles we still can't name. The most likely source, however, was "truck."

Two lines of corroborating evidence support this theory. First, trucks—and there were plenty of them—appeared in a good part of our daily stroll, which may also account for Russell's impressive devotion to big machines that continues to this day, now complete with equally impressive knowledge of what they are and how they work. Second, and more compellingly to his linguist parents, "wuckoo" and "truck" sound suspiciously alike. True, considerable disparities remain: a vowel (oo) was stuck on at the end, and two consonants (t and r) collapsed into an altogether different one. These improvisations are not wild; as we shall see, they fall squarely in line with those made by Russell's friends in the neighborhood:

Neal said "ba" and meant "baby."
Madison said "wock" and meant "rock."
Connor said "tar" and meant "star."
Jennifer said "wawa" and meant "water."

Even though the first spoken words are rarely faithful to their targets, they are sophisticated products of a linguistic system that has been steadily under construction. The one-year-old has come a long way, and we will need a similarly lengthy explanation for how "truck" morphed into "wuckoo."

Before children start talking, they need to figure out what to say. Which is hardly a no-brainer. Spoken words, as you may recall from earlier chapters, don't have pauses in between; they have to be pulled out of speech.[1]

"Truck," however, might have been an easy one for Russell. As well-intentioned middle-class parents, we never left him alone. Everything of interest—what *we* believed to be interesting to *him,* that is—was duly pointed out: "Truck!" The same is probably true for "Bottle," "Rock," "Water," "Mommy," and "Cookie." These sentences are exactly one word long; so at least for these, words do have pauses in between, when we break one sentence before saying another. In fact, almost 10 percent of sentences children hear consist of only one word,[2] which, as a stand-alone item, can be cherry-picked for free.

Well, almost free. Put yourself in a child's shoes and think about it. An isolated word is easy to find only if the child knows it is *in fact* isolated—but how does she know for sure? A baby has no words to begin with, so everything she hears is simply a sequence of sounds. Length of the sequence doesn't provide reliable clues for words: shorter sequences may contain multiple words ("eatit," "Isee"), while long ones may in fact be single words ("refrigerator," "spaghetti"). Alas, the Scandal of Induction strikes again: any string of sounds can always be broken up into many chunks, each of which is a potential word—"cookie" may well be two words ("coo" and "kie"). Just as in the Gavagai dilemma, hidden assumptions bail us out. Children are helped by innate knowledge of how sounds are assembled into words.

Imagine yourself in a foreign land, having to learn words from scratch. Perhaps we don't need to be that harsh: George Lucas's world of *Star Wars* will suffice, but you do need to put your frame of mind back to 1977, when the movie's now familiar dramatis personae made their debut. Recall the first time you heard the sound "Chewbacca."

(Not because it is particularly galactic; as we shall see in a moment, the shaggy giant's name was clearly made up to accommodate English-speaking movie viewers.) We don't have to know anything about its meaning to be certain about one thing: "Chewbacca" is exactly one word. By comparison, "Darthvader," a sound sequence of equal length and novelty, contains exactly two. Such confidence stems from three pieces of fundamental linguistic knowledge, the kind of hidden assumptions that guide us—children and adults alike—to discover new words.

First, the discovery of words requires knowledge of how words are structured from sounds. Much like the making of a sentence, in which a seemingly linear sequence of words is grouped into larger units of phrases, the seemingly linear sounds of words also cluster into larger units of *syllables*. The boundaries between syllables must be respected, even when our language is foul. Sometimes we insert profanities in words: "abso-blooming-lutely," "fan-bloody-tastic," and I trust that you can come up with more vulgar specimens. But notice that the expletive is always stuck in between two syllables. We might have to remind the child not to swear, but syllable integrity is a higher authority altogether: try splitting up the syllable in "abs-blooming-olutely."

Children nowadays often learn to count syllables by clapping along: ti-ger, mon-key, and tur-tle. But the grouping of speech into syllables probably doesn't wait till kindergarten—and needn't be taught. Even four-day-olds, who of course cannot count, measure the length of words in units of syllables rather than sounds. As demonstrated in a series of experiments by Jacques Mehler's research group, babies notice sounds that differ in the number of syllables (*bada* vs. *depiku*), but pay no attention to sounds that differ only in length but not syllable counts (*bada* vs. *teklog*).[3] This is instant good news for the child learner. Larger units means shorter sequences, which translates into fewer possibilities to consider when finding words. Instead of *ch-ew-b-a-cc-a*, which is six sounds, we have *chew-ba-cca*, only three syllables, and the same goes for *darth-va-der*.

The second assumption about syllables is that not all syllables are created equal. In fact, one of the syllables in a word screams out—as the loudest. Every word has a syllable that carries the primary stress, whose vowel is pronounced in a heavier voice than others.[4] This information is lost when spoken words are printed on paper—"Elvis recorded many records"—but it is not lost on the baby. Seven-and-a-half-month-olds pay more attention to the stressed syllables than unstressed ones, and this is critical for finding words.[5] And here is the key: universally, a single word can have only one primary stress. If we hear a sequence of sounds, no matter how short or long, that has only one stressed syllable, then the whole thing must be a single word. Now the "free" one-word sentences really do come for free: the utterance "spaghetti" is only one word, and so the child can proceed to file it away. For the same reason, "Chewbacca" must be one word, "Darth-Vader" must be two words, "ObiWanKenobi" must be three, and "greeneggsandham" must be four.

But we are getting just a little ahead of ourselves. Before we pick out the stressed syllable, a sequence of sounds has to be broken into the right syllables: why darth-va-der, rather than dar-thva-der? The final piece of knowledge about words has to do with the internal structure of syllables in our language, which is on full display in a game of Scrabble. Suppose you have drawn seven tiles: E, L, O, S, T, A, and N. As usual, you find yourself searching for words and scrambling tiles at random—except that it's not random at all. The permutations of seven tiles lead to 5,040 potential words, and no one can handle that many combinations. Before you reach out for *The Official Scrabble Players Dictionary* (unless you are like my office mate in graduate school, who memorized the whole thing) a lot of combinations have to be pruned away. For example, you might wonder if "TOLE" is an actual word (it is), but you would never look up "TSOLE" or "NLAS." The elimination of impossible words is handled jointly by the universal knowledge of syllable structure and the specific knowledge of our native language.

At the core of a syllable is the vowel. Consonants that go before the vowel are called the *onset*, and those that follow the vowel make up the *coda*. The structure within the syllable is not linear, either: the vowel and the coda are closer still, forming the unit the *rime*. Linguists like to use structures like a genealogical tree to denote the togetherness of units. For example, *a* (vowel) and *t* (coda) are grouped together as rime, which is then combined with *c* (onset) to build the whole syllable.

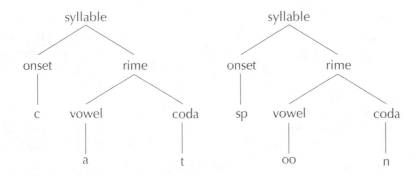

   The integrity of the rime as an inseparable unit is best illustrated, surprisingly, by how speech breaks down. A peculiar type of slip-of-the-tongue is known as a spoonerism, named after the Reverend William A. Spooner, an Oxford don in the nineteenth century.[6] The reverend was famous for misspeaking: "noble sons of toil" came out as "noble tons of soil" and "you have missed my history lectures; you have wasted the whole term" turned into "you have hissed my mystery lectures, you have tasted the whole worm." Freud once proposed that misspeaking reveals suppressed thoughts and desires. This would have left the Reverend with a lot of explaining to do for his most famous slip, "queer old dean" for "dear old Queen." Linguists now know that misspeaking reflects the complex organization of words in the memory, which occasionally goes haywire in real-time execution, and a spoonerism is one of the most frequent failings. The Reverend's errors illustrate the rime as an cohesive unit within the syllable: all involve swapping the onset, leaving the rime—that is, the vowel and the coda together.
   Rimes are also what rhyme:

> Tiger, tiger, burning br*ight*
> In the forests of the n*ight*

Even young children can make up nonsense rhyming words: pight, clight, or zight—yet vlight, dnight, or ptight will never be forthcoming.[7] Only certain consonant combinations, or "clusters," are possible onsets, and only these may participate in word making, real or creative. Pight, clight, and zight can *in principle* become English words, while vlight, dnight, and ptight stand no chance. Likewise, only certain consonants can be codas: di*mg* and te*ln*, for instance, are not possible English words either. For these reasons, darth-vader is darth-va-der, but not dar-thva-der, or darthv-a-der: *thv* is not a possible onset or coda in English, so it must be split up across two syllables. One of the least known job prospects for a linguistics degree is on Madison Avenue in the advertising industry (another is the CIA). In a country where even foreign movie subtitles are anathema, it is critical to come up with product names that sound English (maybe with a pinch of foreign flair): hence we have Excedrin, Zima, and Viagra. But there is no rhyme—not rime!—or reason why English forbids *thv*, *vl*, or many other imaginable consonants from starting a syllable. True, a few consonants squished together could be a mouthful, but many languages do just that: to wit, *Vl*adimir Nabokov, the Russian writer, and *Zb*igniew *Brz*ezinski, President Carter's national security adviser, who is of Polish heritage.

Back to the Scrabble board. The child is again quietly ahead in her own game of building words. To get the words right, the child needs correctly partitioned syllables, which in turn requires knowing what can, and cannot, start or finish a legitimate syllable in English. Peter Jusczyk and colleagues, who made many important discoveries about how children learn words, found that such knowledge is formed sometime between the sixth and the ninth month.[8] Their experiments showed that both Dutch and English babies, before they have said a single word, know what their future words should sound like: when given the choice of made-up English and Dutch words, with respectively English and Dutch onsets and codas, children much prefer their native language.

A word isn't learned until the child puts it into vocabulary storage. Even then, crucial information may still be missing: did Russell's "wuckoo" actually mean "truck," or simply anything large, metallic, and noisy? (We will never find out.) An obvious though not particularly helpful fact about words, courtesy of the influential Swiss linguist Ferdinand de Saussure (1857–1913), is that they are arbitrary mappings between sounds and meanings. *Vache*, *ghwaa*, *niu*, *bagoshi*, and *puluku* all mean "cow," in, respectively, French, Pashto (spoken in Afghanistan), Mandarin Chinese, Navajo (Native American), and Warlpiri (aboriginal of Australia), but none sounds remotely like MOO: they all have to be learned by fiat.

Words are *very* mysterious things. Ever since Plato, some of the most brilliant minds in human history have wrestled with the meanings of completely banal words—"chair," "water," "London"—without much success.[9] A philosophical discursion on the meaning of meanings will take us too far afield, but we shall return in Chapter 6 to some more tangible aspects of word meanings and how children acquire them.[10] The sound side of words, by contrast, is far better studied, and children, in any case, appear to pick up pronunciations of words before meanings.

Even eight-month-olds can memorize sounds of words.[11] Peter Jusczyk and Elizabeth Hohne paid a group of children several home visits. Each time, the children heard three stories that used a set of words that the baby was highly unlikely to be familiar with: "vine," "python," "peccaries," for instance. After a two-week break, the researchers returned with another set of new (and equally unfamiliar) words that nevertheless sounded like those that the babies had actually heard. Both old and new words were mixed up together in random order and read aloud to the babies. The old set of words turned out to hold the babies' attention significantly longer: they had apparently registered in memory through the earlier story sessions. These are not words, mind you. "Word" is a term reserved for instances in which reliable mappings between sound and meaning are established; for "python" and "peccaries," meaning will have to wait.

Even just a few words can be tremendously useful; old words can become seeds for new words.[12] Apparently, the child does some sort of word arithmetic, or subtraction, to be precise. If she already knows the word "big," then "couch" can be stripped out of an utterance for free:

$$
\begin{array}{r}
\text{bigcouch} \\
-\ \text{big} \\
\hline
=\ \text{couch}
\end{array}
$$

Again, revealing evidence comes from children's errors: word subtraction can get a little overenthusiastic. They do say the darnedest things. Was your child "hiccing up"? Does she talk about "yesternight," generalizing from "yester-day"? Many parents have been confounded when the reminder "Behave yourself!" was repeatedly ignored yet the child insisted, "I *was* hayve!" And who can blame them? "Be nice," "Be quiet," "Be gentle," "Be quick"—so why not "Be hayve"?

My favorite examples, naturally, come from Russell. Of the new children in his day-care class:

"Three body came to school today."
"He's a nice body!"

Perfect. Knowing "some," "no," and "any," he had every reason to strip these out and treat "body" as a stand-alone word. Misanalysis of words alone, however, is not solely responsible for his feeling as our equal, and this one will be fondly remembered forever:

"There are three dults in our family!"

Determined to find out how big a role old words play in finding new words, I set up a little experiment. Printed on a card was a picture of tulips, like the one below:

Here is how the experiment went.[13]

Charles: Look! Tulips!
Russell: No! Three lips! And one is just a baby.

With a small vocabulary built up and tucked away in memory, the child is ready to say her first words.

Talk may be cheap but it sure isn't simple. The precise timing, coordination, and movement of articulation rivals even the most sophisticated gymnastic routines. Compare the art of speech to the art of baseball hitting. A major league batter has just 25 milliseconds to decide whether to swing or let the ball fly by, and another 25 to pick a swing (high, low, inside, outside)—and even Ted Williams managed only a lifetime average of .344. By contrast, we top the batting champ every time we open our mouth: 25 milliseconds, as you may recall from Chapter 3, is the delay of vocal cord vibration that turns "*bah*" into "*pah.*" After all, our biology is built for speaking, not for swinging a bat.

To master the gymnastics of speech takes time, even though Nature has done most of the work. To begin with, biological maturation has to be in place before the vocal tract is physiologically flexible enough for the articulation of speech. Greater flexibility of the vocal tract, however, could be a problem. If the acoustic tunnel—in a saxophone or a vocal tract—can be molded into numerous shapes, then the airflow passing through could lead to equally numerous sounds.

Luckily for the child learner, human language employs only a tiny fraction of the sounds that the vocal tract makes, so there are not too many to learn. Grunts, hisses, and whistles, which could be perfectly expressive, are not used in verbal communication in any language: these sounds, unlike consonants and vowels, are not used in a symbolic and combinatorial way. There have been surprises though. The click sounds, which can be approximated as "tsk" in English spelling, play no role in the sound systems of European languages but are used in quite a few African languages, such as Zulu. Even within the range of possible linguistic sounds, languages do a lot of picking and choosing. English uses about forty consonants and vowels, falling on the lower end of the spectrum ranging from about a dozen (Polynesian) to over 140 (Khoisan, one of the click languages in southern Africa). These differences between languages often reveal the origin of "accents." German doesn't have the *th* sounds in "think" and "that" (really two sounds despite the identical spelling); so for a German speaker of English, "this thing" is often "zis sing." English speakers have trouble with French consonants and vowels: more than once have I been humiliatingly corrected by customs officials at the Charles de Gaulle International Airport. And despite its orthography, my last name actually—and still only approximately—rhymes with "song," rather than "sang," but I stopped correcting people a long time ago.

The diversity of sounds across languages is striking (and fun), but even more striking—and fun, at least to scientists—are the deep similarities they share. This, we shall see, further simplifies the child's task of learning to speak; it also eventually helps us make sense of how "truck" morphed into "wuckoo."

One of the crowning achievements of linguistics is the discovery that all speech sounds are in fact the product of very few articulatory organs—lips, tongue, and in some cases, the nose—in independent but coordinated movements. To modern linguists and speech scientists, the vowels and consonants that we have been speaking of have the status of "salt" and "sugar" to a chemist: they are convenient labels of complex substances made of elementary particles (sodium chloride, $C_{12}H_{22}O_{11}$). And we don't need a Bunsen burner to figure out the elements of speech. Much of this insight can be traced back to the 150-year-old work of A. Melville Bell and his sons, including Alexander Graham, the inventor of the telephone.

The Bells were in the difficult business of teaching speech to the deaf, and there were thus professional reasons for their theory of language: *visible speech*. Visible, because the theory holds that much of speech articulation can be directly observed (so the deaf can be taught to speak). In a lecture delivered in 1900, Alexander Graham Bell remarked:

> What we term an "element of speech" may in reality . . . be a combination of positions. The true element of articulation, I think, is a constriction or position of the vocal organs rather than a sound.

Combinations of positions yield new sounds, just as combinations of chemical elements yield new substances. Water is a substance of very different character from either of the gases of which it is formed; and the vowel *oo* is a sound of very different character from that of any of its elementary positions.[14]

We can literally feel how the chemistry of speech works. Consider the consonants in *"fee," "tea," "pea,"* and *"see."* One way of looking at them is that they are arbitrary sounds produced by the vocal tract, just like the four arbitrary symbols in the English alphabet. But this would miss quite a few interesting similarities as well as differences. All consonants are produced with some blockage of the airflow through the vocal tract; where and how such constrictions are formed determine the sound we produce. In *f,* the constriction is made with the lips, whereas in *t,* the air is stopped by the tongue tip pushed up against the hard palate, which is located just behind the upper teeth. These two consonants, then, differ in the place of articulation. There is another dimension in which *f* and *t* are contrasted. In *t,* the air flow first comes to a complete stop, followed by a small explosion; this is unmistakable if you hold a candle directly in front of the mouth and say "tea." In making the sound of *f,* by comparison, there is a little bit of air leakage throughout, creating an audible hissing: *t* is thus a *stop* and *f* is called a *fricative.* (Please consult the glossary if the text gets too jargon laden: I will strive to keep it at a minimum.) Now *p* and *s* start to look interesting—they are hybrids. Like *f, p* uses the lips to form air constriction, and like *t,* it is a stop. Like *f, s* is a fricative, and like *t,* constriction is formed by the tongue tip.

A few more atoms of articulation will be needed for the diverse range of consonants used in human languages, but not too many more: the ways in which articulatory organs interact multiply quickly. For example, another common manner of articulation is voicing— whether the vocal cords vibrate or not—which is the difference between *b* and *p* as you may recall from "bah" vs. "pah" in Chapter 3. This immediately doubles our inventory of consonants: *f, t, p,* and *s* are all voiceless, but by adding the vibration of the vocal cords we can make consonants such as in *"vee," "dee," "bee,"* and *"zee."* For (yet) another class of consonants, the air constriction in the vocal tract is made by the tongue body, pressed upward at the back of the mouth. Viewed this way, $k$ in "key" is a composite of three actions: (tongue body) × (stop) × (voiceless), and $g$ in "gig" is just like $k$, except it is voiced. Finally, the nose is also implicated in speech articulation. For some consonants, the airflow is forced out of the nasal passage, while the articulatory organs in the oral cavity (lips, tongue tip, tongue body) can shift around independently. Putting these together, we get "*m*eal," "*n*eed," and "si*ng*." In the table below, you can find the atoms of consonants, but you can also read the brain directly. As recent work on neuroimaging demonstrates, the auditory cortex shows specific activation patterns that correspond to just these articulatory dimensions.[15]

|  |  | lips | tongue tip | tongue body |
|---|---|---|---|---|
| Stop | voiceless | p | t | k |
|  | voiced | b | d | g |
| Fricative | voiceless | f | s |  |
|  | voiced | v | z |  |
| Nasal | voiced | m | n | ng |

Unlike consonants, vowels are produced with virtually no obstruction of the air, but like consonants, vowels can also be described as coordinated actions among independent articulatory organs. The tongue again figures prominently, but its freedom of movement is again severely limited. Despite the flexibility of the tongue, thanks to the numerous nerves controlling that muscular lump, vowels in human languages use very few positions that the tongue can reach. Feel the vowels in "bit," "bet," and "bat." A moment of probing reveals that for all these vowels the tongue is located in the front of the mouth, but moves from a high position for "bit," to a midlevel for "bet," and hits the bottom for "bat," respectively, at least for most speakers of North American English. Now keep the high-mid-low levels but pull the tongue to the back of the mouth: we suddenly have the vowels in "book," "bought," and "bop," though you might find some dialectical variation here. When the tongue is neither at the front nor back, it is (naturally) in the central area, where we find vowels like those in "but" and "bar," with one higher than the other.

| | Front | Central | Back |
|---|---|---|---|
| High | bit | | book |
| Middle | bet | but | bought |
| Low | bat | bar | bop |

So much for this detour to see the atoms of speech. The modern formulation of the Visible Speech theory was laid out by Roman Jakobson,[16] an intellectual giant of the twentieth century whose influence extends to architecture, anthropology, and literary criticism. (Jakobson, whose first language was Russian, became fluent in six languages but, in his own words, "all in Russian.") It is the combinations of a small number of features that yield the rich and varied range of sounds in human language. In case you have wondered, clicking in Zulu is another manner of articulation, on par with stops, fricatives, and nasals. And like those, it also combines with the lips, tongue tip, and tongue body, producing an ever varied array of clicks.

As the Bells rightly recognized, language instruction ought to start with some understanding of how speech sounds are made by using and combining a universal inventory of speech. But before the development of the X-ray, some aspects of speech articulation were not directly observable: one couldn't, for instance, see where the tongue goes in the back of the mouth for the vowels in book vs. bop. To demonstrate the mechanisms of speech articulation, Alexander Graham Bell had to make do with a rather grotesque talking head: the lips were made out of wires, the larynx was a flexible tin pipe with a rubber sheet stretched over it as the vocal cord, and the whole device was worked by levers controlled from a keyboard.[17] To study the mechanics of vocalization, Bell carried out some dubious experiments on his terrier: the dog was made to growl while he massaged its neck, thereby modifying its vocal tract. Ethics and aesthetics aside, the basic principles of speech production were fairly well understood: the sounds of language are made by combinations of independently moving but precisely coordinated articulatory organs.

As the science of speech progresses, technology has moved forward along the way. It would have pleased the Bells to see the modern incarnation of the visible speech theory serving its original purpose. For example, the speech scientist Dominic Massaro at the University of California at Santa Cruz developed a computer-animated talking head showing the precise mechanics of speech, which has proven to be a fun and effective aid for deaf children learning to speak.[18] I am deeply puzzled, and I'm sure I'm not alone, why students learning a foreign language do not use similar systems as well. Rather than relying on the already specialized perception system (Chapter 3) to discern the subtleties in foreign pronunciations, surely it would be more effective to observe speech articulation in action: seeing is believing.

Babies, on the other hand, require no special devices. From very early on, children have noted the intimate connection between the sounds of language and how such sounds are made. The psychologists Patricia Kuhl and Andrew Meltzoff designed an experiment showing that four-to-five-month-old babies are capable of lip-reading. Two TV screens are set up in front of the baby: on one, someone is silently mouthing the vowel *ee,* for which the mouth is horizontally stretched out, while on the other, someone is mouthing *ah,* for which the mouth is characteristically wide open. When a loudspeaker plays one of these vowels, the baby can reliably turn to the matching face.[19] Although this ear-to-mouth mapping is by no means necessary for learning to speak—blind children, for example, learn to speak just fine—it could help the child to identify the articulatory actions of speech. Full-blown speech, even babbling, takes time, but knowing what to look for is a good start.

Indeed, it will be a long while before this impressive speech engine kicks into full gear. At birth, the vocal tract of an infant is shaped like that of a chimpanzee: the larynx is high, the tongue is big (relative to the mouth), and the vocal tract is therefore short and its movement severely restricted.[20] So the newborn is limited to grunts, snorts, and of course, wails. But these vocal maneuvers are truly baby stuff compared to the complexity of speech. Crying, for instance, requires no movement of the articulators; just keeping the mouth wide open and the vocal cords stiffened will do. Starting from the third or fourth month, profound changes will take place in the baby's vocal tract. The most significant development is the lowering of the larynx, which creates a more spacious vocal tract, a necessary step toward speech.

At about six months, babies start to babble. Regardless of the language they eventually learn, early babbling sounds pretty much the same. Babbles are not words, despite the similarities in their structures. Words, as we discussed earlier, are made out of syllables; so is babbling, which consists almost exclusively of consonant-vowel sequences at the beginning. Some of these are repetitions of a single syllable ("babababa"), while others have more varieties of consonant-vowel combinations ("dabidagu"); neither, however, means anything. This may come as a bitter disappointment to parents who were overjoyed by the first sound of "mama," "baba," or "papa." Quite simply, consonants like *b, p,* and *m* are among the easiest, earliest, and most frequent sounds made.[21] The sequences of syllables in babbling require a rhythmic alternation of opening and closing of the mouth.[22] When the mouth opens, *ah* and *a* (as in "bat") are the most natural vowels to produce. When the mouth closes, labial consonants, including stops (*b, p*) and nasals (*m, n*) are the only kind possible. By contrast, fricatives such as *f, v,* and *s,* which require gradual leaking of the air, are less frequent and appear later when finer control of the vocal tract is in place.

Babbling was once thought to have nothing to do with speech or language; after all, what's babbling good for if it conveys no meaning to serve the purpose of communication? This view turns out to be doubly wrong. First, language does not necessarily involve communication with others. We talk to ourselves all the time, especially children, who are famous for those self-absorbed monologues about, well, whatever comes to their mind. Second, and more important, babbling bears the hallmark of language learning: it is the work of both nature and nurture, the joint product of a uniquely human predisposition for language plus linguistic experience from the environment. Parrots may have the right genes for imitating human speech, but they don't have the right genes to break speech into discrete units of sounds and then put them together again; unlike human babies, parrots do not babble. In other words, parrots can play back perfectly "meaningful" speech; it is the meaningless combinations of sounds that prove impossible.

On the other hand, human children, who do have the right genes for babbling, will not do so when deprived of linguistic experience. While deaf children show some signs of vocalization, they do not produce systematic syllable sequences like hearing children.[23] Yet, deaf children do babble—with their hands—if they are exposed to sign language. The psychologist Laura Ann Petitto and her colleagues found that deaf children spontaneously make hand gestures.[24] These gestures are different from shaking, waving, and other kinds of generic manual movements. They are picked out of the combinatorial sets of signs— specific hand shapes, locations, movements, etc.—in the sign language used by adults around deaf babies. And all the other hallmarks of vocal babbling are present here as well: manual babbling emerges at the same time, is devoid of meaning, but is rhythmic, repetitive, and combinatorial all the while. Finally, manual babbling eventually turns into meaningful manual signs, again at around the same time that words replace babbling in hearing children. Viewed this way, babbling is an essential, and irrepressible, engine of language. All children have the combinatorial system that makes infinite use of a finite set of symbols—be they consonants, vowels, or hand shapes. The senselessness of babbling is the prelude to the infinite senses soon to come.

While babbling doesn't make children understood, it does serve an important purpose; it is the warm-up to speech, as the child tries to figure out how to put the articulatory organs together to make sounds. Soon after the universalist beginning, babbling adapts to the child's native language. This transformation is much like the specialization of the speech perception system: babbling also starts from the universal repertoire and finishes with specific adaptations to the native language.[25]

The specialization of babbling may not be obvious to parents, who, after all, speak the very language. But it becomes clear when babies and parents are switched. The linguist Bénédicte de Boysson-Bardies and colleagues taped babbling from eight-month-old French and Arabic babies; from the recordings alone, French adults can fairly reliably identify French babies.[26] In a further study, the researchers found that the acoustic properties of the vowels in French, English, Cantonese, and Arabic babbling are remarkably similar to those in corresponding adult vowels. The specialization, moreover, is not restricted to sounds; it also extends to syllable structures, as children depart from the universal consonant-vowel template. Most words in Yoruba, the language spoken in Nigeria, begin with a vowel. Boysson-Bardies found that Yoruba babies indeed babble like Yoruba; over 60 percent of their syllables begin with a vowel, compared to about 30 percent in the babbling of French, English, and Swedish, three languages in which most words start with a consonant.[27]

First words replace babbling around the first birthday. Yet, as every parent must have wondered, "Just what exactly is he *saying*?" Could it be that a better question—for a language acquisition researcher, of course—is, "Just what exactly is he *hearing*?" That is, before we blame children for misspeaking, we have to rule out the possibility of mishearing. Learning words would start off on the wrong footing if the perception system gets the signals wrong.

It is a relief to know that mishearing is not usually the problem. The child may say "goat," instead of "coat," but she (probably) doesn't think that we put on an animal on a cold winter morning. By the time a child starts using words, her speech perception system has adapted to the particular consonants and vowels in her language. Indeed, when researchers gave a plastic fish to children who substituted the *sh* sound with *s* in their speech, the following exchange was typical:[28]

Adult: Is this your fis?
Child: No, my fis.
Adult: Is this your fish?
Child: Yes, my fis.

And children often know that they talk funny. Amahl, the son of the linguist Neil Smith (who co-invented the unlearnable language Epun in Chapter 2), used to say "dup" for "jump." Neil's repeated attempts to correct Amahl's pronunciation ("Say *jump*") amounted to nothing, but the two-year-old cheerfully offered an explanation: "Oli daddy gan day dup," or "Only daddy can say jump."[29] For "goat," "fis," and "dup," it is children's articulatory packaging that throws us off.

As if to further frustrate their parents, young children's earliest words are moving targets: the same word does not always come out sounding the same.[30] A child may have said "baba" for the word "baby," but is now saying "bibi," and might well say it perfectly one hour later. My Yale colleagues Louis Goldstein and Michael Studdert-Kennedy, however, managed to find order in this chaos.[31] Children's fickle words obscure the fact that even the youngest has, remarkably accurately, identified the articulators involved in the pronunciations of words. The use of the correct articulators is in fact quite consistent: what goes haywire is the timing and coordination among the articulators, which, like an exquisite clock, require some fine-tuning in the months to come.

Indeed, first words often bear the characteristics and vestiges of babbling. Fricatives, those hissing consonants rare in babbling, continue to be rare among the first words. It is not for lack of trying, though; the child has to make do with the easier sounds. Very often "see" becomes "tee" and "Zach"—a boy's name—becomes "Dak," and we can appreciate children's effort with the atom theory of speech. Instead of stipulating that the child can say this consonant but not that one, we see that she gets part of it right, and part of it wrong:

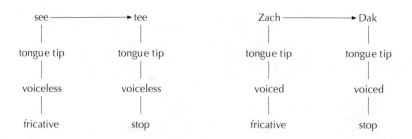

In both cases, the child has substituted the easier stop for the fricative, while the other components of the consonants are perfectly intact.

There are harder sounds still. The "interdental" consonants in "this" and "think," aptly named as you can verify for yourself, are among the most difficult sounds to produce, which is probably why they are quite rare across the sound inventories in the world's languages. The mastery of these doesn't come until the child is three or four years old; until then the novice just has to cut some corners: "thumb" may become "some," "both"—"bof," "though"—"zoe," "that"—"dat." And again, it is a mix-and-match exercise with articulatory atoms. The *th* in both "thumb" and "both," in addition to being interdental, is also fricative, and voiceless; these latter two features are correctly retained in "*some*" and "bo*f*." On the other hand, the *th* in "though" and "that" is voiced, and so are "*z*oe" and "*d*at."

Another challenge—and of particular interest to me—is the consonant *r*, as in "Russell." The main difficulty with this consonant, as well as *l* as in "lake," lies in the delicate curl of the tongue tip during articulation. Fortunately, English has two other consonants, as in "*y*es" and "*w*ater," that provide reasonable substitutes.[32] All four consonants have relatively little air constriction, and particularly so with *y* and *w*, which are referred to as semivowels. ("*A e i o u*, but sometimes *y* and *w*," remember?) Again, corner-cutting happens only in the realm of articulatory proximity: *w*, a labial, and thus easier, consonant, and *y*, a tongue-tip consonant but with no curling, often assume the identities of *l* and *r*. "Rock" becomes "wok," "blue"—"bwoo," and "light"—"yight." Even at the age of three and a half, and after having mastered the consonant *l*, Russell continued to call his room "woom," his friend Ruby "Wuby," and himself "Wussell." (No explanation for "wuckoo" yet, but we are getting there.)

While there are typical behaviors as children utter their earliest words, there is no typical child. All children are different: their vocal tracts have different sizes and shapes, their physiological maturation follows somewhat different schedules, and above all, they have different parents (so they hear different words). Nevertheless, if there were one general law that explains the forms of early words, then it must be the good old K.I.S.S. principle, or Keep It Simple, Stupid. Much of early speech can be explained by the child's tendency to conform to the linguistically neutral structures and articulatorily simple sounds.

Again we see the heritage of babbling, whose influence is not restricted only to the simplification of sounds. The template of consonant-vowel combination, dating back to the "mama" and "papa" days, remains the dominant pattern. As a result, long syllables are often trimmed, or omitted altogether:

cat—ka
soap—so
star—tar
blue—bu

In big words, even whole syllables may be dropped. For a long time, Russell's favorite animal was "Toy Rex," for *Tyrannosaurus rex* (what else!). The following renditions may be familiar to parents:

water—wa
bottle—ba
balloon—loon
banana—nana
telephone—tephone
dessert—zert
helicopter—koter

Indeed, these patterns really ought to be familiar to *all* of us. Adults drop whole syllables: except when we do it, they are not errors but "abbreviations."

laboratory—lab
dormitory—dorm
submarine—sub
nuclear—nuke
cellular—cell

We—both adults and children—are in fact quite picky about what we leave out.[33] In the case of children, it involves more than just the difficulty of saying longer words. For instance, a child may say "zert" for "dessert"; "de," which is still shorter and easier for articulation, will not be forthcoming. At play is our knowledge of word stress—the same information, you may recall, that has been instrumental in finding words in the first place. In general, the syllable carrying the primary stress is kept by both children and adults, as you can verify for yourself. Even children's failings are constrained by their success.

Simplification doesn't always mean leaving things out; children may also improvise under their articulatory constraints. For instance, a child may mean to say "spill" but manage only "fill," where two consonants are rolled into one.[34] This is pure genius. Recall that *s* is a fricative and *p* is a labial; since making two consonants is too hard, the child will have to make do with one—*f* is a labial and fricative *at the same time*.

Making words shorter is not the only way to make them simpler. Children may even make words longer; adding sounds to words can make them conform to the consonant-vowel template. "Duck" may be "duckoo," "car" may be "kaka," and the loud banger in the living room is the "pinano." This finally brings us to Russell's metamorphosis of "truck." First, the two consonants (*tr*) were simplified to just *r*, which was then substituted by a *w*. And finally, an extra vowel *oo* was stuck in for the sake of the consonant-vowel sequence:

"Wuckoo."

We started this chapter with a baby, and let's close it with some American presidents. George W. Bush has been singled out by language guardians for pronouncing "nuclear" as "nuculer," but the habit of cutting corners in speech really is in all of us.[35] "Nuclear" consists of two sticky junctures: the consonant bundle *cl* is a mouthful, while *ear* is really two vowels (*ee* and *er*) rolled together. The K.I.S.S. way, then, is to resort back to the consonant-vowel template—"nuculer" follows. Folks have been saying that for a long time; indeed, the Merriam-Webster Dictionary lists "nuculer" as one of the alternative pronunciations, duly noting, however, "disapproved of by many." Nonstandard pronunciations of "nuclear" could be found in the speech of Eisenhower, Kennedy, Ford, Carter, and Clinton, so perhaps Dubya has a legitimate case that he has been unfairly singled out by the liberal media.

Children's vocabulary size may hover around fifty words six months after uttering the first word. And these earliest words are like pebbles on the beach: although "mommy," "daddy," and the family pet are safe bets, there is no telling what other words might pop into the collection. Stereotypes of boys and construction machines notwithstanding, Russell's "wuckoo" (for *truck*) was a surprise. Some of his other early words included "pepa" (for *pepper*), "duhnt" (for *done*), "wawa" (for *vacuum*), "ya" (for *ear*), and "goosah" (for *goodness*): all perfectly cute, but perfectly unpredictable as well. As such, these earliest words are very much disjointed units of information, scattered around a baby-sized vocabulary: a verb here, a noun there, some starting with nasal consonants, some ending in *t*. But that is about to change. The rate of word learning picks up considerably six months after the first word. And the child is learning more than just more words: she is also starting to connect them.

CHAPTER 5

# Word Factory

How many words do you know?

Don't guess: vocabulary size is not something we mere mortals can intuit. The prolific French writer Georges Simenon—with some 450 novels and stories to his credit—once remarked that his writing style had to be simple because most French people used only six hundred words. Then again, he also claimed to have slept with ten thousand women: perhaps Mr. Simenon was numerically challenged.

More serious offenses have been committed on vocabularies and languages. In the nineteenth century, it was widely held that indigenous languages were primitive, and one of the reasons for supposing so was because these languages were "simple" and made use of very few words. By now such prejudices have largely been eradicated, at least from the scholarly world: we know now that all languages are equally rich, complex, and expressive, and none shows any shortage of words. Nevertheless, vocabulary myths persist. The Eskimos are popularly known to have an unusually large number of words for snow: a hundred, as a *New York Times* editorial once claimed. In fact, the original study on the Eskimo language mentioned only *two* distinct words for snow, but the number somehow snowballed over time as a result of sloppy scholarship and, in some cases, outright sensationalism. Presumably it all made good sense: the Eskimo folks do live in a pretty snowy place and surely they need a lot of words to talk about it.[1] Yet Eskimo probably has no more words for snow than English.[2]

*Probably* is the key word. It is very difficult to measure vocabulary size precisely, be it Eskimo or English. One popular method is to use a big word list of, say, 100,000 unique words taken from a large collection of texts. Since no one can possibly go through the list from A to Z, researchers typically pull out a random sample of, say, 1,000 items. A student then proceeds to check off those he knows. If 600 words out of 1,000 are recognized, then it is reasonable to extrapolate that the student's vocabulary size is at 60,000—which is about the right number for "average" American high school graduates.[3]

The word list approach is not without problems. For one thing, how can we be sure if the student actually "knows" a word? One may have the vague impression that *zakuska* describes some sort of food item, but that's still some ways from its precise meaning (a Russian hors d'oeuvre)—so here a simple yes/no checkoff will not do. Moreover, and more problematic, no word list is big enough to measure our vocabulary size: we can always make new words out of old ones.

Words, like the syllables that make them, have internal structure, and these structures represent a word's *morphology*. The heart of a word is its *root*, where its core meaning is located. In languages like English, the root is often sandwiched between *prefixes* and *suffixes*. Prefixes and suffixes are parasites: they cannot stand on their own— "ing" is not a word—but must latch on to other words. In the process, they create longer words and contribute additional information. The root, then, can be viewed as the core in a family of derivatives, and the example below is an incomplete family portrait:

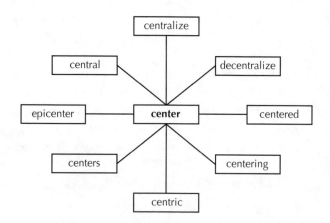

Roots, prefixes, and suffixes are together called *morphemes,* the building blocks of words. Morphemes are combined and recycled by systematic rules, which is why the meanings of derived words are generally predictable from the parts that make up the whole:

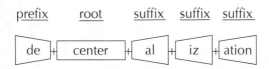

prefix     root     suffix  suffix  suffix

de    center    al    iz    ation

We can pile on as many prefixes and suffixes as we wish, though the meanings of the words become increasingly opaque—take "anti-anti-anti-anti-missile"—and the pronunciation quickly becomes a mouthful. To wit: *floccinaucinihilipilification,* or the habit of judging something worthless, has been claimed to be the longest word in the English language, but I happen to have a pretty *floccinaucinihilipilificational* attitude toward frivolous records.[4]

The failure to distinguish words and their derivatives may have fueled the myth of Eskimo snow words, though it is almost forgivable. Eskimo is a so-called *polysynthetic* language. If you think the term "polysynthetic" reads like the making of a chemical compound, you'd be right on the mark. A word in Eskimo really corresponds to a sentence in English. Nouns, verbs, prepositions, and many other distinct categories of words act the way prefixes and suffixes do in English: they cannot stand alone but may be fused into one very long sequence. For example, *aliikusersuillmamassuaanerartassagaluarpaalli* is one "word," meaning "however, they will say that he is a great entertainer." If we count words this way, then every utterance having to do with snow may add to the tally of snow words in Eskimo, and even the *New York Times* estimate of one hundred would be far too conservative.

This discursion into prefixes, suffixes, and roots is not meant to awaken your painful memory of Latin conjugations. Rather, it is a reminder of the complexity of words, and consequently, how much work it takes to learn them.

One thing that comes out of the analysis of words is that humans probably didn't evolve to be good at math. Words and numbers are in fact computed by similar rules, but only words come to us so effortlessly. We learn in second grade that for expressions such as $2 + 3 \times 50$, multiplication takes precedence over addition. By contrast, we need no linguistics lessons to know that some word-formation rules must apply prior to others. The earlier example of "decentralization" looks like pasting the pieces together from left to right—de+center+al+iz+ation— much the way it's pronounced. If so, why couldn't we stop at "decenter" or "decentral"?

The negative prefix *de-* can combine only with verbs ("deactivate," "dehumidify," "demystify"): using it on nouns ("deaction," "dehumidity," "demystery") or adjectives ("deactive," "dehumid," "demysterious") upsets the spell-checker on my computer. To use it properly, we have to wait until the noun "center" turns into the verb form "centralize," via a stop at the adjective "central." Only after all this can the suffix *-ation* apply, turning the verb "decentralize" into the noun "decentralization."[5] It is as if the mind inserts brackets around prefixes and suffixes—like $(2 + 3) \times 5$—to ensure that "center" must zig-zag its way to "decentralization."

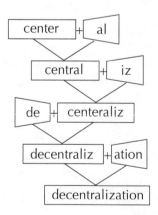

Viewed this way, words in the mind are not listed in a big dictionary. Constructed in a  factory is more like it, and the metaphor is to be taken literally. Words are the product of an assembly line where every stage is critical, as the output of one process feeds as input into the next.[6] What's more, each stage not only changes the meaning of the word, it also changes its pronunciation. For example, verbs are turned into past tense by adding *ed* (*walk–walked*), nouns mark multiplicity by adding *s* (*car–cars*), adjectives reverse meanings by adding *un* (*true–untrue*). Pronunciation changes are not limited to making words longer. When "deep" becomes "depth," the vowel becomes shorter just as the spelling indicates. When "church" becomes "churches," the *s* actually is pronounced like *z*, and a short vowel—indicated by *e* in the spelling—is stuck in between. In the path from "center" to "decentralization," the primary stress goes from the first *e* ("center") to *i* ("centralize") and then to the second *a* ("decentralization"). Distinct sounds may even become similar when new words are formed. For most North American English speakers, *t* and *d* in "writing" and "riding" actually sound the same! Both become a "flapped *d*," where the tongue flaps quickly to build and then release just enough air pressure for articulation: think of it as the regular *d* in fast-forward mode.[7]

This is probably more than you ever wanted to know about your native language, but try to put yourself into a young child's shoes. To be a competent speaker of a language, the child has to construct a word factory—*all the way from scratch*. The biggest challenge the child faces is that she hears only the packaged goods: words that have been piped through her parents' word factory and have come out as speech. In other words, she does *not* hear roots, prefixes, and suffixes as neatly separated packets of information, she does *not* see the intermediate compulsory steps in the formation of complex words, and she does *not* know whether Daddy will "be writing" or "be riding" this Saturday afternoon. To construct a word factory, the child will have to do a massive amount of reverse engineering: harness the packaged goods, unwind everything, and figure out how to make words on her own.

How children build a word factory is still very much a puzzle. A main reason for our ignorance lies in children's unwillingness to share their secrets. A story has it that Einstein did not say anything until age three, when he muttered "The soup is too hot" at the dinner table. When his stunned parents asked him why he had never spoken before, young Einstein replied, "Well, up to now, everything has been fine." Whether Einstein really was a late talker is beside the point, but for language acquisition research, the moral of the story is clear: a child doesn't have to say anything he doesn't want to, and what he actually says may be just the tip of what he actually knows. Moreover, when we do hear children speak, we hear only the packaged goods from *their* word factory: the inner mechanisms of word formation are hidden for both parties. To understand how word learning works, we will have to be reverse engineers as well: we need to unwind words to where they started out.

Pronunciation is the last stage in word formation, so it is the first layer of the package we shall peel off. Again, children's mistakes provide the most valuable insights on the inner mechanisms of the burgeoning word factory. Although the fine-tuning of speech articulation may take years to complete, as documented in the story of "wuckoo," the child is forging ahead with pronunciation rules for words. For a brain teaser, consider some renditions of words from the two-year old Daniel:[8]

| Set 1 | Set 2 |
|-------|-------|
| bump | gug (for "bug") |
| down | guck (for "duck") |
| gone | gig (for "pig") |

The problem here cannot entirely be reduced to articulatory packaging: Daniel was perfectly capable of saying *b, p, d* (and *g*), as the first set illustrates. What, then, explains the proliferation of *g*'s in the second set?

Things become clear when we translate pronunciations into articulatory features, the atoms of speech. The word-final consonant *g* is produced by the tongue body at the back of the mouth. Somehow it manages to *spread* that mode of articulation to the word-initial consonant *b*, thereby turning "bug" into "gug."

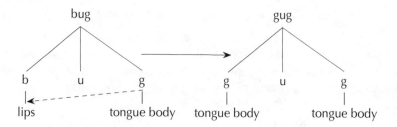

Think of feature spreading as succumbing to peer pressure. Sounds within a word want to sound alike; that's how "duck" became "guck" as well.

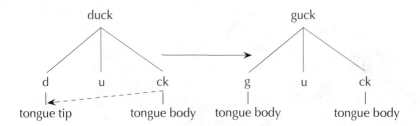

Not an unreasonable move on Daniel's part. By making the two consonants more alike, he avoided a tongue twister. Here we see the vestige of the K.I.S.S. principle from the story of "wuckoo": the biomechanics of a toddler's articulatory system are just not refined enough to handle all the sounds of speech, or handle them all that well. In Daniel's case, the ends justify the means: as if having *anticipated* the difficulties of moving the tongue from front to back, the toddler proceeded to *invent* a rule that makes the two consonants more alike. Those who really suffer are parents: what on earth does he mean when the child says "gig gig"? "Big pig," "pig big," "pig dig," or, for those in Boston, "Big Dig"?

But honestly, parents shouldn't complain. We constantly bombard children with feature spreading and other sorts of articulatory laziness. Consider the pronunciations of *d* in "rocked" and "rolled": despite the identical spelling, they actually sound different. Just to complicate the matter further, the same distinction shows up over and over:

swiped (t)      bribed (d)
scoffed (t)     starved (d)
kissed (t)      seized (d)
kicked (t)      bragged (d)

Add to these the verbs that end in vowels—"played," "fried," "snowed"—which also pronounce *d* in past tense. Dictionaries will overload you with two fat rules for English past tense:[9]

- pronounce *d* as *t* if the root verb ends in *p, f, s, k,* . . .
- pronounce *d* as *d* if the root verb ends in *b, m, n, g, z, v, ay, y, ow,* . . .

Quite a handful. But the rules in the word factory turn out to be different, simpler, and very much along the lines of *bug–gug* and *duck–guck.* As can be readily verified, the past-tense suffix *d* ends up as *t* precisely when it is attached to verbs that end in *voiceless* consonants. Features spread in parents as well as children: this time, the voicing feature goes from the final sound of the verb to the past-tense affix, turning *d* into *t* in the process:

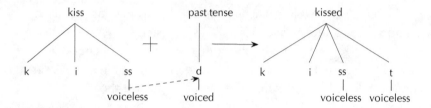

The *d* suffix is under no pressure when combined next to the voiced feature to begin with. These cases include verbs that end in voiced consonants—*bribe, starve, seize, brag*—as well as those that end in vowels, which are always pronounced with the vibration of the vocal cords. So a single rule of spreading, and the spreading of a single feature, completely replaces the plethora of statements in English dictionaries. While we are at it, we might clean up the mess with English nouns as well. When forming plurals, the *-s* suffix sometimes comes out as the voiceless *s* (*tick–ticks*) but sometimes as the voiced *z* (*egg–eggs, bee–bees*). But that's exactly how the past tense works: if the last sound of the noun is voiceless (*s, k, p,* etc.), the feature spreads to the plural suffix.[10]

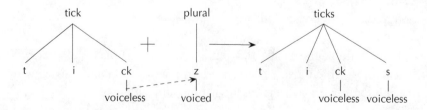

\*      \*      \*

Feature spreading is one of the most common sound patterns in the world's languages: in some cases, features spread like wildfire. Many languages exhibit what is called *harmony,* where all consonants or vowels within a word share a feature and often become completely identical. In the Australian aboriginal language Warlpiri, the last vowel of the first root—*i* in *maliki,* "dog," and *u* in *kurdu,* "child," illustrated in the example below—infects every vowel that follows.

mawliki-kirli-rli-lki-ji-li
"the dogs are with me now"

kurdu-kurlu-rlu-lku-ju-lu
"the children are with me now"

(Warlpiri, like Eskimo, is a language with really long "words." The various parts are demarcated with hyphens for your reading pleasure, but of course there are no pauses between them when Warlpiri is spoken.)

If a child hears his parents economize speech all over the place, it is entirely reasonable for him, like Daniel, to do a little corner-cutting of his own. However, this mode of explanation may get the logic backwards: it is possible that parents simplify speech *because* children do. In other words, we find sound patterns such as feature spreading all over the world's languages because it goes easy on speech articulation, and children are just doing what comes most naturally. Even though Daniel had no problem saying the *d* sound (he did say "down" correctly), articulatory economy proves too tempting. Yet there's got to be a limit on how "natural" a human language can be. If pursuit of articulatory economy runs loose, then all words would end up sounding the same—back to "mama" and "baba" perhaps,[11] the earliest and easiest sounds of babbling. And that would render a language completely useless.

A language must strike a balance between being easy on the speaker and being intelligible for the listener. The resulting compromise is an intoxicating mix of the natural and the arbitrary.[12] Recall the flapping rule in North American English, which homogenizes the distinct sounds of *t* and *d* into the flapped *d* in words like "writing" and "riding." Now this seems like a prime example of articulatory laziness, with the net effect of speeding up speech. But flapping is by no means a matter of necessity: the two consonants in "writes" vs. "rides," for example, do not flap and therefore remain distinct. The precise conditions that do lead to flapping are quite complicated—please consult the endnotes[13]—but the quickest way to recognize the arbitrariness of flapping is to turn to British English, which does not do it. And so far as we can tell, it has nothing to do with their food, weather, or national passion for soccer—even though it does make the language sound a little stiff to us Americans.

Finally, languages have lots of rules that make no sense whatsoever.[14] In Boston, while Nomah Gahciahpahrah is no longer in town, pahking in Hahvahd Yahd will still earn you a ticket. This much-ridiculed dialect, made famous by JFK's "youth and vigah," has a peculiar rule that gets rid of the consonant *r* every now and then, and it is by no means random. To wit, "red" doesn't delete *r*, so it's not pronounced "ed"; "broom" is not "boom." Bostonians drop *r*'s in a very precise way:

If *r* is the last consonant of a syllable, then delete the *r*.

And a *very* arbitrary rule it is. To be sure, the *r*-less speech can be ultimately traced back to a southern British English dialect spoken centuries ago (more on its fascinating fate in America in Chapter 8), but there was no conceivable reason, then or now, that *r*-deletion *must* be part of this, or any other, dialect. All the same, a child growing up in Boston does not ask about the history of her language; she simply has to learn the words and rules in her surroundings. Some of them may be "natural," while others are completely arbitrary, but all must be acquired en route to language.[15]

To understand how word learning works, it is useful to bear in mind how words fit into the overall picture of language learning. The word factory isn't just about words or rules: to run it properly requires turning on every component of language. Take the morphological rule for agreement in English: "I read," "you read," but "she reads." A child needs to learn not only what this rule *is* (add suffix *s*), but also what it is *for.* That is, *s* is applicable only in the context of third person singular present tense, and the agreement holds between the subject and the verb within a sentence. To learn a rule as simple as "add *s*" therefore requires the whole package of linguistic information: what makes a word a verb, where to find the subject, and how the language encodes time, among others. To understand how children learn rules, we cannot treat words in isolation and must jump ahead a bit to peek into their sentences.

Many young children learning English are prone to leaving their verbs bare. What do we make of "he laugh" when a two-year-old boy points to Daddy? Did Daddy just laugh? Should he laugh? Is Daddy laughing at the present time, or is he just a jolly fellow that laughs all the time? This is all very confusing.

Perhaps the boy was just confused. At a tender age, children might have trouble parsing the world into the appropriate linguistic representation. Maybe they don't have the concepts of tense, person, number, that go into the agreement rule: after all, many children don't start counting until they are three or four. But this would not do justice to the toddler. The cardinal sin in linguistics is to jump to a sweeping conclusion about all languages—and children—on the basis of a single language. Sometimes we need to travel around to find just the right language to test children's capacity: in the present case, a visit to a neighbor's house may do the trick. Spanish, whose stature is rapidly rising in America, presents a tough test for the young word learner, as its morphology makes English verbs look pitifully simple. Below is the list of six distinct agreement patterns for the verb *hablar* ("to speak"), and that's just the present tense:

| | | |
|---|---|---|
| yo | habl-o | "I speak" |
| tú | habl-as | "you (singular) speak" |
| él | habl-a | "he/she speaks" |
| nosotros | habl-amos | "we speak" |
| vosotros | habl-áis | "you (plural) speak" |
| ellos | habl-an | "they speak" |

If the two-year-old struggles with the relatively barren words of English, how long would it take him to master the intricacies of Spanish verbs? No time at all, it turns out. Spanish children get the verbs correctly and consistently from day one: about 98 percent of the time, to be precise.[16] In fact, the study of language acquisition has revealed that the more complex the morphology, the better and faster children learn it:[17] for instance, children learning Eskimo use those characteristically long "words" right off the bat.[18]

A global perspective for language forces us to assume that children all over the world are on the same footing—which is just a polite way of saying that learning the English language doesn't make our children stupid. But it does make them drop the agreement suffix. The bareness of verbs in child English is due to, simply, the bareness of verbs in *adult* English. The -s marking for verbs, which shows up only in the context of third person singular in the present tense, actually makes up only a small portion—about 3 percent—of all verbs a child hears.[19] Presumably, this is because children mostly hear things like "I run," "you hide," and "we play," where the verb sounds just like the stem.[20] But if there ever were a contest for verbal bareness, English would be no match for Chinese, which has no tense marking on the verb whatever. Here is how to "speak" in Chinese:

| | | |
|---|---|---|
| wǒ | shuō | "I speak" |
| nǐ | shuō | "you (singular) speak" |
| tā | shuō | "he/she speaks" |
| wǒmen | shuō | "we speak" |
| nǐmen | shuō | "you (plural) speak" |
| tāmen | shuō | "they speak" |

Which is exactly why a young child's English is often bare. Most of the time, when she hears a verb in the present tense, she has no evidence that her language is *not* Chinese. The necessary data for mastering English inflection simply takes time to accumulate. For Spanish children, by contrast, every verb is fully marked with tense and agreement, so every verb represents an opportunity to learn.

\*       \*       \*

Humans are the only creatures that are biologically designed to learn words,[21] though I can hear the protest of pet owners: after all, "sit" may induce obedient behavior in a golden retriever (but perhaps not a terrier). And the media occasionally report the feat of word learning by other species through extensive laboratory training.[22] There is no doubt that these remarkable animals are learning, but there is no reason to believe that what they are learning can be called "words." On the one hand, words are not just concrete objects ("sock," "ball," "banana") or specific behaviors ("fetch," "roll," "hush"); words frequently express abstract thoughts and entities ("stuff," "want," "feel"). On the other hand, no other species has shown any evidence for a word factory: the use of morphology, a hallmark of human language. As Spanish-learning children show us, a word factory can be built quickly, but as English-learning children show us, such a factory still needs raw materials to work with. Words and morphologies can differ wildly across languages, and thus no amount of innate disposition can replace nurture or experience.

It is difficult to quantitatively measure children's knowledge of words. Researchers just don't have a good idea how many words, or which words, a child knows at any particular point of language learning.[23] Given all the problems with the word list approach to vocabulary size, walking an eighteen-month-old through a yes/no list is out of the question. As a last resort, we turn to parents. A list of words that children may be familiar with is submitted to parents for inspection: the words they *think* their children know are then tallied. This method doesn't work perfectly, either. It turns out that many Americans have an inflated sense of their children's linguistic capacities.[24] (Don't even think about asking the grandparents.)

In any case, we can be certain that word learning involves the quiet accumulation of words, occasionally punctured by the emergence of rules: a Eureka moment, so to speak, as children discover rules that can generate more words.[25] This is easier said than done. A famous linguist once remarked, "all grammar leaks."[26] In less colorful terms, rules often have exceptions, and exceptions can throw us off and rock the very foundations of rules. Only very recently did I revise a thirty-

year-old belief that rabbits are as friendly as they look: at least one of
them actually bites.

Nothing illustrates the challenge of learning rules better than those
governing the use of English verbs in the past tense.[27] The regular verbs
are perfectly simple and obedient: as discussed earlier, one suffix -d and
one feature spreading will suffice. Except that this simplicity is buried
within some 150 irregular verbs.[28] Any English dictionary will give you
a laundry list of irregular verbs. Some of these add -d just like the regular verbs but also change the vowel: *sell–sold, tell–told, flee–fled,
say–said*. Some add -t and don't change anything: *burn–burnt,
spell–spelt, spill–spilt*. Some add -t at the expense of the original consonants: *send–sent, build–built*. Some, in addition to having the -t suffix,
also change the vowel: *lose–lost, deal–dealt, feel–felt, keep–kept,
sleep–slept*. Some add nothing at all yet still manage to change the
vowel: *sit–sat, sing–sang, feed–fed, shoot–shot, read–read, rise–rose,
fall–fell*. Some simply stay put: *hit–hit, quit–quit, cut–cut, set–set, let–let*.
And don't forget the few weirdos that (almost) completely abandon
their roots: *bring–brought, fly–flew, are–were*; no sane person could ever
have dreamed that the past of *go* is *went*. In sum: what a mess!

How do children fish the rules out of this chaos?[29] This may surprise
you: we often don't know if children have learned a rule until they
make a mistake. Suppose that a child uses the past tense perfectly: "I
played outside," "He pushed me," "You guessed right." It'd be premature to declare victory: the child could have directly *memorized* the
packaged goods from parents' speech, without having made these
forms on his own.

We know for sure that rules are in place when children start *misus-
ing* them on irregular verbs:[30]

Mommy goed to the store.
Super Grover flied away.
You buyed the truck for me last year.

What's going on?
Irregular verbs are, well, irregular: they are the unpredictables.
For instance, there is no rhyme or reason that "bring," "think,"

"buy," and "seek" form the past tense by replacing everything after the initial consonants with *ought*. They just do, and we just have to memorize them on the basis of repeated exposure.[31] Irregular learning could be a lifelong process, and there are obscure or obsolete ones many of us never learn: who knows the past tense of "cleave" is "clove"? (Who still uses "cleave," anyway?)

Irregular verbs, therefore, pose a problem for young children, but it's not a profound one. A young child hasn't lived long enough, and therefore hasn't heard irregulars often enough. But worry not. It's not as if they are left speechless when the memory for irregulars fails: the regular rule makes a reliable backup. Unlike the mini-rules for irregulars, which apply to a fixed list of words, the "add -*d*" rule is not restricted at all—it slots right in even when brand-new verbs are invented, as "I just *googled* my next-door neighbor." When the child fails to access the special rule for an irregular, the "add -*d*" rule takes over: the irregular verb then gets *regularized*. Only after seeing regularization errors can we say with certainty that children have learned the regular rule.

So children's use of the past tense follows a curious pattern. It starts as good, gets worse, gradually becomes good again, and stays good for the long haul. The very earliest past tense is error free. At this point, children are simply accessing the special memory for irregulars, and there is no regular rule yet to pick up the slack in case memory fails: there is nothing like "Super Grover flied away."[32] Only after the accumulation of a sufficient amount of regular verbs will they discover the rule of "add -*d*," and only then will irregular verbs start to succumb to the regular rule. Gradually, irregular verbs get better again: the memory for irregulars gets stronger over time, and children no longer tell us how they "drawed" a picture.

In a few short years, the word factory will be up and running. By then, children will be able to generalize the rules they have accumulated to make new words: after all, the hallmark of a fully operational factory is an endless stream of products. The psychologist Jean Berko Gleason invented just the right experiment for quality assurance.[33] A group of four-year-olds were given a novel picture and an even more novel word.

This is a wug.

Now there is another one.
There are two of them.
There are two ___.

What would children do? As Berko Gleason observed, "Answers were willingly, and often insistently, given." Seventy-five percent of the children said "wugs"—wug*z*, that is. (Many of those who didn't appeared to have missed the point of the game—four-year-olds are easily distracted.) For first graders, the response of "wugs" rises up to 99 percent.

The last bit on children's speech is for parents—and about parents.

Word learning takes a lot of time. As you may recall, even the prelude to word learning, the adaptation of the speech perception system to the native language, takes up a good part of the child's first year. For the impatient (and sleep-deprived) parents, that seems like an eternity. When words finally arrive, a different kind of worry comes along with them. In a society where vocabulary is the proxy of intelligence and high SAT scores are ostensibly the ticket to the Ivy League, many parents have understandably taken a serious interest in their children's words.

Perhaps they just want to help out. In many middle-class Western cultures, grown men and women often completely lose themselves when talking to babies: they switch to a dialect fondly known as "motherese." This particular style of speech is highlighted by shorter sentences, dragged-out melody, and exaggerated pitches and intonation:

"Sweeetiee baaaby! You're sooooo cute! My goooood boooy!"

There is apparently a literary tradition to this. James Joyce's *A Portrait of the Artist as a Young Man* begins with the father's bedtime story in motherese (or parentese, for the sake of dads):

Once upon a time and a very good time it was there was a moocow coming down along the road and this moocow that was coming down along the road met a nicens little boy named baby tuckoo.

Conceivably, motherese can help children learn language. Accentuating words and dragging them out perhaps gives the baby better examples of the consonants and vowels, and simple words may be the only kind a young child can handle. For babies, at any rate, motherese is music to their ears. Mother's voice—and smell too, apparently—is a favorite from birth. Although mothers probably don't need further convincing, it is nice to have some experiments to back them up.[34] When given a choice, babies tend to favor speech patterns of motherese, even if it is not spoken by their own mothers, and even if it is motherese of a foreign language.

"Your instinct is supported by science" is, of course, just the kind of thing that parents like to hear.[35] But let's get the facts right. Preference for motherese does not establish its necessity, or even its usefulness. Every five-year-old I know ranks pizza and french fries above almost every other food category, but that's not to say that pizza and fries are essential, or even beneficial, for a child's growth and development. Come to think of it, motherese might well have drawbacks. Surely you'd want children to learn English, or whatever the native language is in your environment, rather than a slow, exaggerated, and high-octave version of it with fewer consonants. Doesn't it confuse the child to have multiple words for the same meaning: one for grown-ups, and the other just for me? Looking ahead to the development of grammar, are fragmented sentences and reduced vocabularies what you wish upon your child when she's ready for kindergarten?

If anything, motherese reveals more about parents than children: it is a peculiar cultural phenomenon in modern Western industrialized societies, not part of the universal and biological foundation of language. Speaking in motherese is probably just what some of us do when we see anything cute and cuddly: after all, "Gooood boooooy" is applied to puppies as well as to babies. Many linguistic communities have very different habits of adult-child interactions. In Papua New Guinea, Kaluli parents make a point of not modifying speech when addressing babies, who are regarded as helpless and *taiyo* (meaning "soft"): what's the point of motherese if they don't understand anything anyway? Parents speaking Mohawk, a native language of North America, do treat children as potential conversational partners but make no simplification of language in the process. By contrast, Inuit children are expected to be quiet around adults rather than bubbly, and Inuit mothers generally do not engage in vocal interactions with children at all.[36] Even among middle-class Americans there is a good deal of variation. On the one hand, not all parents use motherese. On the other, parents like myself tend to imitate *children's* speech rather than simplifying or exaggerating our own: when a five-year-old boy is in the toilet humor stage, proper English grammar and correct anatomical terms just don't feel right to me.

Relax. No child has failed to learn language, or has learned it better or worse, because of motherese or the lack of it. In a classic study, the psychologists Elissa Newport, Henry Gleitman, and Lila Gleitman found that most mothers in fact speak whole sentences to even the youngest babies. When tracked over time, children's language development with or without motherese showed no difference.[37]

For all we know, motherese is neither good nor bad for child language learning: it is simply irrelevant. Language learning is remarkably resilient. All you need to do is to talk to children—baby-talk or otherwise—and biology will take care of rest.

Science does not necessarily relieve parents of their worries, however. Doing, or trying to do, the best for the young is an instinct that is impossible to suppress, and that's something I understand. My wife and I—both professional linguists who fully understand the autonomy of language learning—still catch ourselves correcting Russell's regularizations: "you mean you *brought* the book to school?" It makes us feel like good parents, though it's probably pointless. The psychologist Courtney Cazden recorded the following exchange:

Child: My teacher holded the baby rabbits and we patted them.
Adult: Did you say your teacher held the baby rabbits?
Child: Yes.
Adult: What did you say she did?
Child: She holded the baby rabbits and we patted them.
Adult: Did you say she held them tightly?
Child: No, she holded them loosely.[38]

Good intentions are no substitute for patience.

Because words and rules vary from language to language, word learning necessarily takes a lot of time. But parents will have good reason to cheer up as we follow children into the terrain of grammar: some things take no time to learn at all.

# CHAPTER 6

# Colorless Green Ideas

'Twas brillig, and the slithy toves
Did gyre and gimble in the wabe;
All mimsy were the borogoves,
And the mome raths outgrabe.

How are we supposed to make sense of this famous nonsense? As Alice put it,

"It seems very pretty," she said when she had finished it, "but it's *rather* hard to understand."

Yet there is something about Lewis Carroll's "Jabberwocky" that is not quite so jabberwocky. After all, it did impress Alice, however vaguely:

"Somehow it seems to fill my head with ideas—only I don't know exactly what they are!"

The Jabberwocky poem is nonsense, but not gibberish. Alice would have been utterly clueless had it been like this:

Toves the 'twas slithy brillig and
The did and gyre in gimble wabe;
All mimsy were borogoves the,
Raths and mome the outgrabe.

The pathway to enlightenment is that dreaded word: *grammar*.

*     *     *

Many of us shudder at the very mention of "grammar." Along with math, grammar must be the most unpopular class for school children, and for good reason. Grammar, like mathematics, forces upon us a good deal of terminology, not to mention an abundance of dos and don'ts that we have to memorize: do use the active voice, don't split infinitives, do keep participles from dangling, don't ever use double negation. Why do we have to study the constraints of English grammar when we already speak English?

Perhaps we don't—but that's for educators to decide (and more on that later). For us, constraints are the essence of grammar. Make no mistake: "Jabberwocky" is really English with nonsense words plugged in, and it is the structure of English that filled Alice's head with ideas. (The details would have to wait for Humpty Dumpty himself, as Lewis Carroll readers will recall.) We use grammar to translate the combinations of thoughts into the combinations of words, and those who have the same grammar can translate the words back to thoughts. Grammar is Nature's substitute for telepathy: for it to function properly, though, we have to pick a particular codebook and stick with it.

Alice had it easy. She already had a grammar—English—before embarking on her adventure on the other side of the looking glass, and she could use that grammar to read the thoughts of the Red Queen, Tweedledum and Tweedledee, and Humpty Dumpty. How does a young child, who doesn't have a grammar to begin with, decipher thoughts? What is the original code that kicks off the mind-reading process?

The answer is universal grammar: an innately available übergrammar that provides a sketch of all human grammars. As we shall see, universal grammar has its own dos and don'ts, which will be spelled out in two chapters—this one chiefly on the don'ts and the next one for the dos—but they are quite different from those championed by grammar teachers. And they must be. As a statement of the innate linguistic capacity that resides in our biology, universal grammar must be maximally indifferent to the specific grammars it eventually grows into. So let's look at universal grammar from its beginning.

The search for universal grammar was officially launched in 1957 when Noam Chomsky published a slim book entitled *Syntactic Struc-*

*tures,* which revolutionized linguistics and psychology. Actually, one might say that the revolution started with a sentence of the most unusual kind (and which came to be Chomsky's entry in *Bartlett's Familiar Quotations*):[1]

(a) Colorless green ideas sleep furiously.

If Google hits provide a reasonable measure of popularity, then "Colorless green ideas sleep furiously" just edged out the Jabberwocky poem "'Twas brillig, and the slithy toves."[2] Less famous but equally important is a companion sentence that Chomsky invented immediately afterwards:

(b) Furiously sleep ideas green colorless.

Despite their strangeness, the sentences nevertheless will elicit different reactions. Sentence (a) is grammatical, or structurally correct, but doesn't really mean anything. (I suppose if you had enough to drink, some meanings may be concocted; indeed, poems have been written around this famous line.)[3] Sentence (b), by comparison, is just word salad. With the help of recently developed technologies that measure neuroelectrical potentials in the brain, we can now observe the ways that grammar tickles our nervous systems. The brain shows distinct activation patterns when we encounter word salads like (b) even if they are tucked away in otherwise unremarkable prose.[4]

Chomsky's colorless green ideas do not merely prove the existence of a grammar in our heads: more importantly, they show that grammar is *generative.* Few of us can permanently inject a novel word or expression into a linguistic community; such privilege is reserved for celebrities, like Homer Simpson and Yogi Berra. Yet from a finite repertoire of words and expressions, everyone can readily make new combinations of words and expressions that other members of our linguistic community can readily understand. It is certain that "colorless green ideas sleep furiously" was never uttered prior to 1957, but every speaker of English can readily recognize its grammaticality. The grammar, therefore, cannot simply be a list of sentences we have previously heard—not that we could memorize that many sentences in the first place. Rather, the grammar must be a compact device that encodes the regularities of how sentences are formed in our language, one that we can use to create and understand new sentences. In the words of the nineteenth-century philosopher Wilhelm von Humboldt, language makes "the infinite use of finite means." A generative grammar makes this infinite use possible.

It is natural to look at grammar as the arrangement of words: "the cat meows," "the dog barks," . . . But we can do better by abstracting away from the actual words, thereby making the grammar more compact. "The cat meows" and "the dog barks" are different combinations of words, but they are also *identical* combinations of *different* words. Building on this intuition, we can classify words into part-of-speech categories: nouns, verbs, adjectives, prepositions, and so on:

Art = article (a, the, those)
Adj = adjective (good, funky, blue)
N = noun (cat, dog, schools)
V = verb (run, arrive, swing)
P = preposition (on, to, for, from)

Translating words into categories, "the cat meows" and "the dog barks" become the same sequence of article-noun-verb. But when categories combine, they don't do so as equals. The article-noun sequence "the cat" is dominated by "cat," rather than "the." The same goes for every sequence below: they are all about "cat," whereas the other words play second fiddle:

the big *cat*
the *cat* that made a mess
the *cat* in the hat
the hat-wearing *cat*
the *cat* that came back
the *cat* that came back in a hat

Now we can shrink the grammar further. The sentence "the cat meows" is about two things: in grammar-class terminology, the *subject* (who) and the *predicate* (did what). Substituting "the cat" with any of those listed above—"the big cat meows," "the cat in the hat meows," etc.—still gives us only two units of information, though we know more about the cat. Each unit is called a *phrase,* whose meaning and structure are built around the key word, or its *head.* Now "the cat meows" can be broken into a sequence of two phrases, rather than three categories: a noun phrase (NP) headed by the noun "cat," and a verb phrase (VP) headed by the verb "meows" by itself.

Linguists are fond of using upside-down trees to illustrate how phrases are stacked together to make sentences: words are leaves, phrases are branches, and the entire sentence is the root, conventionally denoted by the symbol S for sentence. "The cat meows" can be graphically represented:

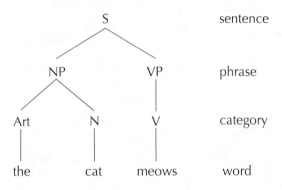

"Colorless green ideas sleep furiously" is grammatical because it follows the grammar of English: a noun phrase ("colorless green ideas") followed a verb phrase ("sleep"), in which the verb is then modified by an adverb ("furiously").

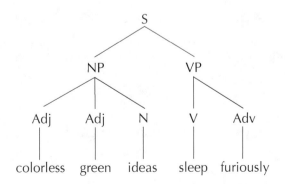

Wait. This sounds *too much* like grammar class, where only nerdy kids (like me) cared about the difference between "predicates" and "prepositions." Even the grammar tree looks suspiciously like those despicable "sentence diagrams." Don't be alarmed. Everyone knows sentences are built out of phrases: how well you did in grammar class depended on whether the teacher found a way to tap into such unconscious knowledge. Phrases, not words, are the building blocks of sentences: you can pluck them out, move them around, combine them together, and, usefully, stand them alone. Movie titles, for example, must pass the phrasehood test:

| | |
|---|---|
| *Vertigo* | (noun phrase) |
| *The Third Man* | (noun phrase) |
| *Kill Bill* | (verb phrase) |
| *On Golden Pond* | (prepositional phrase) |
| *The Lord of the Rings* | (noun phrase followed by prepositional phrase) |
| *Mr. Smith Goes to Washington* | (noun phrase followed by verb phrase) |

Not all blocks of words are phrases, and nonphrases make bad movie titles:

| | |
|---|---|
| *One Flew Over* | (prepositional phrase incomplete) |
| *When Harry Met* | (verb phrase incomplete) |
| *It's a Wonderful* | (noun phrase incomplete) |

That sentences are built out of phrases—not just words—can be viewed as the first principle of universal grammar. And there is *really* no reason to do badly in grammar classes: if there is any doubt as to how to break up sentences into phrases, we can just ask an eighteen-month-old.

For children learning English, the first sign of grammar comes about when they put two (or more) words together. This typically happens at age one and a half, though your child's age may vary.[5] This stage of speech has been characterized as "telegraphic," as if the child picks and chooses when she speaks.

For cookies.
All gone.
That truck.
Like sleeping.

This indeed looks like children are just pulling out sequences of words from sentences, but that's not what happens. We never hear children say, for instance:

Cookies for.
Gone all.
Truck that.
Sleeping like.

That's because the first principle of universal grammar is at work. Both the actual and the impossible telegraphic speech are strings of words from fuller sentences:

The milk is *for cookies*
The juice is *all gone.*
I want *that truck.*
Cats *like sleeping.*

Compare:

Cookie Monster has *cookies for* supper.
Kitty is *gone all* the time.
I don't want a *truck that* small.
You are *sleeping like* a cat.

Again, children's failings reflect their mastery of language. Even at the telegraphic stage—the first sign of grammar—children know that phrase boundaries are not to be breached. For instance, truncating "cookies for" out of "Cookie Monster has cookies for supper" would break the integrity of the noun phrase and the prepositional phrase: two incomplete phrases do not add up to a complete one.

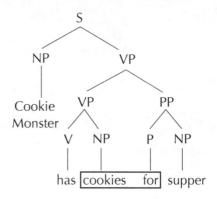

There is in fact a greater issue at the telegraphic stage of speech. Throughout this book, we have presented children's language in the context of their parents' language. Roughly, we start with some theoretical linguistics that highlight some subtle and complex properties of language. This is followed by some developmental psychology, showing that young children have complete mastery of these properties, or at least they come pretty close. But this needn't be. Why don't we describe children's fragmentary language in its own terms, rather than fitting it into the mold of a fully developed language? More concretely, why do we suppose that "for cookies" is the result of plucking off branches from a more complete grammar tree? Why do we attribute to children pieces of grammar we can neither hear nor see?[6]

This is a question that parents can readily answer. As they might have noticed, children understand longer and more complicated sentences than they speak—and thus they must have a more complete grammar than telegraphic speech indicates. This observation can be tested more rigorously. The University of Pennsylvania psychologist Lila Gleitman, one of the world's leading researchers on child language, designed a clever experiment in the late 1960s to do just that.[7] If children in the telegraphic speech stage indeed had an equally telegraphic grammar, then they would respond well if their parents also spoke telegraphically. Right? Not at all. It turned out that children understand fully spoken English, and telegraphic speech actually confuses them. We need no further proof for the futility of motherese.

We may date the emergence of grammar even earlier, but some technology will be needed.[8] In a typical study, a toddler may hear:

Big Bird is washing Cookie Monster.

Vying for attention are two TV screens. The logic in this experiment is the same as in high amplitude sucking for infant speech perception, except now the trick has become high intensity *looking*—the child has to find the screen that matches the sentence she just heard. If she understands that the subject comes before the verb and then the object, the child is expected to stare at the one with Big Bird washing Cookie Monster, rather than the foil video where Cookie Monster is washing Big Bird. Researchers found that even seventeen-month-olds do not disappoint, and these are generally children whose speech is still limited to single words. This finding has massive implications for parents, who ought to watch their language *all the time*: even if children have not strung two words together, it doesn't mean that they don't understand.

A final reason not to underestimate children's grammatical capacity comes from a global perspective: what is amiss for children learning one language turns up perfectly for those learning a different language. Take, for instance, the missing articles in the telegraphic speech. Words like "the," "a," and "an" are often absent in the beginning stages of child English: for instance, "I hit ball." Missing articles are the source of endless confusion for parents. While the meanings of "a ball" and "the ball" both entail that of "one ball," their appropriate usage requires, so to speak, telepathic abilities. For instance, we say "the ball" when the ball is familiar to both the speaker and the listener, for example, the bouncy blue one in the corner of the living room, or the one just delivered by Roger Clemens on TV. Either way, "the" is used for describing specific things in the shared knowledge of both parties. By contrast, we use "a/an" for things unknown to the listener. All the same, the appropriate use of articles requires the speaker in effect to read the listener's mind.

When Russell said, "I hit ball," I had no idea whether he hit *some* ball, or *the* bouncy blue one that he and I bought together at the museum. Perhaps he was just confused, unable to calculate whether my mental state was equivalent to his—or more specifically, whether *I* knew about the particular ball *he* hit. That, however, would be underestimating the toddler. Very often we need to travel halfway around the globe to see children's linguistic ability on full display.

Russian is a language that typically does not use articles. Rather, the function of specificity is taken up by the grammar and sentence structure. Consider the statements about dogs below.

Sobaka      laet
dog          is-barking
"The dog is barking"


Laet          sobaka
is-barking    dog
"A dog is barking"

If the noun *sobaka* ("dog") appears before a verb, then it bears the specific meaning of "the dog." However, if it follows a verb, then it refers to a nonspecific and is equivalent to "a dog." After several visits to nurseries in Moscow, my colleagues Sergey Avrutin and Dina Brun found that Russian children just over a year and a half old apply the specificity rule appropriately.[9]

For English-speaking two-year-olds, whom we must assume to be as capable as their Russian friends, the absent articles do not reflect a confused mind. It is a classic case of "the spirit is willing but the flesh is weak." As you may recall from Chapter 4, the unstressed syllables in words are particularly susceptible to omission:

balloon—loon
banana—nana
telephone—tephone
dessert—zert
helicopter—koter

All articles ("a," "an," and "the") are unstressed: prime candidates to be swallowed up in continuous speech.

*     *     *

The development of grammar in the first three years is nothing short of astonishing. Below is a more or less random sample of Russell's speech over six short months:

| | |
|---|---|
| 1 year and 10 months: | pull Mommy hair |
| 1 year and 11 months: | that my toy truck |
| 2 years: | wanna play Baba glasses |
| 2 years and 1 months: | Mommy help me open door |
| 2 years and 2 months: | You want a bottle of water? |
| 2 years and 3 months: | Put the truck on bed if you don't want me to cry. |

But I was mostly excited when Russell first started reciting the loopy nursery rhyme just before his third birthday:

This is the dog
    that worried the cat
        that chased the rat
            that ate the cheese
                that lay in the house
                    that Jack built

On display is the most potent force in grammar: the infinite use of finite means. Jonathan Swift once wrote:

So, naturalists observe, a flea
Hath smaller fleas that on him prey;
And these have smaller still to bite 'em,
And so proceed ad infinitum.[10]

Grammar works very much the same way: small phrases can be embedded within big ones. Language therefore has the ability of self-reproduction, or *recursion,* to use a term from mathematics: a phrase may beget another phrase, then another, then yet another. There is no limit on the depth of embedding, just like the nursery rhyme can go on forever. In fact, we have already seen a few, though less colorful, examples of recursion. Take the phrase "the cat in the hat." It's still about "the cat," though a more sophisticated one this time, with "in the hat" to dress up its image and modify its meaning. But "in the hat" has its own structure as well: it is a prepositional phrase in which a preposition ("in") combines with *another* noun phrase ("the hat").

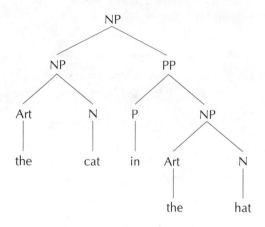

The hat itself may be modified by another prepositional phrase, say, "from the store," and the store may be "beside the street," the street may be "at the heart of the city," and the city . . . ad infinitum.

Recursion pops up all over language: many have argued that the property of recursive infinity is perhaps *the* defining feature of our gift for language.[11] Words, for example, can be arbitrarily long—as long as recursion goes. Take the noun "nation": adding "-al" changes it into an adjective ("national"), and adding "-ize" changes it to a verb ("nationalize"), and adding "-ation" changes it back to a noun ("nationalization") again. If we so please, we can loop back to the beginning and start the process of noun-adjective-verb-noun iteration all over again. Similarly, sentences can be arbitrarily long and infinitely varied. For parents, soon enough endless nursery rhymes will be replaced by endless teenage gossiping, but the grammar of embedding one sentence into another stays the same: "There is a rumor going around that she told me that you told her that I saw you kissing Jim."

But recursion must be handled with care. The following nursery rhyme, while perfectly grammatical, has an increasing level of difficulty for both the speaker and the listener:

The cheese lay in the house.
The cheese the rat ate lay in the house.
The cheese the rat the cat chased ate lay in the house.
The cheese the rat the cat the dog worried chased ate lay in the
    house.[12]

Grammar is powerful, but it's not the only force that governs the use of language. The performance of a computer program is ultimately derived from the efficiency of its design, but in the real world it's also bounded by the processor, hard drive, memory, and other physical resources. For the same reason, when sentences are processed in real time, they are subject to constraints from other parts of our cognitive system, in addition to grammar. In the original nursery rhyme, a noun phrase (NP) is closely followed by the matching verb; what that NP does becomes immediately clear and can be filed away.

dog    worried    cat    chased    rat    ate    cheese    lay

In the twisted version, however the gaps in between get longer and longer; so the noun phrases have to be stacked up in the memory for a long time before they are finally resolved:

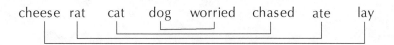

cheese  rat    cat    dog    worried    chased    ate    lay

As the suspense piles on, the brain just gives out.

With this background on phrases and grammars, we're ready to revisit Alice and "Jabberwocky."

'Twas brillig, and the slithy toves
Did gyre and gimble in the wabe;
All mimsy were the borogoves,
And the mome raths outgrabe

Like Alice, we can make some educated guesses about what's going on, and we do so purely on the basis of how words (and phrases) are related to one another. "Slithy" is probably an adjective, "toves" must be a noun, "gyre" and "gimble" are verbs, perhaps on the lines of "jump" or "roll," but can't be "push" or "devour." Of course, massive details are missing, but at least we've got a good start.

The details will be filled in by Humpty Dumpty, who is quite an arbitrator on words and language.

> "When *I* use a word," Humpty Dumpty said in rather a scornful tone, "it means just what I choose it to mean—neither more nor less."

Accordingly, "unbirthday present" is "a present given when it isn't your birthday," "glory" refers to "a nice knock-down argument," "impenetrability" means that "we've had enough of that subject, and it would be just as well if you'd mention what you mean to do next, as I suppose you don't mean to stop here all the rest of your life."

Humpty Dumpty may be a buffoon, but he is remarkably sensitive to the restrictions that universal grammar places on words:

> "They've a temper, some of them—particularly verbs, they're the proudest—adjectives you can do anything with, but not verbs—however, *I* can manage the whole lot of them!"

We can *all* manage. It is coded in universal grammar that words are picky, and some are pickier than others. Adjectives, as Humpty Dumpty correctly notes, are easygoing: you can line up as many of them as you want, such as "the *big, bad, hungry, lying,* and *cheating* wolf." But you can't do that with the "proudest" verbs.

Russell fell.
*Russell fell Zelda.

*Russell pushed.
Russell pushed Zelda.

*Russell gave.
*Russell gave Zelda.
*Russell gave the yo-yo.
Russell gave Zelda the yo-yo.

The star (*) is what linguists use to indicate ungrammaticality: the starred sentences are awful because they have either too many or too few noun phrases to go with the verb. These noun phrases are often called the *arguments* of the verb: just as both values of $x$ and $y$ are required for the function $(3x + 2y)$ to have a value, a verb needs all its arguments to make a grammatical sentence. Think of the arguments as slots: depending on the number of slots, verbs fall into three broad classes:

*intransitive* verb: __ laugh
*transitive* verb:   __ push __
*ditransitive* verb: __ give __ __

The second principle of universal grammar says that all slots must be occupied.[13] Interestingly, there aren't a lot of slots to go around. We can make up a verb, say, "zib" with four arguments: "Russell zibbed Bart the skateboard Lisa" means that "Russell presented Bart with a skateboard on behalf of Lisa." But as far as we know, no such verbs exist in any language: it seems that three arguments cap the number of slots a verb consumes. And this gives the definitive proof that Humpty Dumpty is just making things up as he goes. No language can have a word like his "impenetrability," that means "we've had enough of that subject, and it would be just as well if you'd mention what you mean to do next, as I suppose you don't mean to stop here all the rest of your life." A perfectly fine thought to contemplate, but way too many arguments for any verb in human language.

How many arguments a verb takes is intimately related to its meaning: an intransitive verb often describes self-inflicted events ("Russell *fell*"), whereas a transitive verb typically denotes some relationship between one individual and another ("Russell *pushed* Zelda"), and sometimes, an individual and a proposition ("I *think* that Russell pushed Zelda"). It appears that children must learn the meanings of a verb before using it properly.

Quite the contrary. The psychologist Lila Gleitman and the linguist Howard Lasnik turned the picky verb on its head.[14] Suppose that the child knows, from the second principle of universal grammar, that meanings of verbs are expressed by the grammar in systematic ways.[15] Now, if she notices two noun phrases in the vicinity of an *unknown* verb, then that verb must be a transitive one with two arguments. Consequently, it cannot have the meaning of any solitary action such as "walk," "laugh," or "fall." This way, a simple constraint on the structures of verbs significantly narrows down the possibilities of meanings of verbs. A bit counterintuitive, we might add: the child is exploiting the whole (i.e., the sentence) to learn something about the parts (i.e., the words).

Let's see how grammar helps two-year-olds learn.[16] A duck and a bunny—grown-ups in puppet suits, really—appeared on the TV screen and proceeded to engage in the following strange activities. The duck repeatedly pushed down the rabbit's head, while both swung their arms in the air like windmills. For one group of children, the audio went:

"The bunny is gorping the duck."

For the other, it anounced:

"The bunny and the duck are gorping."

When two events—head pushing and arm wheeling—compete for attention, what is the meaning of "gorping"? To find out, both groups of children were then shown *two* video screens simultaneously: one showing only the bunny pushing down the duck while the other showed only arm-wheeling.

"Now find gorping!"

Remember that all children saw the same video: the same two puppets, doing the same things. But the sentence structures of the verb "gorping" were different. The first group heard it in a transitive form, which means that the two puppets are jointly involved in the activity of "gorping." By contrast, the second group heard it in intransitive form, which indicates "gorping" as an individual activity: the two puppets were just doing the same thing together. And indeed, children who heard the transitive "gorp" stared at head-pushing and those who heard the intransitive version preferred arm-wheeling.

We can look to Humpty Dumpty for further proof. Even his verbal eccentricity is constrained on the grammatical structures of verbs:

"And what's to 'gyre' and to 'gimble'?"

"To 'gyre' is to go round and round like a gyroscope. To 'gimble' is to make holes like a gimblet."

We thought so too: whatever "gyre" and "gimble" mean, they are clearly intransitive verbs, like "jump" and "roll," and cannot involve other individuals, like the transitive "push" or "devour." To be sure, universal grammar cannot tell the child *everything* about word meaning. For example, "walk" and "saunter" appear in almost identical sentence structures, and only further experience can pick out the more leisurely pace of the latter word. Universal grammar cannot replace learning through experience: it only makes it easier.

A *lot* easier, actually. Learning grammar can be viewed as a game that a little boy plays with his father. Daddy talks, the boy listens—perhaps disobeys—and Daddy talks some more. All the while the boy is trying to figure out the grammar that can generate the sentences in Daddy's speech. The boy might occasionally talk back, but there is no guarantee that Daddy will pay any attention. Not that he is a bad father: recall from Chapter 5 that in some cultures, adults do not interact with children until they are socially and linguistically adept. To fully understand the game of language learning, then, Daddy can be assumed only as a rather passive participant.[17] The goal of the game is to learn Daddy's grammar within some finite amount of time: nobody learns forever.

Such a view of learning as a game is by no means restricted to language. The problem of drawing inferences from data and making correct generalizations is extremely important to a lot of people. For us, it's language learning; for Wall Street, it's financial forecasting; for politicians, it's about predicting elections; and for baseball managers, it's selecting just the right pitcher to get someone out. Suffice it to say that there is a lot at stake, but everyone with some vested interest here faces the Scandal of Induction: how do we choose just the right hypothesis out of infinitely many candidates, all of which are consistent with a finite sample of data?

Mathematicians and computer scientists have developed a highly technical field of research that studies the problem of learning more rigorously.[18] There is one and only one strategy that defuses the Scandal of Induction, and it's not surprising: to learn anything successfully, you need insider information about what kinds of hypotheses are possible and what are not. In other words, *some* prior knowledge about the target hypothesis must be available to ensure that one doesn't wander too far afield. To take a trivial example, what is the next city after the following sequence?

Pittsburgh
New York
Brooklyn
Philadelphia
Chicago

Even if you are a dyed-in-the-wool Red Sox fan, it'd be difficult to predict that the next city is St. Louis: these are in fact cities that lost to Boston in the World Series, with an infamously long stretch from Chicago. But you would never guess it right unless someone tips you off. While this may seem like a trick question, it does have practical implications. All corporations are in the business of making money, but they make money in different ways. The accurate prediction of a company's fortune requires not only its past performance figures, but also the inner structures and mechanisms of its business operation: there is no one-size-fits-all formula that works for Google, John Deere, and ESPN.

Universal grammar, however, *is* a one-size-fits-all formula that the child can bring to the task of learning any language.[19] This is why "Colorless green ideas sleep furiously" was as much a landmark in developmental psychology as in linguistics. Before Chomsky's revolu-

COLORLESS GREEN IDEAS 111

tion, linguists used to collect, catalog, and analyze samples of actual speech, much like naturalists who used to run around the countryside collecting beetles and butterflies and sorting the specimens into neatly labeled boxes. But a sample of actual speech, however large, is about the said, not the *unsaid*. To complicate the matter further, the unsaid *could* be said. Language is as infinite as human thought is boundless: after all, creative writers earn their living by saying things that have *not* been said before. In order for universal grammar to prevent children from drifting far from the grammar they are trying to acquire, it must draw a clear distinction between the unsaid and the *in-principle* unsaid.

So linguistics became an extreme sport. The secrets of Nature can be revealed only under extreme conditions, and that's why physicists create experiments—knocking particles around in mile-long colliders, for instance—to observe the laws of Nature that are not observable under normal conditions. In fact, we have done a few experiments, albeit extremely low-tech ones: only impossible movie titles, for example, can highlight the principle that sentences are made out of phrases. By the same token, linguists are obsessed with sentences that are in principle ungrammatical—not only for English or Spanish, but for all languages we can lay our hands on—for only these can tell us about the true limit of universal grammar. The most common response at linguistics conferences is: "Great lecture, but in Basque/Hindi/Warlpiri/Swahili . . .": back to the drawing board. Occasionally, though, we get it right. No one speaks all languages, and the current theory of universal grammar was developed almost exclusively on the basis of a few European and Asian languages—only because these are the native languages of most linguists. To be able to generalize and confirm the theory, we need to study far more unfamiliar languages: for this, we do need friends in faraway places, and sometimes we have to venture out there ourselves.[20]

Some of the structures forbidden by universal grammar, as we shall see, are downright bizarre. But it is useful to keep these in perspective. The goal is to discover the principles that help children learn languages: the more crazy hypotheses universal grammar weeds out, the better the chance a child will have of learning all the complexities in her grammar before learning how to tie her shoes.

The infinity of language lies in recursive combinations of words and phrases, but it also derives from the fact that words and phrases may not lie still. One sentence can be converted into another to add a spin on the meaning.[21] For example, our common complaint "Russell detests vegetables" can be turned into "Vegetables, Russell detests": this is usually accompanied by intonational emphasis on "vegetables," and the net effect is to highlight our frustrations.

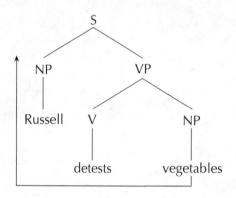

Similarly, the hopeful statement "Russell will eat vegetables someday" can be turned into a doubtful question—"Will Russell eat vegetables someday?"—with the movement of the auxiliary verb "will" to the beginning of the sentence:

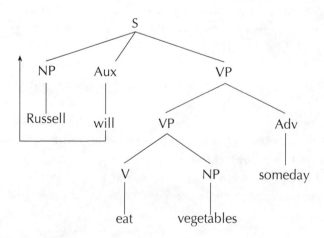

Such grammatical metamorphoses are called *transformations*.[22] Transformations greatly enrich the expressive power of language users, but they are a potential hazard for language learners. As universal grammar keeps the child away from crazy grammars, it must also keep him away from crazy transformations: the nightmare scenario is one in which transformations wreak havoc, dragging anything in a sentence from wherever it pleases to wherever else.

On the surface, at least, languages can be quite flexible when it comes to the freedom of transformations. The most striking examples come from the so-called "free word order" languages like Warlpiri, aboriginal of Australia. Take an activity that frequently takes place in our backyard: "The child is chasing the dog." (I pick this example because the child's mother is an expert on Warlpiri and the languages of Australia.) The English sentence can be translated into Warlpiri as is:

| Kurdungku | ka | wajilipinyi | maliki |
|-----------|-----|-------------|--------|
| child     | is  | chasing     | dog    |

Except that quite a few other permutations of words are equally grammatical:

| Maliki | ka | kurdungku | wajilipinyi |
|--------|-----|-----------|-------------|
| Maliki | ka | wajilipinyi | kurdungku |
| Wajilipinyi | ka | kurdungku | maliki |
| Wajilipinyi | ka | maliki | kurdungku |

So are transformations really wild? Of course not. We may recall the principle of structure dependence from Chapter 2 that moves the auxiliary verb ("was") around phrases rather than strings of words:

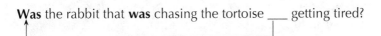

**Was** the rabbit that **was** chasing the tortoise ___ getting tired?

Transformations in Warlpiri follow the principle of structure dependence as well, and the flexibility of word order there is not due to crazy transformations that are radically different from those in English, but to *more* transformations that are exactly like those in English.[23] The word-order variants in Warlpiri, as a result, reflect various ways of phrasing the same message, thereby heightening the various facets of the same meaning. We will not indulge in the intricacies of the Warlpiri grammar, but it suffices to note that the auxiliary verb *ka,* the counterpart of "is" in English, must sit behind one and exactly one phrase: "free word order language" is just a misnomer.

Let's move closer to home and look at some more familiar—and famous—sentences. Groucho Marx (along with George Carlin) must reside on the highest echelon of verbal humorists. Take his memorable "I shot an elephant in my pajamas." It is an ingenious use of grammatical ambiguity. On the one hand, the prepositional phrase "in my pajamas" could modify the verb phrase that denotes the act of shooting, and on the other hand—and thus the funny part—it could modify the noun phrase "an elephant." The ambiguity is immediately resolved in the punch line: "How he got in my pajamas, I don't know."

Try a little transformation on Groucho Marx. In English, we ask questions by moving a wh-phrase ("why," "what," "whose") to the beginning of a sentence. Consider this:

**Whose pajamas** did you shoot the elephant in ___?

Chew on this for a second. The humor is gone, as an ambiguous sentence is turned into an unambiguous question: now the elephant can no longer be wearing anyone's pajamas. The only interpretation of the question has to do with the attire of shooting. What happened? Here we find one of the most exotic constraints on transformations, which I shall call the principle of No Grandparent Left Behind.[24] Transcribing a funny sentence into trees may be humorless but it readily reveals the structure of universal grammar. A pajama-wearing elephant can be graphically described as below, where a small noun phrase "my pajamas" ($NP_1$) is embedded in a larger phrase ($NP_2$). The triangle is the lazy linguist's way of ignoring irrelevant structures.

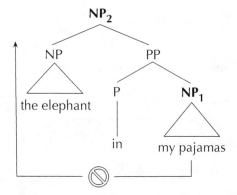

Moving $NP_1$ to form a question, however, would strand the grandparent node $NP_2$ behind. For some reason, no transformation allows that: in general, no small noun phrase can escape the dominance of a large noun phrase. Therefore, when we rewind "whose pajamas" back to where it comes from, the only grammatical tree we draw in the mind would have to look like this:

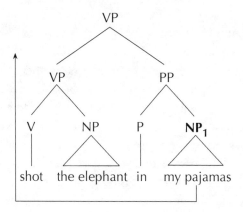

Here we can move "my pajamas" all we want, because the grandparent is of a different type: a verb phrase.

No Grandparent Left Behind has nothing to do with meaning: it is a constraint on *form*, and it's a very general one. In the examples below, we have no trouble understanding the speaker's intention, though all sound repulsively bad:

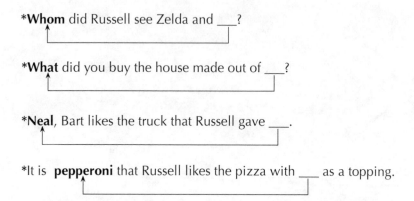

*Whom did Russell see Zelda and ___?

*What did you buy the house made out of ___?

*Neal, Bart likes the truck that Russell gave ___.

*It is pepperoni that Russell likes the pizza with ___ as a topping.

In all cases, the offending noun phrase left its noun phrase grand-parent behind.

Sounds complicated? This is not exactly rocket science, but it does require us to take a hard look at the intricacies of grammar from a brand-new perspective. And there is something peculiar about No Grandparent Left Behind. It is a form of *negative* knowledge, which basically says, "X is bad." Negative knowledge creates some interesting logical puzzles. How do we learn that X is bad? Not, of course, if so far we haven't seen X: X might well turn out OK when someone decides to give it a shot. Just think of the first farmer who boldly ate a piece of moldy milk curd (now known as *cheese*), or recall "Colorless green ideas sleep furiously," which was never uttered before 1957 yet is perfectly grammatical. When weapons of mass destruction failed to turn up in postwar Iraq, Secretary of Defense Donald Rumsfeld famously quipped, "Absence of evidence is not evidence of absence."[25] And on the ground of grammaticality, he would be right.

Generally, we gain negative knowledge only if it is explicitly taught or if we, or someone else, did it and got burned:

Thou shalt not steal.
Red mushrooms are lethal.
Playing with sharp knives can shed blood.
Upgrade Microsoft Windows and the whole hard drive might be
    wiped out.

Removing your star pitcher an inning too late may cost you the
pennant, and not retaining him after winning the World
Series is also a bad idea.

Trial and error, while frustrating and occasionally maddening, is
a luxury unavailable to a child if she were to learn universal grammar from experience. Obviously, no one learns their native language by taking grammar lessons. Even if parents wanted to offer
grammatical advice, most wouldn't know where to start: raise your
hand if you know what a "participle" is. Moreover, when does the
child get a chance for trial and error? The sentences that illustrate
No Grandparent Left Behind are so grammatically repellent that I
am certain that, before the search for universal grammar began
about fifty years ago, no one had even dreamed of them. It seems
that on the grounds of logic alone, universal grammar must be
innate.

Still, it would be reassuring to demonstrate that youngsters do not
indeed leave grandparents behind. To study how children ask questions, the linguist Tom Roeper and the psychologist Jill de Villiers led
a Herculean project—surely the largest experimental study of child
language of all time—involving well over a thousand three- and four-
year-olds.[26] (Those with kids ought to know that even *one* three-
year-old is quite a handful.) It'll be a while before children develop a
taste for Groucho Marx, so they got a G-rated version instead. A dog
broke his leg, but a little girl came along and taped him up with a
bandage.

**What** did she fix the puppy with ___?

As the story goes, the question could have two answers: "She fixed
the puppy with a bandage," or "She fixed the puppy with a broken
leg." As universal grammar goes, however, answering "a broken leg"
would be illegitimate; a small noun phrase takes off and leaves the
grandparent noun phrase behind:

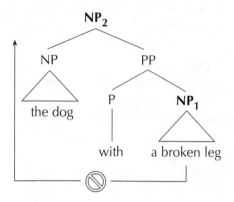

And children answered:

"A bandage."

For all the restrictions and negative knowledge that we all uncon-
sciously follow, the study of universal grammar can be a quietly liber-
ating force. Universal grammar is about what language is: it is to be
distinguished from *prescriptive* grammars, often distilled in newspaper
columns, which tell us what language should be. We are all entitled to
our own opinions of what is appropriate, be it the arrangement of
words or flowers—as long as we keep in mind that these are just opinions. The properties of universal grammar linguists have unearthed,
however, are a useful defense when language "authorities" try to
rationalize their pontifications: none of the don'ts they advertise can be
found in the book of universal grammar.

Take the maxim "Don't split infinitives." To be sure, some linguistic
units cannot be taken apart, and that's why children do not extract "fish
with" out of "The kitty eats fish with rice," which would disrupt phrase
boundaries. But that is already guaranteed by universal grammar: even
eighteen-month-olds know it, so we need no reminding. Unfortunately,
the infinitive is not among the unbreachables. The infinitive "to" specifies, among other things, the *tense* of the verb that follows: it is on par
with "does" (present tense), "is" (ongoing), "did" (past), and "will"
(future). All these tense markers are readily splitable from the verb:

Russell does *boldly* go where no man has gone before.
Russell is *boldly* going where no man has gone before.
Russell did *boldly* go where no man has gone before.
Russell will *boldly* go where no man has gone before.
Russell wants to *boldly* go where no man has gone before.

The tirade about splitting infinitives is a combination of nostalgia and ignorance. It derives from the long-held reverence for the Latin language, which indeed didn't split infinitives. And that's not because Latin is more elegant or precise, as is still held in some quarters; more on that in Chapter 8. Actually, you couldn't split Latin infinitives even if you wanted to. The infinitive in Latin is actually *one* word. For example, "to eat" is *comere,* where the suffix *-re* marks the infinitive: to split it would be like splitting the suffix *-er* from "reader" in English. Languages of Latin descent such as French, Italian, and Spanish still have infinitives like Latin: the speakers of these languages are therefore spared of the unnecessary advice.

More seriously, though, some prescriptive advice still reeks of prejudice from a bygone era. Take African American English, the dialect spoken in, but not limited to, many black communities. A few decades of scholarship have firmly established that African American English is just as systematic and rule governed as any other language or dialect. Yet the linguist Geoffrey Pullum observes, "The majority of English speakers think that [African American English] is just English with two added factors: some special slang terms and a lot of grammatical mistakes."[27]

One such "mistake" is the use of double negatives in African American English and other less prestigious dialects. Apparently on the principles of logic, two negatives cancel each other out and the result is a positive—but universal grammar was designed by biology, not logic. The double negative is the victim of triple doses of prejudice. First, plenty of languages—including the "scholarly" language of Greek—make extensive use of double negatives.[28]

| Dhen | ipa | tipota | (Greek) |
|------|-----|--------|---------|
| not | I said | nothing | |

"I didn't say anything."

| Gianni | non | ha | visto | niente | (Italian) |
|--------|-----|-----|-------|--------|-----------|
| Gianni | not | has | seen | nothing | |

"Gianni didn't see anything."

| Balzs | nem | ltott | semitt | (Hungarian) |
|-------|-----|-------|--------|-------------|
| Balzs | not | saw | nothing. | |

"Balzs didn't see anything."

| John-wa | nani-mo | tabenakatta | (Japanese) |
|---------|---------|-------------|------------|
| John | nothing | ate not | |

"John didn't eat anything."

Second, for those who bemoan the decay of language, English used to make extensive use of double negations; well, make it triple or quadruple at that.[29] In *Canterbury Tales,* for example, Chaucer said of the Friar:

Ther *nas no* man *no* wher so vertuous

Or "there wasn't no man no where so virtuous." When talking about the Knight, Chaucer went one up:

He *nevere* yet *no* vileynye *ne* sayde
In al his lyf unto *no* maner wight.

By this token, African American English would mark the revival of the classical form.

Third, it is possible that *everyone* in America spoke a fragment of African American English at one point. Many children learning English, regardless of their demographics, make frequent use of double or multiple negatives:[30]

Daddy's not being nothing.
I don't want no milk!
He didn't do nothing.

No doubt some of these children will become language pundits when they grow up.

It is difficult to suppress Nature. The prevalence of double negatives is not surprising if we look past the supposed logical design of language and turn to the mechanisms of universal grammar. The double negative is just a specific realization of the very general (and familiar) grammatical process of *agreement,* where some ingredient of grammar is explicated in multiple places in a sentence. In "he laughs" and "they laugh," the singular vs. plural distinction is realized twice: one on the pronoun subject, and the other on the verb.

A last kind of prescriptive rule is not only linguistically groundless but flat-out wrong. Here's another popular tip: use a pronoun only after its *antecedent,* which is literally a thing or event that appears prior.

*Russell* is happy with *his* truck.

But switching these around is perfectly grammatical: apparently, the antecedent doesn't have to come first.

The truck *he* got pleased *Russell.*

Language guardians have often blamed linguists as defenders of bad language: moral and cultural relativism is often tossed in at no extra charge.[31] We as a profession are supposedly promoting the idea that anything goes in grammar, and my counterexample to the pronoun rule would add to their fodder. But no, we have *never* said anything goes in grammar. Indeed, this whole chapter is about the don'ts in grammar. Of course the rules for pronoun use are not arbitrary, but it takes a lot of work to find exactly what those rules are. Twisting my counterexample slightly, "he" preceding "Russell" becomes ungrammatical if they still refer to the same person:

*He* got the truck that *Russell* liked.

The only possible reading here is the disappointing one: the truck went not to Russell but to some other boy instead.

Universal grammar does contain a principle, and a negative one at that, on the *misuse* of pronouns. Following the anthropomorphic tradition we started with No Grandparent Left Behind, the rule for bad pronouns can be called the No Nephews Principle.[32] In the offending sentence, "Russell" is the descendant of the verbal phrase (VP) that is the sister of the pronoun "he," which makes Russell a nephew. According to universal grammar, this relationship is too cozy for comfort:

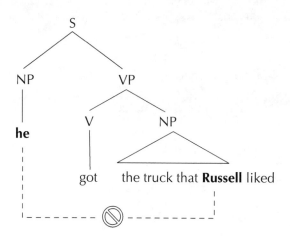

In "The truck he got pleased Russell," "he" is part of the family tree that represents the subject "the truck he got," and that makes Russell a cousin, not a nephew. No violation of linguistic principle incurs.

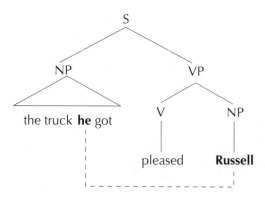

When it comes to the proper use of language, universal grammar is the ultimate authority. It is not about what rules are deemed reasonable or popular; it is about what rules are *true*. And one sign for a true rule is that it appears in young children, long before they are polluted by dubious grammatical advice.

The linguists Stephen Crain and Cecile McKee put a group of three-year-olds through the No Nephew Principle. As usual, puppets were recruited to help out. (Crain in fact popularized the use of puppets in the study of language acquisition, and Jabba the Hutt made an appearance in Chapter 2, as you might recall.) The experiment started out as a show with a familiar cast.[33]

(Eeyore is reading a book, and Pooh walks in.)
P:   Hello, Eeyore! You're reading a book.
     (Turns to the fruits on the table)
     What a fine-looking apple!
E:   No, Pooh. You can't eat the apple—it's my apple.
P:   OK, I'll eat a banana instead.
     (Disappointed; ate banana nevertheless)
E:   I've finished reading. You can read the book now.
     (Pooh starts reading).
     Now that Pooh is reading the book, I can eat my delicious apple.
     (Remorsefully, to self)
     I shouldn't be such a selfish donkey.
     I should let Pooh eat this apple. I should eat a banana.
     (Turns to Pooh and hands over the apple)
     Here you are, Pooh. You can have the apple.
P:   I'm a lucky bear! I can read the book and eat the apple, all at the same time!
     (P eats apple.)

End of story. Enter Kermit.

K:   That was a story about Eeyore and Winnie the Pooh.
     First, Eeyore was reading a book and then Pooh was reading it.
     I know what happened.

The test stage was like a yes-or-no quiz. Kermit would make some observations about the story and children were asked if he got it straight. Three-year-olds are a hard age to work with: they have grown independent and they surely don't like to be judged. But in this experiment, no ego is bruised: it is *Kermit* that is being judged, and children are doing the judging. Another complication in working with youngsters is their tendency to answer "yes" to every question in an experiment. (Why they are so agreeable in the laboratory is a mystery, but whatever it is, I'm sure millions of parents are dying to know.) Here Crain and McKee's experiment design was particularly clever: they made sure that to get the answer right, the child must say "No."

Here we have four versions of Kermit's story:

(a) When *Pooh* was reading the book, *he* ate an apple.
(b) When *he* was reading the book, *Pooh* ate an apple.
(c) *Pooh* ate an apple when *he* was reading the book.
(d) *He* ate the apple when *Pooh* was reading the book.

With "he" referring to Pooh, all four answers from Kermit are *factually* correct: Pooh indeed ate an apple when Pooh read the book. But if the No Nephews Principle controls how we understand language, then only (a–c) are admissible. In the crucial case of (d), "Pooh" is part of the structure that modifies the verb phrase "ate the apple," which makes it the (distant) nephew of "he," and that's a no-go. The only interpretation of (d), then, would take "he" to mean someone other than Pooh, and that makes him Eeyore. But that interpretation would be wrong: Eeyore unselfishly gave the apple away. When Kermit retold the story as in (d), the three-year-olds reliably pointed out, often with glee, that he had erred.

The study of universal grammar is a joint venture between globetrotting theoreticians who worry about impossible grammars and laboratory experimentalists who put young children through these impossible grammars. Perhaps, as in physics, one of these days there will be a grand unified theory of universal grammar. Linguistics today is where physics was in the age of Galileo and Kepler. The collection of principles, like those touched upon here, may one day be replaced by one powerful principle—perhaps just the principle of recursion—that underlies them all.[34] Universal grammar is still waiting for its Newton and Einstein. Whatever it turns out to be, its job is to keep children on the right track to their language.

Innate things needn't be learned, and for this entire chapter, the child doesn't have to do a lick of work. But grammars do differ, however many universal features they may share. Sooner or later, she will have some choices to make.

CHAPTER 7

# Twenty Questions

Animal, vegetable, or mineral?

As much as I enjoyed the game of Twenty Questions as a child, I was never very good at it. It might be that I'm just the worrying type. How come a car is "mineral"? What about pizza, where presumably animal (pepperoni) and vegetable (pepper) are rolled into one? Are olives green or black? It might also be the inevitable complication derived from the question-answer style of the play: the game works only when the minds of the two parties sufficiently match. While I never shared my brother's fascination with Princess Leia—he is three years older, after all—he never quite matched my mental database of baseball stats and stars. A generation later, only Russell knows that the chain of *animal-pet-big-red* leads to Clifford, his favorite cartoon character.

But Twenty Questions really *is* the perfect game, if perfection is measured by information theory, the foundation of modern digital communication. Information theory seeks to quantify (and then minimize) the cost of transmitting information—be it a number, a novel, or the subway map of New York City—which can be measured by the amount of uncertainty that a transmission can eliminate. Each packet of transmission serves to remove some uncertainty; in the sense of Twenty Questions, each packet answers a query from the questioner. Gender, for example, has very low information complexity: there are (in general) only two possibilities, so that one yes-no answer, or one bit in digital communication, would remove all doubts. Greater degrees of uncertainty require more bits. Suppose we are to guess a number between 0 and 7, which is to pick one possibility out of eight. This is a bit—actually, two bits—more complicated than gender informa-

tion. We can of course ask questions exhaustively, though that's clearly
not the smart move:

Is it 0?

Is it 1?

. . .

Is it 7?

If the number happens to be on the large side, we might have to wait
quite a while before asking the right one. A far more efficient strategy
is to fashion the queries in the style of Twenty Questions:

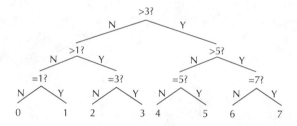

Now regardless of what the mystery number is, three questions can
conclusively settle the matter. Which is exactly how numbers are represented in the computer and transmitted over the Internet, where 0
stands for No, and 1 stands for Yes:

| 0 | 000 | No | No | No |
|---|-----|----|----|----|
| 1 | 001 | No | No | Yes |
| 2 | 010 | No | Yes | No |
| 3 | 011 | No | Yes | Yes |
| 4 | 100 | Yes | No | No |
| 5 | 101 | Yes | No | Yes |
| 6 | 110 | Yes | Yes | No |
| 7 | 111 | Yes | Yes | Yes |

In the best-case scenario, each yes-no question can resolve half the uncertainty that might linger in the mind of the receiving party, so twenty questions can cover a lot of ground: $2^{20}$, or 1,047,576 distinct objects, to be precise. Claude Shannon, the brilliant mathematician who laid the foundation of information theory, proved that the twenty-questions style provides the most economical decomposition of information. But as my own confusion reveals, perfection is prevented not by mathematics but by the world, which does not always break down into neat categories. And on top of that, my categorization of the world may well be quite different from yours.

Languages, however, are perfectly neat for the game of Twenty Questions. In fact, the classification of languages was the central occupation of linguistics in the nineteenth century, much like the classification of biological species. It became clear that many languages bear close genetic relations via common descent. Below is a family tree of the familiar Indo-European languages; most are still living but some are now extinct:

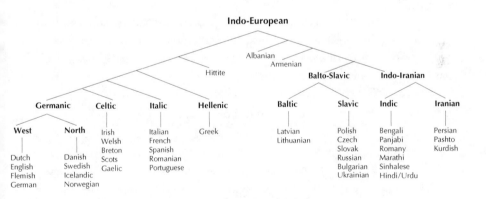

Such a family tree may indeed prove handy for a game of Twenty Questions, but only when the players are well versed in historical linguistics. It is utterly useless when the game is played in Nature; that is, when children set out to find the language spoken by surrounding adults. Telling a child that English is Indo-European/Germanic/West doesn't help with the brute fact that her language starts a sentence with the subject, followed by the verb, and then the object.

As we shall see, Twenty Questions *is* the perfect game of language learning, with no knowledge of linguistic genealogy required. During the past twenty-five years, linguists have come to believe that every child is born with a classification of languages—an altogether different kind—etched somewhere in the mind as a few dozen questions, or *parameters*.[1] The first few years are spent discovering the answers to these questions, finding out the Yes's and No's specific to her native language, and the mastery of a grammar is as simple as that.

But this needn't be. Languages could have been organized differently: the grammar of each language might consist of an arbitrary set of rules, and no two grammars would have anything in common, much less Yes's and No's according to a universal set of parameters. After all, maximum confusion among the peoples, and thus maximum randomness among the tongues, was exactly what God had in mind when he messed things up at the Tower of Babel:

> And the whole earth was of one language, and of one speech. And it came to pass, as they journeyed from the east, that they found a plain in the land of Shinar; and they dwelt there. And they said one to another, Go to, let us make brick, and burn them thoroughly. And they had brick for stone, and slime had they for mortar. And they said, Go to, let us build us a city, and a tower, whose top may reach unto heaven; and let us make us a name, lest we be scattered abroad upon the face of the whole earth. And the Lord came down to see the city and the tower, which the children of men builded. And the Lord said, Behold, the people is one, and they have all one language; and this they begin to do: and now nothing will be restrained from them, which they have imagined to do. Go to, let us go down, and there confound their language, that they may not understand one another's speech. So the Lord scattered them abroad from thence upon the face of all the earth: and they left off to build the city. Therefore is the name of it called Babel; because the Lord did there confound the language of all the earth: and from thence did the Lord scatter them abroad upon the face of all the earth.
>
> Genesis 11:1–9

For all its intrigue, the Tower of Babel remains a speculation. As will be detailed in the final chapter of this book, there is no evidence to suggest that all languages are progenies of a single ancestor. But as far as the biblical account goes, the theory of parameters does make a radical claim: that God's confounding of the languages wasn't quite thorough enough. Indeed, the theory of parameters is charged with two ambitious missions—to provide a theory of the languages of the world and the languages of the child—in a single stroke.[2] On the one hand, the theory of parameters must reckon with the world's vast linguistic diversity: how are the apparent differences across languages charted with a few dozen points of variation? At the same time, as a statement about the human mind, it must meet the challenge from every child: how does a child discover the Yes's and No's for her native language in a short few years?

As we have seen before, the structures of sentences can be visualized as trees, which will also make the working of parameters transparent. The basic word order of English is subject, then verb, and then object, or SVO for short.

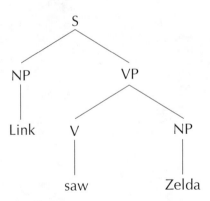

And the same is true of Edo, a language spoken in Nigeria:[3]

Òzó     mién     Àdésúwà
"Ozo    found    Adesuwa."

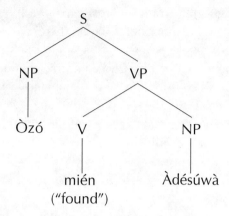

Japanese sentences are typically SOV, where the VP is the mirror image of English:[4]

| Ichiro-ga | Hideki-o | butta |
|---|---|---|
| Ichiro (subject) | Hideki (object) | hit |

"Ichiro hit Hideki."

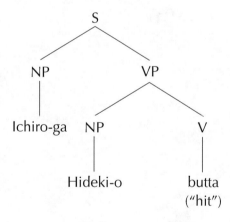

And the same goes for Navajo, a Native American language:

| Ashkii | naaltsoos | yizhjih |
|---|---|---|
| Boy | book | grabbed |

"The boy grabbed the book."

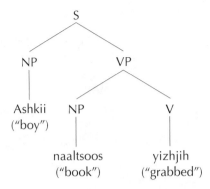

We can easily collapse the two types of rules for VP (V NP or NP V) into a parameter. By treating the head of a phrase as the axis of its orientation—here, the verb in the VP—we could say:

- VP head-initial: English, Edo
- VP head-final: Japanese, Navajo

This seems unremarkable, however. Why would a child pick a two-way switch when she has two ways of writing a rule? Parameters only pay dividends when we look at *other* types of phrases in these languages.

| Òzó | rhié | néné | èbé | nè | Àdésúwà | (Edo) |
|-----|------|------|------|----|---------|-------|
| Ozo | gave | the | book | to | Adesuwa | (English) |

Prepositions such as "in," "at," and "to" are called *pre*positions for good reasons: they precede the rest of the phrase they head:

| to | Adesuwa |
|----|---------|
| nè | Àdésúwà |

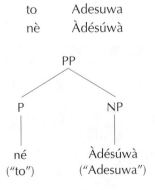

just like the verb in the VPs of these languages:

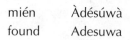

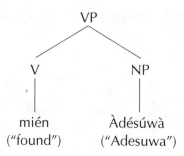

mién       Àdésúwà
("found")   ("Adesuwa")

Fittingly, the equivalent of a preposition in Japanese and Navajo is called a *post*position, for it goes after its NP sister:

**Japanese:**
Hideki-ga  Ichiro  to      kuruma  da  Kobe  ni   itta
Hideki     Ichiro  with    car     by  Kobe  to   went
"Hideki went to Kobe by car with Ichiro."

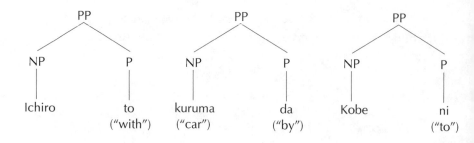

**Navajo:**
'éé'        biih    náásdzá
clothing    into    I-got-back
"I got into (my) clothes."

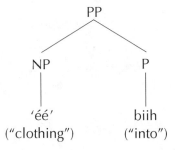

'éé'                    biih
("clothing")           ("into")

And these are precisely SOV languages where the verb follows its sister in the VP as well.

Coincidence? We think not. Our confidence is built on surveys of many languages, which must be the right kind. For instance, given the familial closeness among the Germanic languages, properties of Dutch grammar are likely to be found in Swedish, German, and Icelandic, for they all are descendants of a common ancestor not long ago. This is why we paired English with Edo, then Japanese with Navajo—languages that are spoken continents apart and bear no historical relationship whatsoever. It is as if a language projects a kind of "harmony" among the full variety of phrases, which tend to fix their structures once and for all.[5] If the VP is head-final, then so will be the prepositional phrase (PP), the adjective phrase (AP), the noun phrase (NP), and so on. But this makes sense only if the grammar is equipped with a central control unit—dubbed a "head-directionality parameter"—that controls the assembly of all phrases.

**The head-directionality parameter:**
- Head–initial: English, Edo
- Head–final: Japanese, Navajo

And it is the child who directly benefits: if she can figure out the parameter value for *one* type of phrase, then the rest can pretty much follow the blueprint.[6]

Transformations are also controlled by parameters. Some are obvious, and there are an abundance of examples in a child's linguistic environment. In English, we may ask:

What does Russell want ___?

where a wh-word ("what"; linguists also count "who," "why," "where," "when," and stretching a little, "how") moves to the beginning of the sentence to form a question. By contrast, wh-words stay put in Mandarin Chinese:

Chéngcheng    yào    shénme?
Chengcheng    want   what
"What does Chengcheng want?"

Languages thus fall into two camps:

**Wh-movement parameter:**
• Yes: English, Warlpiri, Mohawk
• No: Chinese, Japanese, Turkish

Quite understably, wh-questions constitute a most common type of sentences when we talk to children, but other transformation parameters are expressed less frequently—and also less transparently.

At first glance, the basic sentence structures of English and French seem to match word for word; both are SVO languages.

Martin    frappe    Milhouse (French)
Martin    hits      Milhouse (English)

The similarity is superficial because French covers its trail well. In comparison to English, French moves its verbs around, but that can be observed only when a stepping-stone—an adverb, for instance—is skipped over:

Je    **fais** *toujours*    mes    devoirs
I     **do**   *always*      my     homework
"I always do my homework."

Martin    **frappe**    *souvent*    Milhouse
Martin    **hits**      *often*      Milhouse
"Martin often hits Milhouse."

By contrast, the equivalent in English is not possible: "Martin hits often Milhouse" is ungrammatical. Yet this peculiarity of French grammar isn't strange at all, at least to our ancestors a few centuries back. Both Old English (circa 450–1150) and Middle English (circa 1150–1500) placed verbs where modern French does, right before adverbs:[7]

Here men **vndurstonden** *ofte*   by this nyght  the nyght of synne.
Here men **understood**     *often* by this night  the night of sin.


Wepyng and teres **counforteth** *not* dissolute laghers.
Weeping and tears **comfort** *not* dissolute laughers.


. . . that is to seyn whil that they **lyven** *both*
    that is to say while that they **live** *both*


Quene Esther **looked** *never* with swich an eye.
Queen Esther **looked** *never* with such an eye.


In previous installments of English as well as modern French, the verb skips over the adverb to land at a position called *tense,* for it is where the temporal information—past, present, and future—is encoded. Languages have at their disposals two ways of inflecting

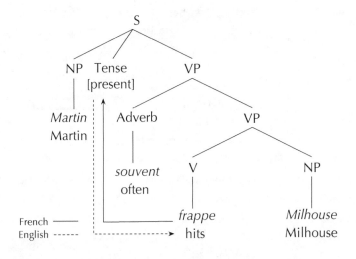

verbs. The French way is to raise the verb "higher" up to tense, bypassing the adverb if it happens to be present. Somehow English lost this habit a few hundred years ago; its current option is to lower the tense information onto the verb, and the adverb again bears witness.

**Verb-tense parameter:**
- Verb raising to tense: French
- Tense lowering to verb: English

English verbs used to travel even further, although this was restricted to questions. In modern English, by contrast, we dislodge the auxiliary to the beginning: the main verb stays put, as in "Did you see my master?" You wouldn't catch that in Shakespeare's plays, written in the period of Early Modern English. The main verb went all the way:

**Saw** you my master? (Speed, *The Two Gentlemen of Verona*, I.i)
**Speakest** thou in sober meanings (Orlando, *As You Like It*, V.ii)
**Came** you from the church? (Tranio, *The Taming of the Shrew*, III.i)
**Know** you not the cause? (Tranio, *The Taming of the Shrew*, IV.ii)
**Heard** you this, Gonzalo? (Alonso, *The Tempest*, II.i)

With this bit of English verbal history in hand, we are set for a language safari. Every language in the world is a combination of parametric choices; each of these may be perfectly familiar, but tossing them together can make an exotic mix. Take Welsh, a member of the Celtic family and a VSO language. (Other VSO languages include Irish; Niuean, spoken by the Niueans in New Zealand; and Zapotec, the language of about half a million native Americans in Oaxaca, Mexico.)

| Brynodd | y | dyn | fara. |
|---|---|---|---|
| Bought | the | man | bread. |

"The man bought bread."

A straightforward way of describing Welsh seems like this:

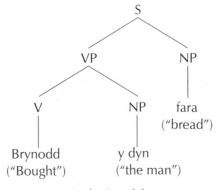

**"Fake" Welsh**

This would make Welsh really odd. In all the languages we have examined so far, the verb always takes the object as a sister, together forming the verb phrase, which in turn is merged with the subject to construct the sentence. In the diagram above, however, the verb in Welsh seems to be paired with the subject first, then the object.

But appearances can be deceptive—and hence science often has to resort to experimentation. The true structure of the Welsh grammar will be revealed only when we look at sentences slightly more complicated than the basic VSO pattern. Welsh is no different from the rest of the world: it does involve an extra step, but even that isn't all that unusual. Welsh is like Shakespearean English on acid: the verb always—not just in questions—moves to the beginning. Alternatively, it can be viewed as taking the French grammar a step further. While the verb stops at tense in French, it moves further in Welsh to a position that traditional grammarians call the *complementizer* (don't ask). This move passes by the subject as well and results in a VSO order—and obscures a further similarity with English and French. Welsh sentences actually start out in an SVO structure, as the following example shows:

| Naeth | y | dyn | brynu | fara |
|-------|-----|-----|-------|-------|
| Did | the | man | buy | bread |

Word for word, this would constitute a question in English, but it is rather emphatic Welsh, meaning "The man *did* buy the car." Since the auxiliary verb *naeth* ("did") has moved to the initial position of the sentence, the main verb *brynu* ("buy") can then stay behind. When the auxiliary verb isn't present, the main verb will have to do the moving to the complementizer. But it cannot get there in one fell swoop: it must pick up the tense information along the way (notice the past tense form of the verb).

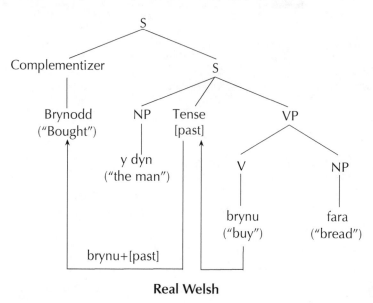

**Real Welsh**

In general, to decipher the parameter system of a language requires grammar gymnastics of this kind, even for properties as basic as word order. As transformations move things around, one needs to find the appropriate data—not just any data—to deduce what has moved, where from and where to. This in turn might take a detour to the study of the morphological system of the language: in the present case of Welsh, we have to figure out how tense is realized on the verb. It's a lot of work, but only then can we safely state another dimension in which languages may vary:

**Verb-to-complementizer parameter:**
- Yes: Welsh, Zapotec
- No: French, English

\*       \*       \*

All vertebrates are built according to a shared body plan, though limbs, wings, or flippers, may stick out at different places. Much the same, all human language grammars are instantiations of a universal blueprint: a super grammar tree, to be more precise, whose parameters control where phrases branch out and how they move around:[8]

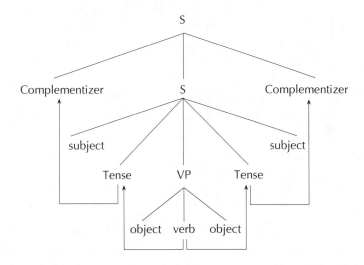

While we are on the tree metaphor, trimming is allowed too. In many languages, selected branches of the tree can be omitted, and these may include subjects, objects, and other important aspects of meanings. At one end of the spectrum, and close to home, we have Spanish, the second largest language in the United States. Pronoun subjects in Spanish are often omitted, yet without any consequences of misunderstanding. Recall from Chapter 5 the complex morphology of Spanish (which a two-year-old learns superbly well). Omitting the pronoun is possible because, as you can see, the verb conjugations unambiguously mark for agreement with the subject.

| (yo) | hab-o | "I speak" |
| (tú) | habl-as | "you speak" |
| (él) | habl-a | "he/she speaks" |
| (nosotros) | habl-amos | "we speak" |
| (vosotros) | habl-áis | "you (plural) speak" |
| (ellos) | habl-an | "they speak" |

This rather economical strategy, called *pronoun drop,* is used in numerous languages ranging from Italian, Catalan, and Portuguese—the European cousins of Spanish—to those scattered all over the globe and bearing no historical relationship with Spanish whatsoever: Mohawk in America, Warlpiri in Australia, Swahili in Africa.

At the other end of the spectrum (and the Earth), we find languages like Chinese, Japanese, and Korean. Chinese verbs cannot be more bare—this is again a review of morphology from Chapter 5—yet the subject can still go AWOL:

| | | |
|---|---|---|
| wǒ | shuō | "I speak" |
| nǐ | shuō | "you (singular) speak" |
| tā | shuō | "he/she speaks" |
| wǒmen | shuō | "we speak" |
| nǐmen | shuō | "you (plural) speak" |
| tāmen | shuō | "they speak" |

The verb bears no agreement with the subject at all, so the Spanish/Italian route to missing subjects clearly doesn't work. Instead, the Chinese strategy, called *topic drop,* is to make extensive use of contextual information. As long as it is mutually understood, the topic of a conversation can be left unsaid.

Speaker A: **Zhāngjiāngjūn** jìngpèi Liújiāngjūn.
General Zhang respect General Liu.
"General Zhang respects General Liu."
(General Zhang is the topic of conversation.)

Speaker B: Danshi ___ gèng jìngpèi Guānjiāngjūn.
But ___ more respect General Guan.
"(He) respects General Guan more."

You may wonder why English is not like Chinese; surely, we can hold a good conversation topic of our own. Moreover, English verbs show at least some agreement, however limited compared to Spanish, but still infinitely more than Chinese verbs. But glossing the above conversation into English results in something that no English speaker will say:

Speaker A:   Link loves Zelda.
             (Link is the topic of conversation.)

Speaker B:   *But __ loved Saria first.

Well, sometimes life just doesn't make sense. Together with a mere handful of languages, many of which are spoken in western Europe, English makes compulsory use of subjects. Illogical, perhaps, but that's the way it is, and we have all learned it without ever asking why. In fact, the requirement is so stringent that we have to stick a "subject" in the sentence even when it is not a typical "subject":

*It* rained.
*There* are toys on the floor.
*There* seems to be a large boulder rolling down the hill.

Words like "it" and "there" are called *expletives* by linguists: the etymology makes perfect sense (and has nothing to do with profanity).[9] "Expletive" derives from Latin, meaning "filled out." Indeed, "it" and "there" fill out the position that is typically occupied by subjects, though they don't bear the usual function of subjects as participants in events and therefore they contribute nothing to the meaning. No one is "doing" the raining, and it is toys and boulders—not "there"—that are on the floor and doing the rolling. In fact, expletives are the telltale signs of a grammar that requires subjects. Revealingly, languages that don't require subjects, like Chinese and Italian, do not have expletives:

Xiàyǔ.          (Chinese)
Rains.
"(It) rains."

Piove.          (Italian)
Rains.
"(It) rains."

Taking all the parameters together, we may compile a periodic table of languages:

| Language | Head–initial | Wh | V→T | V→C | Topic drop | Pronoun drop |
|---|---|---|---|---|---|---|
| Chinese | yes | no | no | no | yes | no |
| English | yes | yes | no | no | no | no |
| French | yes | yes | yes | no | no | no |
| German | no | yes | yes | yes | no | no |
| Japanese | no | no | yes | yes | yes | no |
| Spanish | yes | yes | yes | no | no | yes |
| Welsh | yes | yes | yes | yes | no | yes |

Indeed, parameters have been likened to trigger switches on the universal grammar engine: flipping them one way or another will set the whole language in motion.

If we take the parameters around the globe, we will notice that the geography of grammar isn't exactly symmetrical. For instance, there are just a handful of OVS languages, mostly found in the Amazon basin, and their structures are not very well documented or understood.[10] However, what to make of this grammatical imbalance is unclear. One possibility is that the innate universal grammar, for whatever reason, prefers placing the subject first.[11] Another is that the OVS order is "inferior"—in a sense to be made clear in Chapter 8—to other word orders and got swallowed up when they came into contact. Less interesting, though virtually impossible to rule out, is the possibility that most of the OVS languages simply died out without a trace.

Putting aside genealogically related languages, which bear a certain degree of grammatical similarity by virtue of common descent, we have no idea why a language makes its particular parameter choices to fill out the universal scheme. This may come as a surprise: many, including some leading scientists, still believe that the language and culture of a society are mutually determined—which appears to be a sensible idea, because our language is a main thread weaving together our culture.[12] Take, for instance, the much-discussed Asian values and "thoughts."[13] According to a popular view, the way in which Asians— really East Asians—observe pictures and categorize objects, and their much-noted "group-over-individual" style of social networking, are somehow related to the marking of nouns, word orders, and other features of their native languages. As a Chinese author and *Guardian* columnist opined recently: "The philosophy that informs the structure and system of each language is very interesting. In the English language your subject, verb, and object come first. It's very up-front. This is not the same in Chinese. In China, we had a law from 230 BC to 1912, if you said something wrong, 3,000 relatives could be killed. So Chinese are very careful when they speak, they put the verb at the end of the sentence. It is something deeply ingrained in us."[14]

Nonsense! East Asian languages are quite a heterogeneous bunch, despite the extensive linguistic contact that is prominently marked by the heavy borrowing of Chinese orthography by the Koreans and the Japanese. For the record, Chinese word order is SVO—a Chinese author is not necessarily a Chinese linguist. The word order of Korean and Japanese, by contrast, is SOV. If anything, Chinese ought to think like Americans, for their grammars bear the same basic word order, whereas the minds of Koreans and Japanese would match those of Navajo speakers, who also use an SOV grammar. Moreover, Korean and Japanese, like many other languages, use case markers on nouns; for instance, "-ga" and "-o" in Japanese expressly denote subject and object case ("John-ga" makes John the subject, and "John-o" makes him the object). Chinese, on the other hand, has no morphological marking whatsoever. Finally, and in broadest linguistic terms, Chinese is a part of the Sino-Tibetan family, which also includes Burmese, Vietnamese, and Tibetan, while Korean belongs to an altogether different family, the Altaic, whose members spread across the vast land from the Balkan peninsula to the northeast of Asia: Turkish, Mongolian, Manchu. Japanese is perhaps part of that family as well, though we are not quite sure, but we *are* sure that it has nothing to do with Chinese. It would indeed be remarkable if the residents of Seoul, Korea, and Ulaanbaatar, Mongolia, "think" in similar ways, but that, as far as we know, has never been demonstrated. On the other hand, if there is any "Asian" way of thinking—if it is not merely a stereotype—it probably has more to do with Confucius, whose shadow looms large in, precisely, the East Asian area.

Commenting on the prevailing confusion over the mutual determination of language and culture, the linguist Mark Baker writes:

> As we look at how the different language types are distributed around the world, there is no hint of a significant interaction between language type and culture type. Japanese, Mongolian, Malayalam, Turkish, Basque, Amharic, Greenlandic Eskimo, Siouan, Choctaw, Diegeno, Quechua, and New Guinean languages are all head-final languages. Chinese, Thai, Indonesian, Arabic, Russian, French, Yoruba, Swahili, Salish, Zapotec, Mayan, and Waurá are all head-initial languages. Is there anything in the pattern of cultural interactions or the basic worldview of the first group of people that consistently distinguish them from the second group? Is there any causal relationship between how they order their words and how they experience life? So far as anyone knows, the answer is no. . . . The culture of a group is typically more similar to that of its neighbors than to the culture of people who speak grammatically similar but historically unrelated languages elsewhere in the world. For example, the cultures of the various native groups in California were very similar despite the great linguistic diversity in that area before the arrival of Europeans. . . . Furthermore, ethnic groups seem able to change their language without changing cultures, and vice versa.[15]

Quite so. No event in the Anglo-Saxon history of the past millennium is responsible for the loss of verb raising to tense from Middle to modern English. The search for causal connections between language and culture is bound to fail. By implication, neither chopstick handling nor group thinking guarantees a head-final grammar.

In any case, grammar learning is over well before chopstick handling or group thinking begins. The grammar system of a four-year-old is not significantly different from that of his parents. The later years in a child's life are used to fill in the useful but nonessential details: idioms, more (and bigger) words, nice turns of phrase, the composition of research papers, and the art of talking to the in-laws.

The question of grammar learning can again be approached by the strategy of reverse engineering. Unlike the rest of developmental biology, language learning cannot be studied by cutting up the brain, knocking out genes, or depriving the child of necessary nurture and experience. And hence our survey of the grammatical landscape of the world: by gaining a deep and precise understanding of the end product, that is, the language that children eventually learn, one might be able to piece together the mental mechanisms that lead to that product.

Enter the parameter. The theory of parameters, which is chiefly the result of pencil-and-paper analysis of the world's languages with an occasional field trip to the desert and rain forest, is at the same time a theory of the mental mechanisms children employ to learn grammars. Rather than constructing thousands upon thousands of rules from scratch, each of which is subject to the Scandal of Induction, parameters provide all the questions—complete with all the possible answers—that a young grammar learner may ever encounter. As both students and professors can attest, a multiple choice exam is far preferable to open-ended essay questions.

The problem is, though, the pupil could be in for a *very* long exam.

Imagine the scenario where a child flips the parameter switches at random. Each combination gives rise to a possible human grammar—but it is most likely a pretender, unless it accidentally happens to be one actually used in the environment. Sooner or later the pretender grammar will be contradicted: the child will go back to flip some more switches, and eventually she will stumble on the right one.[16] The trouble is, though, no one can wait that long. Just a handful of parameters can yield a lot of combinations, far more than those on your gym locker. Although we have been talking about "twenty" questions, most linguists would contend that about forty to fifty parameters are required to capture the basic variations across languages. But forty switches translate into $2^{40}$ combinatorial possibilities. Not quite a googol, but an astronomical number nevertheless, with a 1 followed by twelve zeros. (Clearly, only a tiny fraction of these may be spoken on Earth at any time.) Given the fact that a child typically nails down most of her grammar by the age of five, a hit-or-miss strategy could require searching through about five thousand grammars every second, and skipping food and sleep altogether.[17]

If you think the image of a toddler wandering around in the land of parameters seems too abstract, you are absolutely right. So far we have been concerned with theoretical models of grammar learning, and models, after all, have to be squared with reality. If the theory of parameters is correct, then it must be somehow connected to instances of child speech like "Hit ball," "Bunny run," and "Where going?" Here, reverse engineering again proves productive: what children say during the course of learning can tell us a great deal about the mental mechanisms for setting parameters. But here the metaphor of parameters as trigger switches runs into a major problem—even if we assume, for the sake of argument, that the child can somehow steer clear of the pretender grammars and lock in on the target grammar rather quickly.

The hit-or-miss model, or even its magically efficient variant, is at odds with how children actually learn grammars. Indeed, the problem with the elegant metaphor of parameters is that it is too elegant:

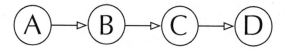

As the child flips the switches, she will traverse through a chain of grammars: A to B, B to C, and then C to D (hopefully the right one). But this means that the child may be using a Japanese-style, head-final, grammar this minute, and switching to an English-style, head-initial, grammar the next—either by randomly flipping switches, or in a more intelligent way, after realizing the Japanese SOV grammar just doesn't work for the SVO sentences in English.

If only language learning in real life were that snappy. As can be readily confirmed by parents, children's grammar does not change radically, and no language is learned overnight. When we keep track of their linguistic development over time, we will find that the term "learning curve" is more applicable to learning grammar than to bike riding.

Let's take a concrete example. Every child learning English shows a curious "subject drop" phenomenon, where omission of the sentence subject is frequent (on average, about 30 percent):[18] "He tickles me" is often reduced to just "Tickles me," leaving out the subject "he" altogether. The omission is actually a bit more general: when the child says "I dropped," the object "it" is dropped along with the ball. This type of error is intriguing because it cannot be blamed on parents, who would never say such a thing. However, if we keep track of the proportion of missing subjects in English-speaking children, we see a smooth curvy decline, tapering off till around the third birthday, when subject use is consistent and comparable to that of adults. Learning by flipping switches just does not bode well over time.

Nor can it deal with the present. Again, take the case of the missing subject. The compulsory use of the subject in English is achieved by the negative settings of two parameters:[19] that is, English is unlike Chinese, which can drop topics in context, or Italian, which, just like Spanish, can drop subjects for the agreement on the verb suffixes. Warlpiri, aboriginal to Australia, allows both options; one rarely finds pronouns at all in this language. The triggers model would have the child wander around the four squares (see the figure below) and eventually end up in English, where [-T, -P] denotes the negative values of the topic-drop and pronoun-drop parameters.

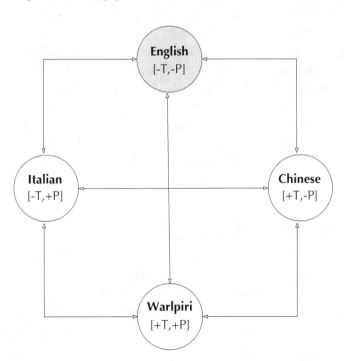

This is an elegant theory, for it gives a precise account of where children's grammar goes astray: when children drop subjects, they might have landed in a wrong circle, which is one parameter or two away from English grammar. But here's the problem: if the child is temporarily stranded in Italian or Chinese grammar, then she would essentially be speaking like Italian or Chinese adults. Yet the numbers don't quite add up. Again, English-speaking children under age three leave out the subject about 30 percent of the time, which is considerably less than Chinese adults (50 percent), and far less than Italian adults (70 percent). Moreover, English-speaking children occasionally drop objects too, in about 8 percent of sentences; this discrepancy cannot be attributed to the Italian grammar, for which missing objects are completely ungrammatical.[20] So the two-year-old cannot be speaking Italian or Chinese and, of course, she cannot be speaking English either: why would she defy the grammar and leave out subjects in one out of four sentences? The child is stuck in a nowhere land of parameters.

The gap between theory and reality is getting too wide for comfort. Are parameters merely elegant tools linguists invented to describe the grammars of the world, or are they embedded somewhere in the child's mind as she embarks on the journey of language learning? A somewhat curious response to the mystery of grammar learning is to say that there is basically *no* learning. It holds that children's language, or more precisely, their grammar, is in fact *perfect* (or at least as perfect as adults'). The errors in their speech are imperfections due to a performance "bottleneck." It is assumed that children don't have the necessary cognitive and perceptual resources to bring out the otherwise perfect grammar.[21] It's another case of the spirit is willing but the flesh is weak.

Under the imperfection theory, one would insist that children learning English really *do* speak it—just not too well, yet. In other words, they know perfectly well that subjects are compulsory in English, but simply fail to use them in practice—and they fail 30 percent of the time, to be precise. This doesn't sound like an unreasonable approach. There are a lot of things that toddlers know but fail to deliver in action. For instance, they understand the concept of a straight line, recognize it when they see one, but can only manage to draw a squiggle; the problem lies in the hand, not the mind. Furthermore, imperfect performance surely is a hallmark of early language; we have seen plenty of examples from earlier chapters. Children know about the specificity of things, but often drop unstressed articles; they know that Nemo is a "fish," but may say "fis" instead. It is not a stretch of the imagination to suppose that children don't have grammar use under perfect control. Perhaps, for instance, the child omits the subject not because she doesn't know the grammar, but because the sentence is getting too long for her tiny language processor, and the subject is dropped to make way for the rest of the sentence.

The imperfection theory is too sensible to dismiss—entirely. After all, children are not very good at a lot of things, and they do get better over time. When the mind still lacks sophistication, "relativity" or "weapons of mass destruction" cannot be part of children's lexicon. It is true, for instance, that young children often start out making short sentences. English-speaking children's earliest utterances may consist of two or three words. In developmental psychology, the progress of language learning is typically measured by the increase in sentence length, presumably as the resources—memory, articulation, lung capacity—for using an otherwise perfect grammar become more available as the child grows.

But the imperfection theory runs into three major problems. First, to say that a child's grammar is as good as adults' says precisely nothing. It says nothing about why English-speaking children learn English, and Chinese children learn Chinese. It merely postpones the question: *how* does a child's language become identical to an adult's? One might well say that immediately after birth, an angel wires the baby's brain to English, which then idly waits for the rest of the brain to develop (and the bottleneck to loosen). The imperfection theory takes nurture, or the experience with language, completely out of the equation.

Second, the imperfection theory implies that children learning different languages ought to produce similar errors, because it is inconceivable, for instance, that an Italian or Chinese two-year-old possesses a better memory and can hold her breath longer than an English-speaking two-year-old. This is of course a radical claim; it is also radically false. Take again the case of dropped subjects. While English-speaking children use subjects imperfectly, Italian and Chinese children use subjects as perfectly as Italian and Chinese adults.[22] Move north a bit and we find that two-year-old Eskimo children are perfectly capable of making long sentences like "Attamamuttakujautsarauqmut" (roughly meaning "It might have been seen by Daddy"); however one measures the linguistic complexity of such a sentence, it easily breaks an English-speaking two-year-old's language bottleneck.[23]

Finally, the imperfection theory is too general: it does not explain why children's grammar errors are what they are, not some other conceivable form.[24] For example, perhaps young children drop words because they can't hold long sentences: this would explain children's omission of subjects, which indeed makes sentences shorter. But doesn't dropping the object make the sentence shorter as well? And why do children drop objects only 8 percent of the time but drop subjects 30 percent of the time? Why don't they drop the verb? The overarching message in this book has been that, yes, children do make mistakes when they learn languages, yet these mistakes are far from random and reflect the very specific ways in which language is represented and constructed. For each of these specific types of errors, the imperfection theory must be amended with a specific repair patch, to keep insisting that the grammar is actually perfect. And this reminds us of the numerous updates, patches, and "service packs" for Microsoft Windows, each of them to be undermined a week later by another Internet worm.

That, however, does not seem to deter Microsoft's dominance of the market. For all these vulnerabilities, the imperfection theory has come to occupy a central position in the field of language acquisition and developmental psychology. As we read about the supposed stages of child language learning in parenting books, the single-word stage is usually before one and a half, followed by the two-word stage, which lasts until the second birthday, when the multiword stage takes over. The child supposedly just "picks up" her language—"like a sponge," as it is often colorfully put—and maturation and growth take care of the rest. While these statements may be reassuring to parents, they bury the mystery of language learning ever deeper. One may add that for the unfortunate few who do experience language learning problems, getting a detailed understanding of how language learning takes place is probably well worthwhile.

Yet perhaps we shouldn't be surprised by the popularity of the imperfection theory. Such a view of language and children comports with how we see the world.

From Plato and Aristotle on, the commonsense conception of Nature, dubbed *essentialism* by philosophers, has been a negotiation between idealization and imperfection. We are naturally inclined to divide up the world into categories and kinds, and these are defined by certain essential characteristics of their constituent members, which are imperfect realizations of the idealized essence. Triangles offer a good illustration of the essentialist perspective. All triangles share a defining feature (namely having three straight lines and three angles), and all triangles are sharply delimited from circles, rectangles, and other geometric figures. There can be nothing in between, and every three-year-old knows this. Often there is an idealized archetype of the triangle family: when asked to draw a triangle, most people will probably supply an equilateral. As the great biologist Ernst Mayr (1904–2005) forcefully argued,[25] essentialism is also a dominant perspective in our intuitive understanding of the biological world. Winged flight is the essence of the bird class; sparrows and robins are therefore closer to the archetype, or are "better" birds, than ostriches. And history has never been short of essentialist definitions of ourselves, starting with Plato's tortured notion of man as a featherless biped—and the great philosopher was soon presented with a plucked chicken. More dignifying and closer to home, Benjamin Franklin, in the perceptive words of the historian Gordon Wood, "has represented everything Americans like about themselves—their level-headedness, common sense, pragmatism, ingenuity, and get-up-and-go,"[26] which at least in part explains his enormous popularity among Americans and his presence as the only non-president on U.S. paper currency. Nevertheless, archetypes often lead straight to stereotypes. Ernst Mayr notes that essentialism is a premise of racism, for it enhances the conception of human populations as internally homogeneous but mutually exclusive groups, each of which is defined by a certain set of physiological or mental attributes. From here it is a sinister leap of faith to suppose further that these attributes can be preserved or even purified, as the eugenics movement and Germany's Nazis made horrifically clear.

There is nothing intrinsically right or wrong about essentialist thinking, which may well be an innate trait of the human psyche.[27] When it leads to absurdity, we must be prepared to reject it. But it is an open question whether the world, or a specific part of the world, can indeed be partitioned into groups of essence. For triangles, rectangles, and other geometric figures, essentialism works perfectly, and it would also seem to work for language. After all, there is a widely spread opinion, reinforced by preachy language columnists, that every one of us speaks an imperfect approximation of some idealized "English." We can try to perfect our language, much as golfers strive to imitate Tiger Woods's swing. Children are, by extension, perfecting their language as well, and their imperfections are just a matter of degree. If you listen to English speech carefully, you may hear occasional lapses of the compulsory subject requirement:

Speaker A:   Let's go see a movie.
Speaker B:   Nah, (I) don't want to.

Still works in progress, children will inevitably drop subjects en route to perfection, or at least betterment.

Viewed this way, the imperfection theory, though conceptually natural, is still empirically awkward. The perfect grasp of grammar is merely asserted, and we are not told just how the child gets to the target in the first place. And it wastes the theory of parameters, an elegant, precise, and vigorously tested theory of the world's languages. If the errors in children's language are blamed on imperfect use of grammar, rather than on grammar itself, then we will need an equally elegant, precise, and vigorously tested theory of language use—and that's not kosher. All scientists go into the business expecting that, as Einstein famously remarked, "things should be as simple as possible, but not simpler." The parameter theory alone can fully explain children's language, but the essentialist perspective has to be dropped.

Perhaps it's time to switch to Macs.

Had essentialism persisted in biology, the Darwinian revolution would never have materialized. Evolution is, by definition, the changes in a biological population that result from differential reproductions of individuals. Ernst Mayr has argued compellingly that this very conception of evolution was not possible before Darwin, because "virtually all philosophers up to Darwin's time were Essentialists. . . . They considered species as 'natural kinds,' defined by constant characteristics and sharply separated from one another by bridgeless gaps."[28] It was Darwin's genius to realize that every individual is a genuinely different entity with unique properties; individuals are not imperfect reflections of some idealized archetype, contrary to the essentialist beliefs. (This was all the more remarkable when the underlying basis of the variation, the genes, was not widely known or understood at his time.) Only after the uniqueness of an individual was recognized could one develop the theory of natural selection. Natural selection requires that individuals have genuine and hereditary differences so that they respond to evolutionary pressure in different ways, and will duly pass these differences to their offspring. Once essentialist thinking was dispensed with, evolutionary thinking became possible.

For me, this detour to evolution came when I was a graduate student at MIT's Artificial Intelligence Laboratory. One semester, I opted for a short subway ride to the famous course Biology 17 *Evolution* at Harvard University, co-taught by the two greatest evolutionary biologists of our time: Stephen Jay Gould and Richard C. Lewontin. As the son of two biologists, I have always been fascinated by evolution but— let's be honest—it was Gould's skillful (and fun) exposition on biology and baseball that dragged me out of bed at 8:30 in the morning. Another major attraction was a field trip to the American Museum of Natural History in New York City, for which Gould promised to be a personal guide. He did arrive, albeit half an hour late, but it was well worth the wait. First, the tour was hugely informative and entertaining, despite his all too frequent references to the Yankees. Second, while waiting for Gould in the museum's Dinosaur Hall, I pulled out a paper written by Lewontin in 1983. The result is my Darwinian footnote to Chomsky's theory of language and learning; in less romantic terms, the whole thing was a pure accident.

As Lewontin observed, Darwin not only gave us a brand-new theory of biological evolution, he also introduced a brand-new way of looking at the world:

Before Darwin, theories of historical changes were all *transformational*. That is, systems were seen as undergoing change in time because each element in the system underwent an individual transformation during its history. Lamarck's theory of evolution was transformational in regarding species as changing because each individual organism within the species underwent the same change. Through inner will and striving, an organism would change its nature, and that change in nature would be transmitted to its offspring.

In contrast, Darwin proposed a *variational* principle, that individual members of the ensemble differ from each other in some properties and that the system evolves by changes in the proportions of the different types. There is a sorting-out process in which some variant types persist while others disappear, so the nature of the ensemble as a whole changes without any successive changes in the individual ensembles.[29]

Both kinds of change take place in nature. While the evolution of life is variational, as Darwin recognized, the evolution of a star follows a transformational path, going from the stage of nuclear fusion (where the Sun currently is), to the cooled red giant, then on to the white dwarf, and finally the black dwarf in demise. So there is nothing inherently right or wrong about either perspective; we simply have to look at the individual case. The child hopping around in parameter land is transformational, as his speech supposedly mutates from one grammar into another, from one instant to the next. But that runs into problems. As we have seen earlier, when English-speaking children drop subjects, they clearly cannot be equated to Italian or Chinese. So it was asserted that English-speaking children do in fact know English—the 30 percent of missing subjects must then be dismissed because "the flesh is weak."

What if we drop transformational thinking altogether, and contemplate a variational child? What if the child is born with an ensemble of grammars that includes all the possible grammars, and "there is a sorting-out process in which some variant types persist while others disappear"? Rather than speaking exclusively English, or exclusively Chinese, why can't the child speak *both*?

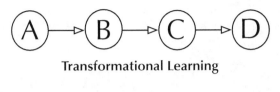

Transformational Learning

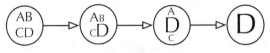

Variational Learning

In other words, rather than having A, B, C, and D mutually exclusively, suppose the learner has access to A, B, C, and D at the same time—D, the presumed target, will eventually persist while others disappear, all thanks to the "sorting-out process" of the linguistic environment in which a child is born. In Kansas, for instance, the English grammar will gradually, but surely, eliminate Chinese.

Now the 30 percent of missing subjects are no longer regarded as an inconvenience; we again draw insights from Darwin's revolution. Lewontin wrote:

> [Darwin] called attention to the actual variation among actual organisms as the most essential and illuminating fact of nature. Rather than regarding the variations among members of the same species as an annoying distraction, as a shimmering of the air that distorts our view of the essential object, he made that variation the cornerstone of his theory.[30]

To wit, the first chapter of *On the Origin of Species* is a detailed documentation of variation in domesticated pigeons: to demonstrate the reality of evolution, Darwin first had to demonstrate the reality of variation. To find the equivalent of Darwin's pigeons, we also need to focus on variation. If the Chinese grammar is still around, the child will make sentences with it, and it would be perfectly grammatical to leave the subject out. Variation in a child's language, where she deviates from her parents, will also be the cornerstone of our theory of learning by natural selection. Children's language differs from ours not because they occasionally speak imperfect English, but because they occasionally speak perfect Chinese.

Now we have come full circle to the subtitle of this book: children learn a language by unlearning other languages. Viewed in the Darwinian light, all humanly possible grammars compete to match the language spoken in a child's environment. And fitness, because we have competition, can be measured by the compatibility of a grammar with what a child hears in a particular linguistic environment. This theory of language takes both nature and nurture into account: nature proposes, and nurture disposes.

Cast in a mathematical model—indeed a very simple one, which I sketched out with a brown crayon the museum had kindly made available for dinosaur coloring—grammar competition is a form of probabilistic learning.[31] While we are mostly unaware, the mind is constantly cranking out and sorting through probabilities (likelihood, tendencies, trends, hunches). For example, I had to reboot Microsoft Windows yesterday, and it crashed all by itself today; yet based on the experience from the past two months, my current estimate of its reliability is that it probably dies every three days. Now this estimate is subject to change as more (or less) annoyance accumulates: if it doesn't crash for another week, my confidence estimate may be boosted to four days, and if the software crashes again tomorrow, my estimate will probably drop to two. (It really *is* time to switch to a Mac.) We can all do this by adaptively modifying our beliefs from experience, without resorting to an explicit log of the actual events.

Children use exactly this type of silent bookkeeping when they select grammars; or more accurately, parameters. The value of a parameter for her language may be Yes or No, but the child doesn't have to make up her mind right away. If the transformational child learns by hopping between alternative values of parameters, the variational child learns by taking a drunkard's walk between the two ends. If you are inclined to think in numbers (see Note 31 if you want all the mathematics): the child assigns a probability—say, $p$, a real number between 0 and 1— to Yes, and the probability for No would be $1-p$. In other words, sometimes she thinks this parameter is set to No, and the rest of the time she thinks it is Yes. Now imagine a language where this parameter is set to No. Concretely, take the verb-to-tense parameter: No for English, but Yes for French. Even if an English child believes that verbs in her language work like French, it doesn't mean that she will always be wrong; the word orders in the sentences below are perfectly fine for both English and French.

| Martin | hits | Milhouse. | (English) |
| Martin | frappe | Milhouse. | (French) |

The moments of truth will come if Martin makes it a habit:

| Martin | *often* | **hits** | Milhouse. |

This type of sentence is compatible only with the English option; if she happens to have picked the French option, she would be expecting "Martin **hits** *often* Milhouse." In much the same way that I silently downgrade the reliability of my computer, the child will punish the French option—in mathematical terms, by decreasing its probability. That is, she will be edging a bit closer toward English. Over time, with the accumulation of these informative sentences, the French option will diminish further and further, and the English option will be the one left standing: survival of the fittest.

Now you may be burning with questions. First, what happens when no grammar is the fittest? This situation arises when the child is exposed to two, or multiple, languages, such that, unlike in monolingual environments, no single grammar works perfectly. Second, why does learning follow "the law of higgledy-piggledy," as the astronomer John Herschel famously remarked about Darwin's theory of natural selection? Why doesn't the child resolve the parameters more decisively, for surely one instance of "Martin often hits Milhouse" ought to get rid of the French option for good? Excellent points. These two questions are ultimately related, and will be dealt with later in Chapter 8 when we discuss how language changes and how the ability for language learning might have evolved in the first place—and it has to do with how rodents outsmart Yale students.

*      *      *

While learning by natural selection sounds exotic, and its application to universal grammar novel, research in developmental biology has provided an independent body of evidence converging on the very same idea.

As we all know, the brain is made of billions of relatively simple neurons, and the brain does its work through billions upon billions of intricate connections among the neurons called synapses. Unlike the cells in other parts of the body, which continue to grow and divide throughout the lifetime of their human hosts, brain cells are formed in the fetus, and most of them are made in the first four months of gestation. As one can imagine, this takes place at an incredibly fast and furious pace, but the main event—the formation of synapses among neurons, hence development of brain functions—is to come later. Building neural connections is a long-term project, but the first few years are again the most active period, during which up to 1.8 *million* connections are formed every second.

Given such size and complexity, it is inconceivable that genes completely determine all the circuitries in the brain: at least some are used to build kidneys, eyes, and toes, and there is just not enough DNA to go around. So the brain compensates by overproduction, which is followed by competition: it generates an enormous pool of synapses, and only those that are sufficiently active as stimulated by neural signals are retained. The understimulated connections will slowly regress into a state of permanent disarray. By adolescence, about half the synapses formed when we were a few months old are gone altogether.

The earliest, and still the best, evidence of neural development comes from the study of the visual system. In the 1960s, biologists David Hubel and Torsten Wiesel, in the work that ultimately led to a Nobel Prize, made pioneering discoveries of how competition and selection take place in the brain.[32] They identified specific nerve cells in cats that respond to specific visual information such as angles, moving spots, horizontal and vertical lines. In addition, and more pertinent to us, if the kitten is raised under visual deprivation, say, inside a box painted with only vertical stripes, only the neurons that respond to vertical stripes will remain active, while the rest, those that are responsible for other aspects of visual information, become inactive, and the kitten never develops normal vision. It is a classic case of "use it or lose it."

Recent years have seen more general and ambitious theories of neurological development based on the notion of Darwinian selection, for which the French neuroscientist Jean-Pierre Changeux and the American biologist Gerald Edelman are among the most prominent advocates.[33] Edelman's work on molecular immunology won him a Nobel; if he's right about the brain, Stockholm will surely be beckoning again. And there are deep connections between Edelman's work on immunology and neuroscience. For a long time, scientists were interested in how antibodies were produced to fight viruses and bacteria, and a leading theory held that the antibody molecule "learned" the shape of the intruder and molded around it. However, Edelman and his colleagues showed, confirming the theory of MacFarlane Burnet and Niels Jerne (both Noble laureates), that animals are born with a totality of antibodies: only the matching kinds are selectively brought out, or activated, by specific invaders. In other words, the immune system has weapons against all potential foes: now *that* is preventive warfare.

In his work on neurological development, Edelman and his colleagues discovered certain chemicals called "cell adhesion molecules," which guide the growth of synapses to build groups of nerve cells in the embryo. This process is presumably controlled by the genes. All sorts of neuronal groups are produced, only for nurture, or experience, to pick up the pruning scissors later on. The latter process, Edelman conjectures, is carried out in a process of competition and selection: hence his theory of *neural Darwinism*. The connections that are used frequently are more likely to be maintained, and those that are not will regress, or will be co-opted for other functions. It is important to keep in mind that selection cannot be the only mechanism for neural development. The brain is not a static object: as long as we learn, be it partial differential equations or a new face, the brain will continue to alter its organization. At least some connections must be triggered by experience, rather than dictated by the genes.

I would love to tell you that there are neural populations in the brain that control the use of the subject in grammar, and if we take a brain imaging snapshot of the head of an English-learning two-year-old, we find it to be in some intermediate formation between a mature brain that speaks English, and one that speaks Chinese. Unfortunately, while no one questions the brain as the ultimate seat of mental activities, we have not even the slightest clue where to look for subjects or sentences inside—or even a noun or a verb, for that matter. Currently, to study how the brain gives rise to the mind, particularly the higher mental functions such as language, the most productive approach remains to first understand the mind on its own, which is far easier to observe and far less expensive to work with than its neurological underpinning.

More direct evidence for learning by natural selection comes from the development of behavior in other species, in particular those for which there is a limitation on what could be learned (specified by the genes) and what is actually learned (determined by the environment). Natural selection learns not only grammars, but also songs. In the first chapter of this book, we noted some strong parallels between how birds learn to sing and how babies learn to talk. Songbird chicks go through various stages before they become fluent in their local dialect, one of which is characterized by overproduction. At this point the chick may have quite a few different songs; all are potential adult songs but only one of them will eventually be retained. If the melody and rhythm of all bird songs can be compared to a universal grammar, then the potential songs overproduced are the equivalent of the Chinese-like grammar in an English-learning child, not yet eliminated by trial and error.

In the end, though, metaphors, analogies, and similarities, while boosting the credibility of our theory, are just metaphors, analogies, and similarities. The most direct evidence possible, and the strongest support for the natural selection of grammars, comes from children's words themselves.

No two-year-old would confess that she is really harboring an alien language, alongside the native grammar that is gaining prominence through natural selection. Toddlers won't tell us whether a sentence is grammatical or not, either. We did try. Once, the Harvard psychologist Roger Brown asked the three-year-old "Adam" (one of the first children in the modern study of language learning; another child has been known as "Eve"), "Now tell me, Adam, is it 'two shoe' or 'two shoes'?"; the reply was quick and cheery: "Pop goes the weasel!"[34]

It suffices to say that a more indirect route of inquiry is needed. We may subtract out the sentences that do belong to the native grammar; if our theory is correct, then the remainder can be attributed to the competing grammars. Except even this approach is not that easy. While missing subjects (e.g., "Tickles me") *can* clearly be attributed to a Chinese grammar, it is harder to show that they *must* be. To show that English-speaking children really do speak Chinese—by which we of course mean the child is exercising a particular parameter value found in the Chinese language—we need to find unmistakable marks of adult Chinese in child English: "Tickles me" is just not good enough.

Fortunately, children can be accommodating—at least when they are curious. If we look carefully at a two-year-old's questions, a peculiar pattern emerges. A good many children will ask:[35]

Where __ going?
Where __ eat?
Where __ find pliers?
How __ do it?
How __ play that game?
How __ get it on?
Why __ working?
Why __ laughing at me?
Why __ drink tea?
When __ go home?
When __ wash hands?

The missing subjects here generally cause no confusion, as they are inferable from the context. For example, "Where going?" may be a response to "We're heading out"; "How do it?" may have followed "You can feed the fish yourself": and "Why laughing at me?" may be asked right after they said something funny, as children often do. But almost never—parents are encouraged to pay attention to their toddlers—would children ask these:

What __ eat?        (= "we," in response to "We are having
                              supper now.")
Which __ pick?     (= "you," asking Mommy to read a story.)
Who __ going with? (= "I," wondering about who's taking him
                              to the park.)
Who __ hit?         (= "he," regarding Dennis, who was behav-
                              ing badly.)

Here the subject also seems in principle inferable from the context; however, children refrain.

These possible and impossible questions are in fact neatly partitioned. On the one hand are questions of When, How, Why, and Where, concerning *modifiers*; for these, children often drop the subject. On the other, we have questions of Who and What, which are *participants*—specifically, objects—in the event denoted by the verb; for these, leaving out the subject ceases to be an option. Why English-speaking children drop some subjects but not others may seem mysterious, until we have a look at Chinese adults.

While Chinese can frequently leave out the subject, it is not "anything goes." A subject can be left out only if it is old and familiar information from the previous conversational context. Consider the following scenario regarding the Simpsons. The minds of two Chinese speakers and the flow of information in the context are depicted by diagrams.

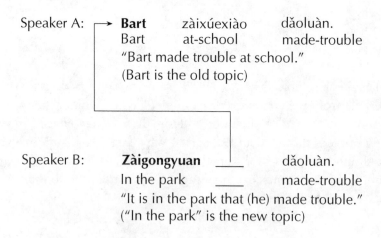

Speaker A:  → **Bart**     zàixúexiào     dǎoluàn.
              Bart       at-school     made-trouble
             "Bart made trouble at school."
             (Bart is the old topic)

Speaker B:     **Zàigongyuan** ____     dǎoluàn.
             In the park    ____     made-trouble
             "It is in the park that (he) made trouble."
             ("In the park" is the new topic)

Speaker A's statement establishes the troublemaker Bart as the topic of the conversation; Speaker B can then leave him out and the context suffices to make his identity clear. Of course, one doesn't have to talk about Bart forever. In all languages, a new topic can be introduced by moving it to the prominent initial position of a sentence. In this case, Speaker B offers the correction that Bart's mischief actually took place *in the park,* a prepositional phrase, but the old topic of Bart is still accessible and Speaker B can therefore leave the subject (the equivalent of "he") out.

This is not to say that the topic drop in Chinese can go unchecked. Consider another imaginary dialogue:

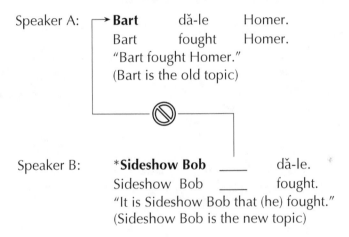

Speaker A:    →**Bart**        dǎ-le        Homer.
                     Bart          fought        Homer.
                     "Bart fought Homer."
                     (Bart is the old topic)

Speaker B:        *__Sideshow Bob__        ____        dǎ-le.
                       Sideshow  Bob        ____        fought.
                       "It is Sideshow Bob that (he) fought."
                       (Sideshow Bob is the new topic)

Again, Speaker A establishes Bart as the protagonist, and again, Speaker B thinks that A got the facts wrong: Bart didn't fight Homer but fought Sideshow Bob instead. As before, Sideshow Bob, the new topic, was placed in the beginning of the sentence. But now the topic-drop strategy ceases to work: leaving out the subject Bart (or the corresponding pronoun "he") results in severe ungrammaticality. This makes perfect sense: the old topic is accessible only if the new topic doesn't trump it. In the previous example, the new topic is about the park, a *modifier* of action, which cannot be the subject, a participant in the action. By contrast, the new topic here is Sideshow Bob, a person and thus potentially the subject, a *participant.* When two topics of the same type compete to dominate the conversation, the new one takes over.

This detour to Chinese grammar is interesting because the subtle restriction of topic drop is imported wholesale in American children's English. The only difference is that in Chinese, a new topic is established by fronting.[36] English questions concerning new information like "Where __ going?" and "How __ do it?" are about *modifiers*: they are altogether different from participants and do not stand in the way of contextual linking. According to our theory, the child can drop the subject just as Chinese adults do. By contrast, "Who __ going with?" and "What __ see?" are about *participants*; again like Chinese adults, English-speaking children must leave the subject intact.

We stress that English-speaking children "speak Chinese" insofar as they, probabilistically, exercise the topic-drop option, of which the Chinese language is a standard example; many languages in the world use topic drop.[37]

There you have it: we all spoke Chinese when we were little.

Once we bring natural selection to children's language, everything they say makes sense—biological sense, that is. A number of my colleagues in the field have been independently pursuing similar lines of research: these include experimentalists Tom Roeper at the University of Massachusetts, Roz Thornton and Stephen Crain at Marquarie University in Sydney (whose work featured Jabba the Hutt and Kermit the frog, discussed earlier), the historical linguist Tony Kroch at the University of Pennsylvania—more on this in Chapter 8—and others.[38] But the results from these diverse approaches are converging. In Chapter 6, we have already made observations that young children's English verbs are often bare as Chinese, and their double negatives resemble African American English. When children deviate from the language they are learning, they are exercising *some* option in universal grammar, part of the innate biological endowment. Chances are that we may find exact replicates in the language of adults, though continents or even centuries away.

Despite their unwillingness to share toys, English-speaking children take a long time to grasp the linguistic expression of "self." Specifically, when they think that Tigger is narcissistic, they often end up saying "Tigger likes him"—which is not what adults would say. For grown-ups, "him" in a sentence like "Tigger likes him" can refer only to Eeyore, Christopher Robin, Piglet, or indeed any other (male) individual but crucially not Tigger himself. How do we know what children *mean* when they *say* something different? Not by reading their minds. The linguist Ken Wexler and colleagues told three-year-olds that "Mama Bear washes her" while showing them an incorrect picture of the mother bear washing herself and a correct one of her washing a cub. Three-year-old children picked Mama Bear half the time, while grown-ups would have picked the cub instead.[39]

Here we literally see history playing out in front of our eyes. During the mastery of the -self expressions ("himself," "herself," etc.), children have trekked through a few hundred years of the English language. In Old English, sentences like "John like him" in fact meant "John likes himself," as an excerpt from that time period shows:[40]

| . . . hweðer | he | hine | gefreclsian | wolde |
|---|---|---|---|---|
| . . . whether | he | him | set-free | would |

"whether he would set himself free" (circa AD 971)

Words like "himself" were fairly recent inventions that stabilized only around 1600. Before that, "self" was a stand-alone word that linguists call an *intensifier,* which denotes not self-reference but importance: think of its function as speaking in ALL CAPS.

hwæt Crist self tæhte and his aposolas on þære niwan gecyðnisse
"what Christ self and his apostles taught in the New Testament"

Starting around 1200, a fusion took place. It was as if the space between words disappeared. Pronouns and "self" became a single word, presumably because they were right next to each other. And gradually, the joint product took on the modern meaning of self-reference:

| bute | þane | mete | þat | hie | hire | self | et |
|---|---|---|---|---|---|---|---|
| except the | | meat | that | she | her | self | ate |

(circa 1150–1200)

| He | him | self | wurð | | ðanne | | circumcis |
|---|---|---|---|---|---|---|---|
| He | him | self | was | | then | | circumcised |

(circa 1250)

In modern English, we say "Tigger likes himself" rather than "Tigger likes him" not because the latter is wrong. It was "right" for Old English; in modern English, we don't use it because there is a better and more precise way of saying it: with the word "himself," whose designated function is self-reference.[41] In this sense, the use of "himself" is not unlike that of the irregular past tense. There is nothing wrong with "weared": indeed, "weared" used to be the appropriate (and regular) form for "wear," which became irregular only in the past few hundred years. As in the learning of past tense, where children often overuse the regular form (*hold–holded*; Chapter 5), the preference for "himself" over "him" takes repeated exposure to learn, and it will take a while to eliminate the competitor.

The competitor grammars are not always on display. A three-year-old's world is, after all, fairly simple; many complex aspects of the grammar are not often exercised, and even more rarely are they caught on tape by language acquisition researchers. For example, children ask a *lot* of questions: too many in fact, but most of them are short, simple, and linguistically boring. "Who ate my cheese?" for instance, does not invoke the use of recursion in the formation of the sentence. Something like "What do you think Goron eats?" by contrast, recursively embeds one sentence (about eating) into another (about thinking), and "who" undergoes long-distance movement:

> You think Goron eats what for breakfast.
> What do you think Goron eats for breakfast?

It looks like the wh-word travels to the beginning of the question in one fell swoop. But the linguists Stephen Crain and Roz Thornton caught something strange in English-speaking three-year-olds.[42] Because long-distance questions are fairly infrequent in a child's speech (or adults', for that matter, at least when we are talking to children), Crain and Thornton once again recruited puppets. A story is played out in front of a group of children, who are then instructed to check if the puppet was paying attention. Here's a sample of children's questions:

*What* do you think *what* Cookie Monster eats?
*Who* do you think *who* is in the box?

Although a child may use the correct form as well, these "doubling" questions are intriguing. They run against the imperfection theory, which holds that small children use small sentences because they can't handle sentences that are too long. Here, though, small children are *adding* words to perfectly grammatical sentences as if they are not long enough. But the mystery goes away if we look beyond the local language and turn to the parameters in universal grammar and the theory of learning by natural selection. Many languages, including German and Hindi, show intermediate steps in long-distance questions. Below is an example from German (note that "wer" appears only at the beginning of sentences—either the main or the embedded—rather than at any random place):

| *Wer* | glaubst du | *wer* | die | Bücher | hat? |
|-------|------------|-------|-----|--------|------|
| Who | think you | who | the | books | has? |

"Who do you think has the books?"

The coexistence of English-like and German-like forms is not surprising: we are witnessing grammars in competition. A child born in New York, for example, needs to learn that the way in which questions are raised in her language is *not* the German option. To do so, she will have to hear long-distance questions from her linguistic environment. And this then brings up a final line of evidence for the theory of parameters and the theory of learning by natural selection.

So far we have been dealing with children's failings en route to their language; we also need to account for their success. After all, many parameters of children's grammars *are* virtually perfect as soon as they start speaking, and some are probably in place well before that. It is unlikely that these parameters are intrinsically easier to learn than those learned late (compulsory subjects, for instance): in all cases, the child is making a binary choice. The explanation for such disparities is actually straightforward along the thinking of natural selection in biology—in fact, a good deal more straightforward than the Darwinian version.

For a long time, biologists have likened natural selection to an organism inching up an alpine slope, aiming for the peaks of adaptive fitness. Biologists have also known for a long time that the reality is more complicated. On the one hand, inching up the hill works only if the slope is smooth; in a jagged terrain, which corresponds to, say, slight changes in the environment, the climbing might be stalled in a local valley and never reach the peak of optimality. For instance, being nearsighted is probably less adaptively fit than having perfect version, but being nearsighted could get one out of the draft in a time of war—a change in the environment—thus avoiding premature death. The other side of complexity has to do with multiple peaks in the adaptive landscape; even in the same environment, the outcome of selection is not necessarily the same every time. In a classic experiment in the 1950s, geneticists selected for changes in wing size in two separate populations of fruit flies: it worked, but one population changed the size of cells that make wings, while the other changed the number of cells. In other words, there are multiple solutions to the challenges posed by Nature.[43]

Natural selection in the world of linguistic parameters is far simpler. First, if linguists are right, then there is a finite (and fairly small) number of parameters that gives the complete range of possible grammars. This space appears to be the same for children of all races and cultures, as any infant can learn any language if placed in the corresponding environment. Second, language acquisition is rapid. All major parameters of grammar are set by the fourth or fifth year of a child's life; it is therefore reasonable to assume, for the most part, that the linguistic environment for the natural selection of parameters is a stable one. (Interesting questions arise when no grammar fits the learning data perfectly, as in the case of bilingualism; we will address this topic in Chapter 8.) Third, while genes work together in incredibly complicated ways and their functions can only occasionally be teased apart by modern technologies, the interaction among the parameters is undeniably simpler. It still requires a lot of training and hard work, but with a sufficient amount of immersion in any given language, any linguist worth her salt can take an intricate pattern of that grammar and pinpoint the relevant parameter or parameters, and place it in the typology of languages established from more familiar languages.

These properties of the parameters lead to a straightforward transplantation of evolutionary models to language learning. Evolution is measured by the change of gene frequencies in a population due to evolutionary forces: the greater fitness advantage that a gene holds over its competitor, the faster will it rise to dominance. In mathematical models of evolution, fitness is represented by a real number between 0 and 1, though this value is often difficult to measure in the real biological populations. In the case of language learning, the fitness of a parameter value in a linguistic environment can be explicitly and precisely determined. One could, in principle, record *everything* a child hears until her fifth birthday. This is hardly necessary: the existing data is already sufficiently voluminous and representative, and we can fairly accurately estimate the frequencies of sentences that are required to push the parameter values one way or another.

While we cannot make statements like "Four hundred questions are enough for the wh-movement parameter," we can, like biologists, make *relative* comparisons. That is, all things being equal, parameters that are expressed by *more* sentences in the environment will be learned *faster*, because their competitors will be punished more often. Take the verb-to-tense parameter (No for English and Yes for French), which is expressed by the ordering of the finite verb and adverbs. There are about 7 percent of such sentences in the speech heard by French children, who very rarely err on this parameter, starting with their very first multiword utterances. Now, any parameter that gets more than 7 percent of evidence ought to be learned even earlier, and this is indeed the case. For instance, the head-directionality parameter (Initial for English and Final for Japanese) is manifested in the order of verb and object and prepositional phrase, and the wh-movement parameter (Yes for English vs. No for Chinese) is marked by whether the wh-word skips to the beginning of the sentence. These types of confirming evidence are very frequent in the adults' speech (both over 30 percent), and consequently, children never get these parameters wrong. The compulsory subject parameter (Yes for English and No for Chinese) is supported by expletive subject sentences such as "There came a blue train"—a mere 1.2 percent of the learning data, and the use of subjects becomes consistent only when the child is around three years old. The wh-copying parameter in long-distance questions (Yes for German and No for English) fares even worse: the decisive evidence consists of sentences like "Who do you think ate the cheese?"—about 0.2 percent of the sentences English-speaking children hear; they may be speaking German for a long time. Modeled after those baby growth charts published by the National Center for Health Statistics (and proliferated by parenting books), we can offer an approximate "parameter growth chart" for the time course of how parameters are learned:

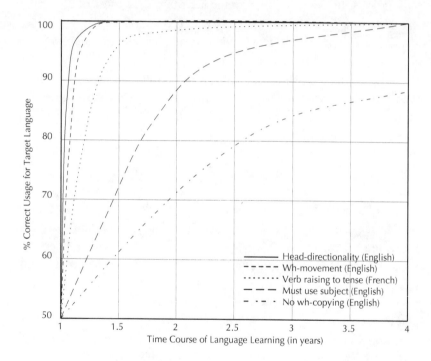

We end the discussion of parameters and natural selection on a more serious note. Some children suffer from some form of language learning deficit: there is no consensus on exactly what percentage of the population is affected, and the symptoms have so far defied a unifying diagnosis. Critical decisions had to be made when educators and therapists designed a battery of language assessment tests. Until very recently, however, the science of how children learn languages has played virtually no role at all in this process. And this area is one in which essentialist thinking reigns supreme. A child may be diagnosed as having language deficits if he shows systematic divergence from the oracle: that is, the grammar he is expected to eventually acquire.

But these conventional methods for language assessment are doubly disturbing. On the one hand, the oracle is often assumed to be the socially dominant "standard" English. Failing to take dialectal variations into account makes children from certain social and economic strata particularly susceptible to misdiagnosis. On the other hand, under the view of grammar learning by natural selection, children's language is *expected* to deviate from the oracle. Before rushing to conclude that a child has a language deficit, we need to recognize the inevitability of grammatical "errors." Maybe that child doesn't have trouble with language: he could simply be a somewhat slower learner for whom the elimination of the Chinese or the German grammar takes a little more time.[44] Perhaps there is reason for concern, and maybe we should talk to him more often, but surely there is no need to panic.

I am pleased to report that some of the world's leading child language researchers are already on the case.[45] To understand how language learning fails will need an understanding of how language learning succeeds.

Linguists' pencil-and-paper dissection of exotic grammars turns out to paint a remarkably accurate landscape of how children learn languages. The parameters serve to partition the mental space of grammars into a number of dimensions, along which the child can gradually inch up to the peak of her language: "Tickles me" is the record of her explorations in parameter land.

What if this exploration goes slightly astray? Actually, scratch "what if." Language learning *must* go astray. If the parameters contain all the answers to language learning, and if children are so good at picking out the right ones, wouldn't children end up talking exactly like their parents?

The answer is no. Language *changes,* and has changed enormously. In this chapter alone, we have seen the shift from Old English to Middle English, from Shakespeare to Cookie Monster. For our theory of language to withstand the test of history, universal grammar and natural selection must be taken back in time.

# CHAPTER 8

# The Superiority
# of the German Language

On a castaway island arrive two populations, one speaking English and the other German. After a few generations, which language is going to be the survivor?

I'm sorry to report that the capitulation of English to German would be all but guaranteed—at least in theory. Theories are always abstractions from reality, and our thought experiment hinges on a number of assumptions. All worldly matters must be put aside. The Blitz of London, the disputed goal that handed England the 1966 Soccer World Cup over Germany, and all other historical grudges have been laid to rest. (This is no *Lord of the Flies.*) The two communities of speakers are supposed to make nice and play together, and more important for our purposes, talk to each other. But can we really take language matters out of social reality and indulge in such desert island fantasies—predicting the superiority of the German language over English? A long argument is in order.

This chapter deals with the subject of language change and continues to explore the parallels between human language and biological evolution. But it may be said that the parallels between these two fields preceded the fields themselves (at least in their modern inceptions). Darwin, in developing the theory of common descent and the classification of species on the basis of their evolutionary relations, made an explicit analogy to language change over time:

If we possessed a perfect pedigree of mankind, a genealogical arrangement of the races of man would afford the best classification of the various languages now spoken throughout the world; and if all extinct languages, and all intermediate and slowly changing dialects, were to be included, such an arrangement would be the only possible one. Yet it might be that some ancient languages had altered very little and had given rise to few new languages, whilst others had altered much owing to the spreading, isolation and state of civilisation of the several co-descended races, and had thus given rise to many new dialects and languages.[1]

We may do well by following the master—and our mission is far simpler. Tracking changes in English grammar, for instance, hardly threatens traditional belief systems in the same way Darwin's revolution did. A few language "traditionalists" aside, linguists have never been subjected to the abuse and ridicule suffered by the early Darwinians: no linguist, so far as I know, has ever been caricatured as a giant ape in leading newspapers, and no Intelligent Designer in his right mind would have come up with expletive subjects or No Grandparent Left Behind. There would be no seasickness aboard HMS *Beagle* either, which the young Darwin had to endure. To gather raw data for language change, a trip to the old manuscript section in the library usually suffices. Finally, evolutionary changes generally take place at a glacial rate, which makes direct observation virtually impossible. By contrast, linguistic changes take place right in front of our eyes.

Word changes are most obvious. Nobody in the 1980s could have known "blog" or "metrosexual." Perfectly familiar words like "spam" have taken on new meanings in this information age. Other aspects of language change are less obvious, yet a few snapshots over time make them unmistakably clear. Consider *Matthew* 26:73 from four Bible translations over the past millennium:

**Old English** (The West-Saxon Gospels, c. 1050)
þa æfter lytlum fyrste genēalǣton þa ðe þær stodon, cwǣdon to petre. Soðlice þu eart of hym, þyn sprǣe þe gesweotolað.

**Middle English** (The Wycliff Bible, fourteenth century)
And a litil aftir, thei that stooden camen, and seiden to Petir, treuli thou art of hem; for thi speche makith thee knowun.

**Early Modern English** (The King James Bible, 1611)
And after a while came vnto him they that stood by, and saide to Peter, Surely thou also art one of them, for thy speech bewrayeth thee.

**Modern English** (The New English Bible, 1961)
Shortly afterwards the bystanders came up and said to Peter, "Surely you are another of them; your accent gives you away!"[2]

Old English looks altogether like an alien species but orthographies (spelling systems) are not audio recording devices: what did Old English *sound* like? When it comes to dead languages, orthography is all we've got. Worse yet, old manuscripts are often incomplete or damaged (the earliest specimen of Old English was recorded on parchment, for instance), and our ancestors were just as prone as we are to spelling and copying errors. Fortunately, the English language happens to have a fairly revealing orthography.[3] Old English was first written in the runic alphabet, which was used in northern Europe but no one knows much about its origins (or what exactly the word "rune" means, for that matter). The orthography we see in the West-Saxon Gospels, while deviating from modern English by more than a few letters, was nevertheless drawn from the Latin alphabet that arrived in the British Isles along with Christianity. It is fairly safe to assume that the importation of the Latin spelling closely followed the adoption of the Latin pronunciation, about which linguists know a great deal from independent sources.

Poetry is another clue in the reconstruction of ancient sound systems, on the grounds that poems generally rhyme. Rather than putting ourselves through a crash course on *Beowulf* (Old English), we can appreciate the use of poetic evidence with the more familiar Early Modern English of Shakespeare, who stopped writing for the stage in 1611, the year the King James Bible was published:

You spotted snakes with double tongue,
Thorny hedge-hogs, be not seen;
Newts, and blind-worms, do no wrong;
Come not near our fairy queen.[4]

This passage from *A Midsummer Night's Dream* suggests that half a millennium ago, "tongue" rhymed with "wrong" rather than "wrung."

None of these cues are foolproof: as we all know, poems don't always rhyme. To make old languages talk requires a good deal of detective work: one must gather multiple sources of clues and hope they collectively point to a single direction. Old English actually didn't sound that strange; at least that's what linguists were able to piece together. Many letters in modern English spelling were used back then and probably sounded the same. Even the few odd ones can find counterparts in modern languages. Take, for example, the passage from the West-Saxon Gospels: æ sounds like "a" in "hat," þ sounds like "th" in "through," ð sounds like "th" in "other." While we have lost ǣ and ē, these sounds are still employed in the relatives of the English language: ǣ is pronounced like the ê in "bête" (French for "animal") and ē is like the first "e" in "Leben" (German for "life").

Once we go beyond the looks and sounds of Old English, we see more linguistic continuities running straight to the present day. The line from the West-Saxon Gospels, if glossed into modern English, reads like this:

then after little first approached they that there stood, said to Peter.
Truly thou art of them, thy speech thee makes clear.

The internal structure of many phrases remain unaltered. From "to Peter" and "thy speech," we see that prepositions and articles come, then as now, before the noun, and a relative clause comes after the noun it modifies ("they that there stood"). But the order in which these phrases are arranged into sentences has changed considerably: it was a lot more flexible back then. For example, Old English had two ways of saying "the woman saw the man," as if word order were irrelevant:[5]

| sēo | cwēn | geseah | þone | guman |
| þone | guman | geseah | sēo | cwēn |

Freedom in grammar is paid for with restrictions on words. Old English has rich morphological markings that directly encode grammatical functions. For example, the article "the" has two forms above: "sēo" is feminine and nominative (designating the subject) and "þone" is masculine and accusative (the object). If we switch the roles around, "the man saw the woman" would be:

| se | guma | geseah | þā | cwēn |
| the-mas-nom | man | saw | the-fem-acc | woman |

Note the masculine nominative form "se" and the feminine accusative form "þā." Switching the orders of the subject and object does not change the meaning:

| þā | cwēn | geseah | se | guma |
| the-fem-acc | woman | saw | the-mas-nom | man |

This is rather like Japanese, where nouns are also tagged with nominative and accusative markers (-*ga* and -*o* respectively). While the basic word order is SOV ("John-ga Mary-o mikaketa," or "John saw Mary"), an OSV variation ("Mary-o John-ga mikaketa") causes no confusion. Again, morphology is not decorative ornamentation on words; one of its chief functions lies in spelling out grammatical relations. Morphologically rich languages tend to have greater flexibility in the assembly of sentences because morphological marking alone often suffices to make clear who did what to whom.

The deterioration of morphology is a major theme in the history of the English language over the past millennium. The period of Middle English witnessed much of this erosion. A large set of suffixes, with designated grammatical functions, used to latch onto nouns; they have all but disappeared over time. As illustrated below, of the various forms that a noun (meaning "stone") could bear in Old English, by Late Middle English only the singular vs. plural distinction was retained.

| Old English | Early Middle English | Late Middle English |
|---|---|---|
| stān | ston | stoon |
| stān-e | ston-e | |
| stān-es | ston-es | stoon-(e)s |
| stān-as | | |
| stān-um | ston-en | |
| stān-a | ston-e | |

Similarly, a single article "the" in modern English has supplanted all the gender-sensitive case-marking forms in Old English (se, sēo, þa, þone). While there is no consensus why these morphological changes took place, the end results are perfectly predictable: as informative morphological marking disappeared, word order freedom went with it. The side effects of morphological change in languages, however, are more difficult to comprehend.

Morphological "deterioration" or "impoverishment" sounds like a serious charge—an aesthetic statement, to say the least. But rest assured that no value judgment is meant here, and the choice of words is due to the limitation of our vocabulary as well as the somewhat dubious tradition of nineteenth-century linguistics.

To properly understand language change requires us to peel off a pervasive layer of social and cultural misconception about language and language change. Even the master had succumbed to this. Darwin's belief in progress, be it a manifestation of the Victorian values of the time or shaped by his own theory of natural selection, led him to endorse the eminent German philologist Max Müller: "A struggle for life is constantly going on amongst the words and grammatical forms in each language. The better, the shorter, the easier forms are constantly gaining the upper hand, and they owe their success to their own inherent virtue."[6]

Is language actually getting better, shorter, and easier? Nowadays we often hear exactly the opposite. Teenager slang is awful, students no longer learn Latin, our children—not to mention our president—cannot put together a grammatical sentence. The whimsical poet Ogden Nash was at least half serious in his "Laments for a dying language":

Coin brassy words at will, debase the coinage;
We're in an if-you-cannot-lick-them-join age,
A slovenliness provides its own excuse age,
Where usage overnight condones misusage.
Farewell, farewell to my beloved language,
Once English, now a vile orangutanguage.[7]

Snobbery or nostalgia: whatever it may be, complaining about kids is nothing new. Many nineteenth-century intellectuals were convinced of society's eroding moral values; language change would of course be a downward spiral, for it directly reflected the decadence of the younger generation at large. The great German linguist Jakob Grimm (1785–1863), better known for the fairy tales he collected with his brother Wilhelm, once protested that "six hundred years ago every rustic knew, that is to say practiced daily, perfections and niceties in the German language of which the best grammarians nowadays do not even dream." Historical linguistics, as a discipline that studies and reconstructs the languages of the past, was seen in a therapeutic light, as one scholar remarked: "A principal goal of this science is to reconstruct the full, pure forms of an original stage from the variously disfigured and mutilated forms which are attested in the individual languages." If the past was full and pure, the present must be fragmented and contaminated: language change is bad.

Well, one would not want to push this argument too far: moral degeneration as the cause for language change can lead to awkward moments. You may recall Henry Higgins, the pompous linguistics professor in *My Fair Lady*—we are a much nicer bunch in real life—who pronounced the Queen's English the superior language of England. However, Professor Higgins would be dismayed to learn that even Her Majesty no longer speaks the Queen's English.[8] Merely half a century ago, the United Kingdom was still a society with rigid class demarcations, which in turn led to "model" accents such as the Received Pronunciation. As social barriers broke down, classes of speech crumbled as well, apparently all the way to the Crown. Thanks to the BBC's excellent audio facilities, Queen Elizabeth's annual Christmas message broadcasts have been meticulously preserved. Using these materials, a team of linguists and speech scientists from Australia detected a gradual drift in the Queen's pronunciations, where the changes in short vowels (*i* in "hit," *a* in "had," *e* in "bed," *o* in "Bob," etc.) were among the most significant. For example, in the 1950s, the Queen's "had" more or less rhymed with "bed," but by the 1980s, it had begun to rhyme with "mad." To be sure, the Queen still doesn't sound quite like Ali G or David Beckham, yet the Australian researchers conjectured that the changes in her pronunciation could be traced to the speech of the younger and lower classes, whose cultural influence has become more prominent over the past half a century; indeed, many are BBC broadcasters themselves.

So is language change progress or degeneration? It is neither, of course. To assert that language change is for the better or worse requires some measure of what a "good" or "bad" language is, and the issue of language change needn't come into question here. But no coherent criterion has ever been given: upon examination, the pronouncements of the self-appointed pundits are always a mix of cultural biases, half-understandings of languages, and an obvious compulsion for telling people what to do. Many linguists have written about these fallacies and we briefly touched upon this issue in Chapter 6 on African American English and linguistic parameters, but the psychologist Steven Pinker's exposé of the so-called "language mavens" remains the most informative and entertaining read.[9]

Let's take a specific case in the context of language change. A by-product of morphological deterioration in English is an inferiority syndrome manifested in the admiration of the Latin language. The mastery of Latin is still regarded as a considerable intellectual achievement: this surely has to do with Latin's traditional role as the lingua franca of scholarly and religious discourse, but also stems from the complexity (and "precision") of its rich morphological markings. It is therefore a mystery why no such respect has ever been extended to the speakers of Eskimo or Turkish. These languages, in somewhat different ways, readily cobble up a dozen morphemes on a single word, and their morphological systems mark a far richer set of meanings than Latin's. Moreover, it is a mistake to think that the scholarly use of Latin and its morphological complexity are somehow causally related.

There are languages, like Chinese, which do not have any morphological marking, and yet this did not prevent the Chinese from developing a rich literary and cultural tradition. Either way, the supposed prestige for complex morphology evaporates.

Furthermore, we, as speakers of English, have even less reason to marvel nostalgically at the beauty of Latin: it's plainly none of our business. Contrary to still prevalent beliefs, English does not bear any direct historical relation to Latin. Being a member of the Germanic family, English is rather like a distant nephew of Latin. So if one did want to mourn the degeneration of English, looking over to Latin isn't the way to do it.

Leave that to the Romance languages. French, Italian, Spanish, Catalan, Romanian, and Portuguese are the direct descendants of Latin, which would make a more appropriate comparison. But here we have to qualify the term "direct." Romance languages did not split off from Latin at the same time. In fact, they are all derived from various dialects of what is (derogatorily) known as Vulgar Latin, suggesting that some form of deviation from the classical Latin had already taken place by then. But are Romance languages really Latin degenerates? It is true that a great deal of Latin morphology has been lost in its descendants. For example, Latin has several case endings on the noun, depending on its grammatical role:[10]

| | | |
|---|---|---|
| nominative (subject) | *porta* est magna | "the gate is big" |
| genitive (possessor) | frons *portae* | "the front of the gate" |
| dative (goal) | *portae* similis | "similar to the gate" |
| accusative (object) | *portam* aperuêrunt | "(they) opened the gate" |
| ablative (source) | prô *portâ* | "in front of the gate" |

All these distinctions have disappeared in Spanish (and most other Romance languages):

| | |
|---|---|
| la *puerta* es grande | "the door is big" |
| el frente de la *puerta* | "the front of the door" |
| parecido a la *puerta* | "similar to the door" |
| abrieron la *puerta* | "(they) opened the door" |
| delante de la *puerta* | "in front of the door" |

However, in some aspects Spanish has increased its linguistic complexity—if that is the right way to put it—a fact that seems to get less attention from the guardians of language. For instance, Latin has only one word for the meaning of "to be":

| | |
|---|---|
| Fessus *sum* | "I am tired" |
| In domô *sum* | "I am in the house" |
| Rômânus *sum* | "I am a Roman" |

Spanish, by contrast, has added a new dimension of being: while being tired and being in the house are both temporary events, being a Roman is permanent. Thus, Spanish uses different verbs for temporary-being versus permanent-being. Viewed in this light, then, Spanish has enriched Latin:

| | |
|---|---|
| *Estoy* cansado | "I am tired" |
| *Estoy* en la casa | "I am in the house" |
| *Soy* romano | "I am a Roman" |

Other very useful additions to Spanish are the definite and indefinite articles:

| *un* | perro | ladró | | *el* | perro | ladró |
|---|---|---|---|---|---|---|
| a | dog | barked | | the | dog | barked |

Latin lacks these, and must resort to an alternative strategy to make the definite/indefinite distinction: like Russian (see Chapter 6), Latin places a definite noun before the verb, and an indefinite noun after the verb:

| latrâvit | canis | | canis | latrâvit |
|---|---|---|---|---|
| barked | dog | | dog | barked |
| "a dog barked" | | | "the dog barked" | |

This may just seem like an inconvenience, but don't tell that to Winnie the Pooh. When the classic children's story was translated into Latin—a 1991 *New York Times* bestseller, no less—the title came out as *Winnie Ille Pu,* or "Winnie That Pooh." That is the best one can do in a language without definite articles.

The great American linguist Edward Sapir once wrote, "A linguist that insists on talking about the Latin type of morphology as though it were necessarily the high-water mark of linguistic development is like the zoologist that sees in the organic world a huge conspiracy to evolve the racehorse or the Jersey cow."[11] Languages, both old and new, are no better or worse; they are just different.

The fact of biological change was first noticed by ancient Greeks and was already apparent to nineteenth-century naturalists.[12] But it was Darwin, through his theory of common descent and natural selection, who supplied explanations for the path of evolutionary change. Language change is also plain for all to see, but we may, following Darwin, ask the deeper questions. Could the languages of the world be traced to a common origin? What causes language to change? Can we develop a theory of language change with the simplicity and elegance of Darwin's natural selection?

First, the question of common ancestry: do all the world's languages ultimately go back to a single origin? That is, was there an Original Tongue, which subsequently begat all of the world's languages, from Ainu to Zulu? Was there a Tower of Babel where "the whole earth was of one language, and of one speech"? If so, how can we know? And if not, how did the enormously diverse array of languages come about?

The primary means of deriving genealogical relations among languages is the *comparative method,* which is perhaps the oldest gadget in a linguist's toolkit. In 1786, Sir William Jones, a British scholar stationed in India and an expert on the Sanskrit language, made a remarkable observation:

> The Sanskrit language, whatever may be its antiquity, is of a wonderful structure; more perfect than the Greek, more copious than the Latin, and more exquisitely refined than either, yet bearing to both of them a stronger affinity, both in the roots of verbs and in the forms of grammar, than could possibly have been produced by accident; so strong indeed that no philologer could examine them all three, with-

out believing them to have sprung from some common source, which, perhaps no longer exists.[13]

Hence a unified Indo-European language family was born. One doesn't need to be a linguist to see the striking similarities between languages within the family, and the marked differences from languages outside the family. This is clear when we look at the number words in Latin, Greek, Sanskrit, Gothic (an ancient Germanic language that survived primarily in the form of a Bible), and Old English, and contrast them with Mandarin Chinese, which is from an altogether different family, Sino-Tibetan:

| Latin | Greek | Sanskrit | Gothic | Old English | Chinese |
|-------|-------|----------|--------|-------------|---------|
| ūnus | heis | eka | ains | ān | yī |
| duo | duo | dvau | twai | twēgen, twā | èr |
| trēs | treis | trayas | threis | þrīe | sān |
| quattuor | tettares | catvāras | fidwor | fēower | sì |
| quīnque | pente | panca | fimf | fīf | wǔ |
| sex | hex | sat | saihs | siex | liù |
| septem | hepta | sapta | sibun | seofon | qī |
| octō | oktō | astau | ahtau | eahta | bā |
| novem | ennea | nava | niun | nigon | jiǔ |
| decem | deka | dasa | taihun | tīen | shí |

It is also plain that within the Indo-European family, some languages are clustered more closely than others. Among the first subgroups recognized by linguists is the Romance family, consisting of French, Spanish, Italian, Portuguese, Catalan, and others, which are all known to be descendants of Latin. Again, one needn't be a linguist—or know Latin—to see that the overwhelming affinities within these languages must trace back to *some* common ancestor.

| French | Italian | Portuguese | Spanish | Catalan | Romanian |
|--------|---------|------------|---------|---------|----------|
| un | un | um | uno | un | unu |
| deux | due | dois | dos | dos | doi |
| trois | tre | três | tres | tres | trei |

| French | Italian | Portuguese | Spanish | Catalan | Romanian |
|--------|---------|------------|---------|---------|----------|
| quatre | quattro | quatro | cuatro | quatre | patru |
| cinq | cinque | cinco | cinco | cinc | cinci |
| six | sei | seis | seis | sis | saşe |
| sept | sette | sete | siete | set | şapte |
| huit | otto | oito | ocho | vuit | opt |
| neuf | nove | nove | nueve | nou | nouă |
| dix | dieci | dez | diez | deu | zece |

More interesting questions arise, and quite a lot of linguistics train-ing would be needed, when we look beyond the obvious cases and attempt finer classifications of languages on the basis of historical rela-tion. Who is related to whom—and how closely? There are many log-ically possible ways of grouping just two languages: Are they siblings (family *a* below), aunt-nephews (family *b*), distant cousins (family *c*), or something even more remote, like leaves hanging on two branches of a bush? The problem is complicated by the fact that those interme-diate steps in language change—the gray dots—that ultimately led to A and B might have gone extinct and left no record behind.

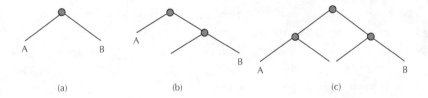

(a)          (b)          (c)

The reconstruction of the historical relations of languages resembles that of evolutionary phylogeny. But linguists may feel they deserve more credit; it is quite likely that the intellectual priority was the other way around. The work of historical linguists probably influenced the evolutionary thinking of Darwin, as he was gracious to acknowledge. In the discussion of the genealogical arrangements of species (and in reference to the only diagram in the entire *Origin*), he noted the lin-guist's methods for reconstructing historical relations among lan-guages:

The various degrees of difference between the languages of the same stock would have to be expressed by groups subordinate to groups; but the proper or even the only possible arrangement would still be genealogical; and this would be strictly natural, as it would connect together all languages, extinct and recent, by the closest affinities, and would give the filiation and origin of each tongue.

In Darwin's time, the most important clue for evolutionary relations could be found in *homologies*: traits that could be traced back to a single origin despite, in some cases, major physiological and functional divergence. The whale's flippers and the human's hands are strikingly similar in skeletal and muscular structures, which suggests that they are both derived from a shared ancestral body plan. At the same time, the striking differences—no small matter, considering that we can type and whales can't—would be attributed to the distinct evolutionary paths: the whale's ancestor apparently forsook life on land and readapted its front limbs for swimming. Moreover, the "various degrees of difference" among homologous traits can be used to deduce the timing of evolutionary branches: the greater degree of similarity between human and chimpanzee hands suggests that humans and chimpanzees split off much more recently than when the whale left the land mammals and returned to the aquatic world.

The linguistic equivalent of homologies are *cognates*: words in different languages that are derived from the same etymological root. The meanings of cognates are generally similar, if not the same, but their pronunciations may have diverged: such "various degrees of difference" may tell us how languages drifted apart over time. For example, "padre" (Italian/Spanish), "père" (French), "pai" (Portuguese), and "pare" (Galician) all mean "father," and it can't be just coincidence that they sound similar. Indeed, all these can be traced back to the Latin word "pater," which means "father" as well. This then makes them cognates, which in turn gives justification for lumping Italian, Spanish, French, Portuguese, and Galician in a single family (Romance).

Note that this method of tracing the natural history of languages can be applied iteratively, starting from the bottom of the family tree and working upward. By 1861, the linguist August Schleicher was able to synthesize a family history of the Indo-European languages:[14]

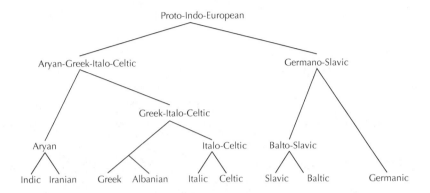

Though modern scholars will find much to disagree with in this particular version of the Indo-European history, it nevertheless represents a milestone in historical linguistics and was built on the basic principles of the comparative method still in use today.

Perhaps the more interesting consequences of linguistic comparison and reconstruction lie not so much in the histories of languages themselves but in the history of the peoples who spoke them. Who *were* the Proto-Indo-Europeans? How did they expand over the vast land from Europe to Central and South Asia, yet somehow miss out on the pockets of Basque, one of the few European languages that are not Indo-European?[15] Did they spread materials through peaceful cultural exchanges or violent warfare and conquests? These questions, often fueled by nationalistic or even racist fervor—think of the Nazis' obsession with a pure "Aryan" language—have traditionally generated fierce controversies among linguists, anthropologists, and archaeologists. Some of these may have been settled in recent years thanks to advances in modern biology. For example, geneticists have discovered a high concentration of certain genes in the population of what is now Turkey, a concentration that gets gradually diluted as one moves westward toward Europe. Moreover, the geographic distribution of the genes shows what the human geneticist Luigi Luca Cavalli-Sforza described as the typical migration patterns of farming populations.[16] Taken together, these findings lend support to archaeologist Colin Renfrew's theory that the Proto-Indo-Europeans originated in Anatolia, which today is indeed part of Turkey, and spread to Europe in parallel to the diffusion of agriculture.[17] What of the Basques, who speak a language very different from modern European languages? Cavalli-Sforza and colleagues found an unusually high frequency of the gene for the blood group Rhesus-negative in the Basque population. Quite possibly, Basque, because of its relative isolation in the mountains of northern Spain and southwestern France, is the only survivor of the "original" European language of the hunter-gatherers, while the rest of Europe was taken over by the invading farmers—and their Indo-European language. It must be said that many questions still remain open. After all, bones, tools, and genes do not bear the direct traces of language. Nevertheless, the fact that we can raise these questions is a testament to the achievements of historical linguistics.

But the success of historical linguistics has not yet reached biblical heights—the Tower of Babel, to be specific—and perhaps never will. There is no reason to believe, one way or another, that all languages of the world can be traced back to a single source, and there is no prospect of reconstructing the Original Tongue that would have been spoken in Africa.

Why not? Why couldn't one connect the dots as usual, with the same methods and principles used in the reconstruction of the Indo-European family, only this time with languages all over the world and leading to a much larger family tree? We must realize that linguistic comparison and historical reconstruction are only as good as the raw materials available to be compared and reconstructed, and this is where the analogy between the natural history of languages and that of species breaks down. In modern biology, the reconstruction of evolutionary history has gone beyond homologies like hands and flippers. The evidence that links all human groups together is the DNA, specifically, the DNA that makes mitochondria, those tiny bacteria-like bodies residing in and providing energy for our cells. The ordinary DNA that makes our body is, of course, obtained from the combined genes of our parents, which can quickly obscure genetic lineage. By contrast, the mitochondria replicate by self-division; since their DNA is passed down from only mothers, it is hence not subject to paternal contamination. However, mitochondrial DNA *is* subject to mutation. Using empirical estimates of mutation rates, which are assumed to be constant (the so-called "molecular clock"), geneticists have been able to compare the degree of divergence for mitochondr-ial DNA across human races and groups and thereby trace the begin-ning of our ancestry to Africa some 150,000 years ago.

Unfortunately, there are no comparable markers for the phylogeny of language. This, however, has not stopped a few maverick scholars from aggressively grouping languages into ever larger language fami-lies of the distant past.[18] In the view of most linguists, however, these theories are based on very scanty evidence and are therefore extremely speculative. It is generally agreed that the historical reconstruction can be extended back ten thousand years but not earlier.[19] The reason is simple: we run out of useful cognates. A number of factors have con-tributed to this limitation. Cultural contact and exchanges may easily supplant cognates and thus trample evidence of linguistic genealogy. For instance, if judged on lexicon overlap alone, English would be most closely related to French, thanks to massive borrowing of words (by the thirteenth century, over ten thousand French words had invaded English). To add insult to injury, what look like cognates may well be fake ones: languages are known to have words that mean and sound like cognates—but are not. *Manhi* in Korean means "many," *namae* in Japanese means "name," *faj* in Thai means "fire," *dog* in Mbabaram (an aboriginal language of Australia) means, well, "dog"; none of these languages, however, is related to English. In fact, given the relatively small number of consonants and vowels used in human languages, and the syllabic restrictions on word structures (see Chapter 4), it is not too surprising to find accidental convergence of fake cognates.[20] Finally, let's not forget that all comparisons and reconstructions presuppose that at least some of the ancient words were preserved in some form of record. Yet this may be too much to ask for: humans might have had the instinct to speak 150,000 years ago, but writing and reading were relatively late inventions of the Sumerians around 4000 BC.

Tough luck: it would have been fun to know what Adam and Eve said to each other back in Africa.

If the past is forever beyond our grasp, what about the future?

To learn about the future, as they say, we must first understand the past and the present. This, then, requires us to get down to the finer details of *how* language change takes place in real time, not just snapshots of *what* has taken place. Again, we can draw inspiration from Darwin's masterpiece. Those looking for the meaning of life in *Origin of Species* may be in for a mild shock: the first chapter reads like a pigeon fancier's manual, but that's precisely how Darwin developed his revolutionary theory. Making use of his numerous sources, including his own membership in two London pigeon clubs, Darwin showed that the great diversities of domestic pigeons could be traced to a shared ancestor, and were gradually modified by pigeon breeders' artificial selection. Given the glacial pace of evolution in nature, pigeons provided the ideal laboratory materials for direct observation.

Not long ago, linguists also considered language change too slow to be caught in action. Charles Hockett, an influential linguist around the mid-twentieth century, asserted in 1958 that "No one has yet observed sound change; we have only been able to detect it via its consequences. A more nearly direct observation would be theoretically impossible, if impractical, but any ostensible report of such an observation so far must be discredited."[21] A few years later, however, this claim was conclusively refuted. Direct observation of language change is possible. No, sophisticated technology is not a prerequisite, as in the case of the Queen's vowels, but one does need to know where to look. The linguist William Labov at the University of Pennsylvania is among the first and most prominent scholars in the modern study of language change, and he started out by, literally, comparing notebooks.[22]

Martha's Vineyard is the well-known island off the coast of Massachusetts. A cluster of fishing villages not long ago, it has since been transformed into a popular vacation spot and the summer home of America's rich and famous. When Labov visited the Vineyard in the early 1960s, he discovered that the native inhabitants' pronunciations differed significantly from the records of a survey, *Linguistic Atlas of New England,* conducted a mere thirty to forty years before. And it again had to do with vowels, a longer kind. Of particular interest were the vowels *au* in "out," "house," and "loud," and *ai* in "mile," "eye," and "light." Those vowels are called *diphthongs*; each is a composite of two simpler vowels, with the tongue sliding from one position of the mouth (*a*) to another (*u* and *i* respectively). In Chapter 4, we noted that all speech sounds can be split into a bundle of features, which specifies the location, manner, and other aspects of articulation.

Under that view, *a*, the first part of the two diphthongs, starts at a low (and middle) position, and then rises to a high back position, *u*, or a high front position, *i*. However, for the native Vineyarders, *a* in *au* and *ai* was centralized, the tongue starting out in a middle, rather than low, position, resulting in a sound like the reduced vowel *e* in "the."[23]

Curiously, according to the *Linguistic Atlas* a few decades back, the centralization of diphthongs was in fact on the wane: it had virtually disappeared in *au*, and survived only marginally in *ai*. What drove the Vineyard residents back to their old habits? Well, something very like the Parisian contempt toward American tourists. The Vineyard natives did not care for intruders either, who were disparagingly known as the "summer people." Centralizing diphthongs gave the natives a way to assert their identity as true islanders, the bearers of old Yankee values of independence and hard work, in opposition to the consumer culture of the summer tourists. It was particularly revealing that the propensity for centralization was highest among the age group of thirty-one to forty-five who still carried on fishing and thus carried a stronger sense of island identity; by comparison, centralization was much lower among those in the service industry for the vacationers. One native inhabitant opined:

> You people who come down here to Martha's Vineyard don't understand the background of the old families of the island . . . the rest of America, this part over here across the water that belongs to you and we don't have anything to do with, has forgotten all about . . . I think perhaps we use entirely different . . . type of English language . . . think differently here on the island . . . it is almost a separate language within the English language.[24]

Unlike Parisians, however, the natives stopped short of correcting the visitors' pronunciations.

The vowels on Martha's Vineyard demonstrated the ongoing reality of language change; they also pointed to the inherent complexity of language change and, by implication, the difficulties we face when trying to understand language change. Since long before the days of "You say tomato, I say tomahto," language has been an integral part of who we are, who we want to be, and how we relate to others, and these are precisely the factors that determined the course of vowels on Martha's Vineyard. To a large extent, language changes like fashion, as both are influenced by a complex array of cultural and social forces and identity politics. While confessions like that of the proud Vineyarder are hard to come by, we all are quite aware of the ways that the language we speak reflects who we are. The classic example again comes from William Labov's pioneering work.[25]

A distinctive characteristic of American English has to do with its *r*-ness. Most dialects of American English are *rhotic,* which means the sound *r* in "car," "bar," and "dart" is pronounced, as opposed to British English. The notable exceptions—for once, something Red Sox and Yankees fans are in agreement with—are found in the dialects of Boston and New York, or New Yawk, as New Yorkers would have it. (But recall from Chapter 5 that these *r*-less dialects drop the pronunciation of *r* only when *r* follows a vowel: "car" becomes "cah," but "rat" does not become "at.")

The history of the *r* and *r*-less speech is a long and interesting one. Around the time of the founding of America, the pronunciation of social prestige in British English was in fact rhotic, which naturally spread from the mother ship to the colonies. (As the United States gained prominence, cross-Atlantic exchanges became more like two-way traffic: even the French now regularly bemoan the Americanization of their language, e.g., "le weekend.") While social barriers are often difficult to break, particularly in those days, dialects and accents are easily imitated. So, just like any other fashion trends, once the mass catches on, the elite moves ahead. By the 1800s, *r*-lessness had emerged as the prestigious pronunciation in England and has remained so to this day, even though some regional dialects of British English are still rhotic. But most of America missed this flip-flop of prestige: the westward migration to the interior brought the *r*'s with it, and the rhotic pronunciation became the dominant speech pattern of American English. The only cities that kept up with the trends were Boston, New York, and a few other East Coast port cities, which imported the *r*-less speech through their continued extensive contact with England. So Bostonians and New Yorkers ended up with an accent that is standard across the Atlantic, but substandard at home.

No one enjoys being the odd one out, not even those proudly independent New Yorkers. We all are quite aware of the social connotations of our language. Labov's investigation of New York speech was simple but ingenious. He visited three department stores, on three echelons of the socioeconomic hierarchy: Saks Fifth Avenue for the rich folks, Macy's for the middle class, and Klein's, now defunct, but popular then among bargain basement shoppers. Labov would ask a salesclerk where to find some item that he already knew was on the fourth floor; this offered a first opportunity to observe the use or nonuse of *r* in the clerk's speech. "Excuse me?" Labov would say, to which the clerk would respond with another utterance of "fourth floor," now more carefully articulated than earlier. Of course, when he actually arrived on the fourth floor, Labov got another chance: "What floor is this?" Then he quickly dodged out of sight and jotted down the data on his notepad.

Labov found that the stratification of *r* and *r*-less speech was as clear as that of wealth and social prestige. The Saks clerks pronounced *r*'s almost three times more often than the Klein's clerks, with Macy's falling in between. Also of interest were the differences in styles across the three department stores. Klein's salesclerks pronounced *r*'s more than twice as often in careful speech as they did when speaking more casually, while there was virtually no difference at Saks. A reasonable explanation is that the speakers of the *r*-less pronunciation were aware of its lower status, and strove to imitate the more prestigious accent in careful speech. The upper class, on the other hand, had nothing to prove.

The linguistic variations in New York City and on Martha's Vineyard are immensely important findings, but they cast doubt on the feasibility of a science of language change. A hallmark of science is the ability to make predictions: a successful theory should not only explain what is at hand, it must also make reliable predictions about (currently) unknown or unobservable phenomena. In the present context, we would like a theory of language change to predict, for instance, whether a language will necessarily take a particular path. Or, more retrospectively, we would like to know whether certain linguistic changes that did in fact take place *had to* take place. Unfortunately, the outlook for such a theory isn't too bright. Language change is, first of all, a product of our biology, which gives us the very material that could change in the first place. At the same time, language change is also a product of our cultures, societies, and histories, which determine the course by which language actually changes. While the study of the biological basis of language (universal grammar) may be precise and deep—great progress has indeed been made in the past fifty years—we will need an equally precise and deep theory of cultures, societies, and histories to complete the picture. But there are reasons to believe that the picture will never be complete.

Again, take the case of *r*'s in American speech. We can probably predict, with some confidence, that the mass tends to follow the trendsetters. The problem is that we have no idea what makes something trendy in the first place. Even social prestige is not necessarily a blessing. After the Soviet Revolution in 1917, the previously desirable pronunciation of the Russian upper class was denounced (along with the upper class itself) such that people tried to disguise it. Our point here is that fashions and trends are not generally predictable. (We'd be rich if they were.) By implication, if the course of language change mirrors that of fashions and trends, as in the case of *r*'s in England and New York City, then a science of language change is hopeless. The ups and downs of *r*-less pronunciation had to do not with the pronunciation itself, but with the unique social environment, and the unique time period. After all, while the English elite ran away from the *r*'s in the 1800s, they put up with the *r*-less pronunciation among the masses in the 1900s. In other words, no one could have predicted the fate of *r*-less speech.

Moreover, language change is part of human history—a unique sequence of events littered with contingencies, surprises, and unpredictability. Which is why "What if" contemplations are so easy (and so much fun). What if Joan of Arc had failed to pick out Charles, the Dauphin, from the crowd? The Dauphin would have remained the Dauphin, rather than King Charles VII of France. What if the winter of 1812 had been warmer? Surely Napoleon's venture into Russia might have been less miserable. The bullet that killed Archduke Franz Ferdinand in Sarajevo set off an explosive chain of events, culminating in the breakout of World War I, but what if he had dodged the shot, or the assassin had missed? History often is the dramatic consequences of random events. Language change, a necessary by-product of human history, can be equally dramatic, and it does not always make for pleasant reading. When Europeans arrived in the Americas, equipped with superior weapons, deadly germs, and genocidal greed, the native inhabitants were virtually eliminated or "assimilated," along with their languages and cultures. After about eighty years of forceful imposition of Russian as the official language, many indigenous languages of the former Soviet Republics are now on the brink of extinction. While the elite and the powerful tend to dominate, the flow of linguistic influence is by no means unidirectional. Take English. With the dominance of the British and American Empires, propelled by modern communication technologies, English has become a truly global language. One doesn't need to look far to see how languages around the globe have actually influenced the more prominent English language. It is well known that many English words are borrowed from French and German, but the following list may hold some surprises:[26]

| | |
|---|---|
| Arabic: | admiral, assassin, mask, mattress, racket, syrup, zenith |
| Chinese: | junk, ketchup |
| Czech: | robot |
| Gaelic: | dad, slogan, trousers |
| Greek: | biology, coma, method, science (and many other scientific and technical terms) |
| Hebrew: | camel, ethnic, jubilee, paradise |
| Hindi: | bungalow, pundit, shampoo |
| Italian: | balcony, ballot, jeans, traffic, volt |
| Native American: | caucus, cockroach, squash |
| Persian: | arsenic, lilac, pajamas, sherbet, talisman |
| Portuguese: | buffalo, caste, port |
| Russian: | bistro, disinformation, mammoth, sputnik |
| Sanskrit: | candy, jungle, swastika |
| Spanish: | banana, cannibal, cork, potato, sherry |
| Swedish: | gauntlet, slag, weld |
| Turkish: | coffee, kiosk, scarlet, sorbet, yogurt |
| Yiddish: | bagel, chutzpah, kosher, schmooze, schmuck |

The fun with etymology is that every word has a story. For instance, "sherry" started out as "Xeres" (now "Jerez") in Spanish, made it into English as "sherris"; our ancestors, quite logically, figured this must contain a plural -s suffix and thus extracted "sherry" for the singular. But very little can be said beyond such a descriptive natural history. There was no rhyme or reason why "Xeres" must be imported into English; it just was.

What does this leave us with? The social, cultural, and historical dimensions of language change may lead one to suppose that language change is *really* like fashion, completely lawless and unpredictable, but that would be throwing in the towel too quickly. Linguistics is not the only discipline that must grapple with the uncertainties of history; we may do well by taking a look at others.

In the book *Wonderful Life,* the late evolutionary biologist Stephen Jay Gould proposed a thought experiment of "replaying life's tape":

> You press the rewind button and, making sure you thoroughly erase everything that actually happened, go back to any time and place in the past. . . . Then let the tape run again and see if the repetition looks at all like the original. If each replay strongly resembles life's actual pathway, then we must conclude that what really happened pretty much had to occur. But suppose that the experimental versions all yield sensible results strikingly different from the actual history of life? What could we then say about the predictability of self-conscious intelligence? or of mammals? or of vertebrates? or of life on land? or simply of multicellular persistence for 600 million difficult years?[27]

Gould was concerned with the fate of the creatures fossilized at the Burgess Shale in the Canadian Rockies. These creatures, some of which looked as if they came straight out of science fiction, emerged after the Cambrian Explosion about 570 million years ago, an era of great biological diversification. Then, it seemed, most of these creatures went extinct rather suddenly, leaving no descendants behind. Gould contends that the survivors were no more adaptive than their extinct contemporaries and that chance, or a cascade of chances, often plays a decisive role in the course of evolutionary history. As a cautionary note on the difficulties in understanding the past, he surely is right. Perhaps a better known example is the demise of dinosaurs. According to a widely accepted theory, dinosaurs' reign of terror abruptly ended 65 million years ago, when a meteorite ten kilometers wide rammed into the Earth off the coast of the Yucatan peninsula. The heat from the impact and the materials ejected into the atmosphere set off massive changes in the environment—a nuclear winter, so to speak—eventually (and pretty quickly, in geological terms) wiping out dinosaurs and up to 70 percent of plants and animals living at the time.

But Gould's point should not be overstated, either. While his account rightly recognizes the complexity of evolution, if pushed to the logical extreme, it amounts to the admission that whatever happened happened: nothing more can be said, for everything is contingency. Indeed, the interpretation of the Burgess Shale has become one of the more hotly debated topics in evolution. Armed with fossils recently unearthed from comparable sites, Simon Conway Morris at the University of Cambridge, one of the original interpreters of the Burgess Shale fossils, has in fact proposed an alternative account, one that stresses the deterministic characteristics of evolution.[28] The fate of the Burgess Shale creatures was sealed because they were less adaptive. So if Gould's tape of life were rerun, Conway contends, the end result would be the same.

While we needn't be concerned with the details in this paleontological debate—nor am I a qualified guide—it is clear that evolution is not entirely contingent. Life does have omnipresent laws: natural selection, Mendelian inheritance, constraints on embryonic development, and so on, all remain operative before, during, and after chance events. Biologists, then, must separate the necessary consequences of immutable laws from contingency effects. True, dinosaurs were wiped out by a chance event, but a more positive outcome was the rise of mammals to dominate the land, which eventually led to us humans. Now, one might ask, was the rise of mammals a matter of necessity, once the chance event of the meteorite had already taken place? Were our mammal ancestors 65 million years ago particularly suited for survival after the impact? Were they poised to assume the ecological vacuum left by dinosaurs? More generally, evolutionary biologists are often interested in the *predictable* evolutionary changes in a population, given that new genes have been introduced or the environment has changed. This may not give a complete account of what happened: for instance, the manner in which the new genes arrived, be it random mutation or migration, or how and why the environment changed. These altogether different problems are often put aside. This is so not because they are unimportant or uninteresting, but because in the end they may be unanswerable: there may be purely chance events that can never be explained. Moreover, the separation of necessity from chance is warranted because the question of predictable changes may be answered independently, which is interesting enough in its own right.

If we wish to understand language change, we must hope that language change, just like evolutionary change, is not all about chance events. There surely have been many chance events that dictated the course of the history of languages. The equivalent of meteorites would be the Anglo-Saxon Invasion, the Industrial Revolution, the birth of the Internet, and so on: all are previously unforeseeable incidents that brought massive changes to languages and indeed, the world. Yet just like biologists, linguists have been searching for the immutable laws that affect language change, which in turn requires a division of labor between chance and necessity. In our context, this means that the external forces in language change—the social elements of language—must be separated from the internal factors: how language works, how it is processed, and how it is learned.

It is fairly safe to assume that internal factors do form a core of immutable elements in language change. When old languages are deciphered and analyzed, they are invariably found to follow the same linguistic principles drawn from modern languages. Both Chaucer and Austen used consonants and vowels, nouns and verbs, categories and phrases, both built sentences with the head-directionality parameter, and both moved things around in strict accordance with the principle of structure dependence. Moreover, we really have no reason to suppose otherwise: since the past is not always directly observable, there can be no science of history unless we assume that the principles and laws that govern the world today were equally applicable yesterday.

For our purposes, this is no more than assuming that our ancestor's brain was wired for language more or less the same way as ours. And if our theory of language learning by unlearning is also correct, our ancestors all learned their languages by the process of natural selection; the possible grammars available to them in universal grammar but not used in their language were eliminated. These two theories further help with the separation between chance and necessity. Language changes when there is divergence, qualitatively or quantitatively, in the speech of successive generations, and this must be because successive generations of speakers have learned, in their heads, different grammars (by which we mean the broad knowledge of language not limited to sentences). Therefore, no matter how intangible social forces push the population one way or another, the child is the sole vehicle that propagates language change over time. Now the picture of language change strongly looks like that of evolutionary change. Children acquire grammar by attending to sentences in the environment; after they have grown up to be parents themselves, it will be their turn to make up the linguistic environment for the next generation. The transmission of language is just like the propagation of human phylogeny; of course, the transmission of genetic materials is faster, and more fun:[29]

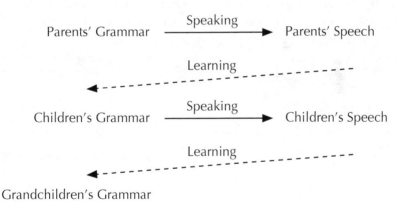

Hence, a theory about our ancestors' languages must turn on a theory of our children's languages.

Parallels abound between language learning and language change; in fact, many of the ideas we have invoked to explain child language in the previous chapters were first proposed for understanding language change. The word "scant" was once upon a time "skamt": *m* became *n* under the pressure of the neighboring *t*. Recall that speech sounds (consonants and vowels) can be further split into more atomic units of actions, and this change can be understood as a plain instance of feature spreading:

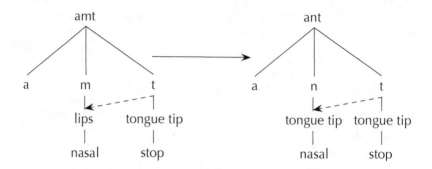

The invasion of *t* into *m* is quite justified. Rather than rapidly switching from the lips (*m*) to the tongue tip (*t*) in the original pronunciation, "scant" unified the places of articulation: *n* is produced with the tongue tip just as in *t* while still maintaining the nasality of *m*. This process of assimilation is one of the most common patterns in pronunciation changes, and is also one of the most common patterns in children's first words. Recall how "bug" morphed into "gug" in the toddler Daniel's English (Chapter 5):

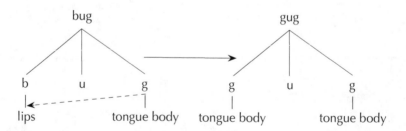

The articulatory motion of g, which uses the tongue body against the velum in the back of the mouth, has infected its neighbor *b*. Again, an economy of articulation has been achieved.

When a young child says "tar," "boo," and "fy"—for "star," "blue," and "fly"—she is traveling down a well-trodden road. As we have seen in previous chapters, the child is simply cutting corners: two consonants are obviously harder to say than one, so some parts of "star," "blue," and "fly" are omitted. Just the same, once upon a time "knight" and "knee" were pronounced with a *k* and "castle" and "Christmas" were pronounced with a *t*. Our Middle English forebears took the easy route, and we are stuck with these useless letters in the spelling system. None of this had to happen. For the German cousins of these words, the *k*'s in *Knie* ("knee") and *Knecht* ("knight") are spoken as well as written; articulatory simplification is merely a tendency, not an absolute law of language change.

Simplification isn't the only form of economy: complexification is another option as long as the end result adheres to the most natural structure of speech. My son Russell's first word "wuckoo" (for "truck"), for instance, resulted from appending *oo* to complete the CV template ("ckoo"). In another rendition, "piano" became "pinano" when a consonant was inserted, again for the sake of the natural CV syllable structure. Adults may do the same: for many speakers, "koala" is "kowala," with the insertion of a *w*, "Dvorak" has become "Devorak," with the insertion of a reduced vowel (a schwa, like the *e* in "the"), and "please" sounds like "puhlease"—at least when begging.

Indeed, many changes in the history of languages look like stabilized innovations or errors in children's language. This may happen because children don't get enough experience to eliminate the erroneous conjectures. For example, irregular verbs used to be more abundant—and in fact, more "regular"—in Old English. There was once a rule that reliably produced *ew* for a verb that ended in *ow*: *Mow, sow,* and *row* behaved like *know–knew, grow–grew,* and *blow–blew*. But to stay that way, *mew, sew,* and *rew* had to be used frequently enough;[30] otherwise, they would drift to the regular rule, and they did. The work and time our children put in to learn irregular verbs therefore result from the failures of learning by our ancestors.

Another reason that children's errors are preserved is because they are reasonable ones, the kind that adults are prone to as well. Who can blame a child for thinking that "behave" is "be have," "hiccup" is "hicc up," or "adult" is really "a dult"? Not those who thought "hamburger" was "ham burger." The word "hamburger" came from German, meaning a meat patty from the city of Hamburg. (By the same token, or the same suffix *-er*, "frankfurter" and "wiener" are products from Frankfurt and Vienna, respectively.) Even though there was no ham in a burger, English speakers still broke the word as a compound consisting of two independent words, the same way in which "blackboard" is the sum of "black" and "board." Innovations of "turkey burger," "veggie burger," "tofu burger," and yes, "beef burger" soon followed. Another food item with a history of misanalysis is *pea–peas*. "Peas" came from the Middle English "pease," a mass noun, which did not change form from singular to plural. Most mass nouns in English refer to substances; it's hard to count "water," "air," or "honey." But there are also intermediate cases: "sand" and "rice" are mass nouns, so treated as substances, even though they are countable at least in principle. "Peas" also falls into this intermediate class; our Middle English ancestors treated "pease" as a substance, yet it was perfectly natural for later speakers to extract out a plural suffix *-s*, leaving "pea," a countable noun like *carrot–carrots*. Peas are, after all, easier to count than rice. Similarly, "orate," the verb, derived from natural reanalysis of "orator" and "oration," which are both nouns. This process is dubbed *back formation* in historical linguistics because, in general, verbs come first, before noun-making suffixes such as *-or* and *-ion* are attached. We might well call these word-learning errors.

Still, the parallels between the words in the past and present are at best approximate, and cannot be molded into a predictive theory of language change. For one thing, had the principle of economy been absolute, all language would have converged to some optimal form: as far as we know, that has never happened. For another, as noted in the discussion of children's early words, there may be many ways to simplify speech, and there is no telling which route will be taken. For instance, "bug" could have turned into "bub" rather than "gug," "star" could have been reduced to "sar" rather than "tar," and individuals may opt for different solutions. Finally, any economy principle, even if it were an absolute one, must have a specific phonological system to optimize. But that phonological system—whether it is rhotic or not—is, once again, another bag of contingencies and unpredictabilities.

The outlook for a predictive theory of grammar change is brighter. First, a grammar can change all it wants, but it can never step out of the closed space defined by its parameters. In other words, a grammar may be a string of 0's and 1's at one time, but changed into a different string sometime later. As long as we can pin down the parameter space, grammar change can have no surprises. Phonological change does not have this luxury: while the verb-to-tense parameter is probably coded into universal grammar, no one would wish to claim, for instance, that the decidedly language-specific rule of adding -d for past tense is hardwired in the brain.

Second, we can learn a great deal about grammar change by studying grammar learning. In fact, combing through old manuscripts to track grammar change is much like reading transcripts of baby-talk. To put it simply, grammar learning is like grammar change on steroids. But both need time. A child doesn't hop from one set of parameter values to another, altering her grammar overnight; rather the emergence of the native grammar is gradual, as nonnative grammars are slowly eliminated by the mechanism of natural selection in a few short years. Grammar change takes longer—much longer—but it is the same process. Take a specific parameter in the history of English that we discussed in Chapter 7. Old English and Middle English moved inflected verbs to tense, bypassing negation and adverbs, but modern English has ceased to do so. Instead, tense lowers onto the verb in modern English:

**Middle English:**
Quene Esther **looked** *never* with swich an eye. (Chaucer, *Merchant's Tale*, 1744)

**Modern English:**
Queen Esther *never* **looked** with such an eye.

Like gene hunters, the linguist Tony Kroch and his colleagues at the University of Pennsylvania have meticulously tracked the natural history of English verbs from AD 1400 onward. They found that the changes in many apparently independent sentence structures could all be traced to the flipping of the verb-raising parameter from Yes to No.

But this didn't happen overnight. It is not the case that one generation of English speakers were happy moving these verbs to the tense position, and the next generation abruptly gave it up. The change in this single parameter value stretched out over three hundred years.[31]

Indeed, all major cases of grammar change are gradual: three hundred years is really a long blink. The record time on documented changes might be found in the history of Chinese grammar. In English, the prepositional phrase follows the verb, as in "I cut the cheese with a knife." Archaic Chinese worked the same way, but modern Chinese has flipped them around: the prepositional phrase must go before the verb, or "I with a knife cut the cheese." The flipping, however, took well over a thousand years to complete.[32]

What is it like to be in the middle of language change? That is, what can we say about the linguistic knowledge of English speakers between 1400 and 1700? If the new grammar does not replace the old one outright, then it must be the case that those on the ascending portion of the curve had access to both grammars simultaneously. And that means, yes, they were English *bilinguals*.

This notion of bilingualism is admittedly unconventional, for bilingualism typically refers to the native (or near native) command of two "conventional" languages: English plus Chinese, German and Russian, Hindi with Italian. These languages are conventional precisely because they are defined by social, political, and historical conventions. From a linguistic perspective, though, these languages are merely labels for different instantiations of the parameter system. But if we think about it, (conventional) bilingual speakers today are no different from the Middle English speakers who also had command of two different instantiations of the parameter system: specifically, one that has the negative value for the verb-to-tense parameter and the other, positive. (Make up some names if you wish: how about Foo and Bar? Then Middle English speakers would be Foo-Bar bilinguals.) Perhaps they ought to be called "bi-parametricals," for they had probabilistic access to opposite values of a single linguistic parameter, but that sounds like a mouthful.[33]

Viewed in this light, the Middle English bilinguals—and hundreds of years of them—were like children for whom language learning never quite finished. Here we will have to dismantle another conventional term about language. When we speak of "learning English," we pretend that there is a single language in the environment to be learned, and when we speak of "having learned English," we mean that the child has attained the language of surrounding adults. But this is clearly an idealization.[34]

The child, then, is actually exposed to a composite of many grammars that are mutually incompatible to some degree, however minute, as no two individuals' languages are exactly the same. But what if the grammars are really incompatible? What if, for example, 60 percent of the sentences that children hear didn't raise the verb to tense, while 40 percent did? Which grammar would the child pick when neither is perfect?

Apparently both, if judged by the language of Middle English speakers. But now we have a puzzle. Why isn't learning winner-take-all? Why wouldn't the grammar that is supported by more linguistic evidence knock out its competitor that is supported by less? Learning would be far more efficient: the child could rapidly zoom in on the dominant grammar while ignoring "noises" in adults' speech, be it slips-of-the-tongue or visiting relatives with funny accents. But once again, how we learn language (or anything else) is determined by our biology, not some mechanism concocted on the principles of logic. If natural selection is a general neurological mechanism of learning, then we may find it in action in other tasks of learning or even in other species. (Indeed, while for us the evidence comes from children's speech, the other scientists who suggested similar theories drew support from neurological studies on cats and monkeys.) So let's downgrade the high art of parameter competition to something far more primitive: how about a multiple choice puzzle for a rodent?

The psychologist Randy Gallistel, while doing his graduate work at Yale in the late 1960s, regularly antagonized undergraduates with the following experiment.[35]

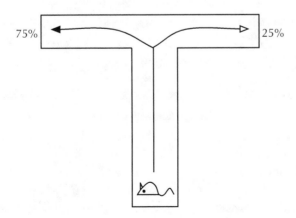

The so-called T-maze is a standard device for the study of animal behavior. Where the path splits, the mouse could turn either left or right to the end of the tunnel. On either side there may be a pellet of food waiting for it—with a probability of 75 percent on the left and 25 percent on the right, to be exact. After being let loose for dozens of trials, how does the mouse adapt to this environment?

Quite impressively, it turned out. If the goal is to maximize reward, the optimal strategy clearly is to turn left all the time: food is guaranteed 75 percent of the time, while turning right at all can only decrease the payoff. And that's exactly how Gallistel's mice performed in the experiment. But that's also exactly what irked Yale undergraduates. The mouse and the T-maze were covered with a large piece of glass: the students could observe the different outcomes of turning left versus right, and they were instructed to compare their own strategies against the rodent's. Disappointingly, Yale students chose the left side approximately 75 percent of the time, and the remaining 25 percent, they chose the right.

I can personally vouch for Yale students' brilliance, but they weren't using their brains; it was an old instinct at work. Many species—fish, pigeons, mallards, in labs as well as in nature—exhibit this behavior of matching the probabilities of events or outcomes in the environment. (The mouse in Gallistel's experiment was somewhat of an anomaly, although a different experimental setup could coerce it into probability matching like other species.) Why would Nature prefer such an obviously irrational strategy if critical resources such as food are at a premium? On second thought, this is not irrational at all. Conceivably, probability matching works like the old adage "Don't put all your eggs in one basket." If everyone goes where the payoff is maximal, as dictated by the "optimal" strategy, everyone will presumably get less of a share while many other (and smaller) resources may remain unexplored. But if everyone keeps their options open and explores among various sites, then all sources may be tapped into and everyone gets to eat a little more. In other words, probability matching does what your investment adviser has been saying: diversify your portfolio; some short-term gain may be sacrificed for long-term stability. This is something evolution might have favored, which would explain its prevalence all over the biological world.[36] When the

Middle English speakers settled on a probabilistic combination of verb raising and not verb raising when the linguistic environment was exclusively neither, it was the same principle at work.

*Now* we are ready for the alleged superiority of German.

What's so great about German? If anything, German is better known for its grammatical horrors, thanks to Mark Twain's famous essay "The Awful German Language":

> Surely there is not another language that is so slipshod and system-less, and so slippery and elusive to the grasp. One is washed about in it, hither and thither, in the most helpless way; and when at last he thinks he has captured a rule which offers firm ground to take a rest on amid the general rage and turmoil of the ten parts of speech, he turns over the page and reads, "Let the pupil make careful note of the following exceptions." He runs his eye down and finds that there are more exceptions to the rule than instances of it. So overboard he goes again, to hunt for another Ararat and find another quicksand.[37]

German words, or more precisely, German morphology, are indeed treacherous. For example, the noun plurals in German employ five suffixes: *Kind-er* ("children"), *Wind-e* ("winds"), *Ochs-en* ("oxen"), *Auto-s* ("cars"), and *Daumen-ø* ("thumbs," where ø indicates an empty suffix, making no change to the noun, just like *sheep–sheep* in English). One cannot predict which suffix a noun takes, and any partial generalization—usually conjured up by desperate students and teachers—must be augmented with a long list of exceptions. Hence the noun-suffix associations are more or less established by brute-force memorization, and there are thousands of these: the horrors of German are real.[38]

But German grammar is a thing of perfect regularity.[39] German grammar consistently reserves the first position of the sentence for the topic, a phrase that best captures what the sentence is about. Anything can be a topic: a noun phrase, a prepositional phrase, an adverb, depending on what the speakers would like to highlight. The second position, however, is resricted to only the verb or auxiliary. Indeed, this strategy appears to be how Yoda, the Jedi Master, puts his topics in perspective:

[A teacher] *will* I be.
[Sick] *have* I become, old and weak.
[Nothing more] *will* I teach you today.
[A long time] *have* I watched.

So do the Germans. They even have a linguistic parameter for it: verb second, or V2 for short. That is, every sentence must have a topic phrase that occupies the first position, and this topic must be followed immediately by the verb, in the second position. This property gives the language both regularity and a great deal of word order freedom. All the variants below have roughly the same meaning in German; although the highlighted topics are different, the verb is always second:

(a)   [My friend] *gave* the man the book yesterday. (Subject first)
(b)   [The man] *gave* my friend the book yesterday. (Direct object first)
(c)   [The book] *gave* my friend the man yesterday. (Indirect object first)
(d)   [Yesterday] *gave* my friend the man the book. (Adverb first).

Sentences like (a), where the subject precedes the verb and the object (SVO for short), contain the most frequent word order, and constitute about 70 percent of German sentences. Sentences like (b) through (d), where the subject follows the verb and some arbitrary phrase precedes it, make up the remaining 30 percent. So far as we can tell, these numbers are remarkably stable throughout the history of the Germanic languages.[40] This is presumably just the way we talk: the "doer" subject is the most likely topic of conversation.

For an English parallel, we need only look to Chaucer's *Canterbury Tales,* written when English and German were a bit more alike (though English was never quite the same as German):[41]

[This tresor] *hath* Fortune unto us yeven.                (Object first)
this treasure has Fortune unto us given
"This treasure, Fortune has given us."

[Wel] *koude* he rede a lessoun or a storie.          (Adverb first)
well could he read a lesson or a story
"He could read a lesson or a story well."


[Into the blisse of hevene] *shul* ye gon. (Prepositional phrase first)
into the bliss of heaven will you go
"You will enter the bliss of heaven."


[No neer Atthenes] *wolde* he go ne ride      (Negative phrase first)
no nearer Athens would he go nor ride


The first three of these examples are clearly at odds with modern English grammar, but are reminiscent of modern German. In these, the topic, be it an object, adverb, or prepositional phrase, comes in first, the verb second, and the subject a distant third. In the last example we see a modern remnant of the pattern—even in modern English, a verb-second pattern is still possible if a negative phrase is first. (We are like the Germans only when we are naysayers.) Sentences like these reveal the Germanic heritage of the English language.

It is the V2 parameter that provides German the edge on our imaginary desert island. In (modern) English, the canonical word order is subject-verb-object (SVO), representing approximately 90 percent of all sentences. That is, someone using a German V2 grammar can nevertheless understand English 90 percent of the time. He would fail, of course, when English sentences deviate from the verb-second constraint. Occasionally in English something—a prepositional phrase, an adverb, a clause, or some other modifier—can be placed at the very beginning of the sentence, (a), stuck between the subject and the verb, (b), or both, (c):


(a) [At Moe's]        you    find    [the same crowd] every day.
    PP                S      V       O                Adverb


(b) [The monkey]      always         teases           [the piggy].
    S                 Adverb         V                O


(c) [In the evenings] [the Darwins] always            played backgammon.
    PP                S             Adverb             V        O

In these cases, the verb is demoted to the third position or even further down: let's call these V≠2 sentences, for they all contradict the V2 grammar of German.

The castaway island in our thought experiment is a T-maze of language learning. Children born to such mixed heritage—and languages—are just like rodents, pigeons, and Yale undergraduates placed in an uncertain environment: picking the German grammar is akin to making a left turn in the maze, and using the English option corresponds to taking a right. Both hypotheses are made available through the innate universal grammar, but neither will work out perfectly on our bilingual island. So the biology of playing it safe takes over, and children may speak German at one instant and switch to English the next.

But this is not an equal partnership. Recall that Yale undergraduates turned left roughly three out of four times if food was available on that side 75 percent of the time. An uncertain environment typically results in a mixture of strategies, proportionally represented according to their payoffs. On our island, the German and English grammar also have differential payoffs. The vast majority of English sentences, about 90 percent, have the word order of SVO, which is very straightforward compared to German grammar, where word order is quite flexible— as long as the verb is in the second position. In other words, if the child picks the German grammar during the natural selection of language learning, it will work most of the time even when she has just heard an English sentence. In contrast to English, only 70 percent of German sentences are SVO, which means 30 percent of German sentences will contradict the English grammar. Statistically speaking, the payoff of the German grammar outweighs that of the English grammar, so our hypothetical language learners would learn "more" German than English. A chain reaction follows, as the first generation of children become parents, grandparents, great-grandparents, . . . (The mathematically inclined should consult the notes for a precise formulation of the problem.)[42] The higher fitness of the German grammar ensures the demise of English when both languages are let loose on our virtual island.

It is important to keep in mind that the German advantage is relative. What would happen if you pitted German against say, Korean, is anyone's guess. But the method we have provided here can be applied to any two languages. Step 1: Write down two contradicting sentence patterns, one from each language. Step 2: Take a large sample of sentences from these languages, and count up the frequencies of the mutually incompatible patterns (30 percent for German over English, and 10 percent for English over German). It's survival of the biggest.

Thomas Watson, the chairman of IBM, thought five computers would be more than the world would ever need. Bill Gates claimed that 640K of RAM ought to be enough for everybody. And everybody was saying in 2004 the Red Sox would choke, before they went on to win the World Series (though now that seems like an abberation). Predicting the future can make one look remarkably foolish—so why are we in the game of predicting a hypothetical one, on an imaginary island? How does such simple number crunching have anything to do with language change, whose social, historical, and linguistic complexity we have been at pains to unravel?

Here we are again taking cues from biology. Every biologist is keenly aware of the complex array of forces in evolutionary change; Darwin himself was "convinced that natural selection has been the main but not the exclusive means of modification." Yet natural selection is among the first hypotheses that biologists test out, and that is precisely because natural selection is the simplest explanation possible. Indeed, the basic dynamics of natural selection can be described by a simple set of equations involving the relative fitness values of competing genes; our mathematical model of language change, where numbers represent the mutual incompatibilities of grammars, is in fact a direct adaptation into linguistics. (See Note 42 if you are interested in the details.) But how do we put our number game and thought experiment to an empirical test? The proof of the pudding is in the eating.

The eating has had to be done in the past: ultimately, our theory can gain support only from scenarios of language change that have already occurred, and ethics prevent us from experimenting with the future. Yet the superiority of German over English in our thought experiment is just a dramatic setup, for in an interesting twist, a demonstration of language superiority actually took place in the history of French.

We first need to wrap our minds around what it means for grammars to be in competition. There is actually no need for speakers of different grammars to come together as in the thought experiment. The English grammar and the German grammar are in fact competing all the time—in every toddler learning her language. As the gradual changes in Middle English show, two grammars—both are mental objects whose properties are specified by universal grammar—may be in competition within a single conventional "language," and stay in coexistence in the transient stages of language change. After all, every instance of language learning is just a bunch of parameters jousting for supremacy. So let's drop terms like "German" and "English" altogether. Fighting for supremacy are two grammars with different parameter values: "German" is +V2, "English" is -V2. The superiority of German is really the superiority of the + value of the V2 parameter: it places the topic—what the sentence is about, often S (subject)—at the beginning, as long as the verb goes second.

If the superiority of German is surprising, what follows is a paradox. Our theory asserts that a +V2 grammar can *never* lose to a -V2 grammar, and that means that had a language had a +V2 grammar, it would not have been possible to change it into a -V2 grammar. But this prediction would seem flat-out false. A number of languages actually took the plunge.[43] For instance, Old French is a +V2 grammar, but modern French no longer is. What happened?

The culprit was a familiar friend. The grammar of Old French turned out to be a cross between modern German and modern Spanish. Like German, Old French must put the verb in the second position, and like Spanish, Old French could leave the subject pronoun out. But if the subject was omitted, the advantage of the +V2 grammar (read: German) over the -V2 grammar (read: English) vanished along the away.

Take the unambiguously German-like sentence (and Yoda one more time), where the verb is in the second position after the noun phrase

[A long time] *have* I watched.

Had Yoda spoken Old French, thanks to the option of omitting the subject pronoun "I," the sentence would have turned into:

[A long time] *have* watched.

This is no longer decisively German (or +V2, to be precise). Since an omitted subject cannot be heard anyway, it could have appeared on either side of the verb (and subsequently been dropped):

[A long time] (I) *have* watched.

[A long time] *have* (I) watched.

And "A long time I have watched" could be proper English (or, the -V2 grammar. In other words, the advantage of +V2 grammar over the -V2 grammar was eroded by omitted pronouns. Ian Roberts, a historical linguist at the University of Cambridge, found that by the beginning of the thirteenth century, the balance of power had shifted toward the -V2 option.[44]

The castaway island is a mental exercise about the hypothetical future, but it guides us to the source of language change that took place in the actual past. It reveals the *impossibility* of a German-like grammar morphing into an English-like grammar: when we are confronted with an apparent counterexample from the natural history of the French language, we know that we have to look elsewhere for the cause—so subject-pronoun drop, a seemingly unrelated facet of the Old French grammar, was not let off the hook. Our theory is further bolstered by French's Romance cousins. All Western Romance languages had V2 in medieval times, perhaps a vestige from some ancestral language.[45] *All* these languages, however, lost V2 later on, and *all* of them were pronoun-drop languages. Many, such as Italian, Portuguese, and Spanish, remain pronoun-drop languages to this day. French today is no longer pronoun-drop, but French lost pronoun drop too late to save V2, which had been dead for at least a century before pronoun drop vanished. By contrast, *all* Western Germanic languages maintained Verb Second, and *none* of these ever had pronoun drop.

This is not a complete theory of language change: such a theory doesn't exist, and cannot exist, as we discussed earlier. Rather, it is a demonstration that one needn't be bogged down by the intangibles in the social and historical web of language: simple hypotheses of language change can be formulated—and lead to simple and elegant explanations of historical events—on the basis of the eminently tangible theories of universal grammar and language learning. This is also an invitation. The modern theory of evolution was not complete until the first half of the twentieth century, when Darwin's natural selection and Mendel's principles of genetic inheritance were forged together into a set of mathematical models with predictive powers. If we regard principles and parameters as genes and the theory of language learning by natural selection as the inheritance and transmission of genes, then a similar synthesis may also be possible.[46] On the offer is a call to arms for linguists, mathematicians, and biologists: it is time for the ancient field of linguistics to join the quantitative world of modern science.

# The Infinite Gift

Language is often said to be a window to the mind, but that means we must step out of language and the mind to get a peek inside. A famous Chinese poem, composed almost a thousand years ago, aptly describes the difficulty of visualizing a mountain while you are on it. You go up a slope or around a bend, and the mountain keeps changing as your own perspective changes.[1] The same can be said about the study of language. We think in it, talk with it, and are constantly surrounded by it: the difficulty is to step aside to see what language is really like.

Once we do step aside, we see that language, even in the hands of a child, is full of complexities and surprises. Some of these, I hope, have been adequately communicated in this book, and many puzzles and mysteries still lie ahead. Underneath every utterance of baby-talk, or every turn of phrase in Shakespeare, lies an elegant, intricate, and infinite engine that forms our thoughts, expresses our feelings, and shapes our mental life. Moreover, if we look beyond the superficial differences across languages that are shaped by accidents of history, we see that all languages are fundamentally variations on a universal theme, and that human minds are fundamentally the same. And if we look closely enough, we might catch children experimenting with this gift of language. As a linguist and a parent, these are moments I most cherish.

# Notes

## Chapter 1: The Greatest Intellectual Feat

1. Maynard Smith & Szathmary (1997).
2. Goodall (1986), Hauser (2000), de Waal (1989).
3. Anderson (2004).
4. Descartes (1662/1969).
5. The Chimpanzee sequencing and analysis consortium (2005).
6. Chomsky (1964), Marler (1991), Gould & Marler (1987).
7. Lane (1979).
8. Gesell (1941). See Curtiss (1977) for the tragic case of "Genie."
9. Jacob (1977), Chomsky (1995). Hauser, Chomsky, & Fitch (2002).
10. Chomsky (1959).

## Chapter 2: Mission Improbable

1. Quine (1960), Goodman (1955). For the first reference to the Scandal of Induction in the context of language learning, see Macnamara (1972).
2. A recent example is the language Wôpanâak (Wampanoag). Once spoken in eastern Massachusetts, it has not had a speaker for over a century. The Wôpanâak Reclamation Project began in 1993 as a collaboration between Jessie Littledoe Baird, a member of the Mashpee Wampanoag Tribe, and the linguists Ken Hale and Norvin Richards at the Massachusetts Institute of Technology (MIT). After obtaining a master's degree at MIT, Baird returned to Mashpee and is now teaching classes to the members of the tribe. A dictionary containing approximately 6,500 words has been compiled as a result of this project.
3. Zue et al. (1989).
4. Carey & Bartlett (1978), Markson & Bloom (1997), Bloom (2001).
5. The Scandal of Induction does not only strike language. Making explicit connection to Chomsky's theory of an innate grammar, the vision scientist Donald Hoffman (1998; p. 13) observes:

Kids aren't taught how to see. Parents don't sit down with their kids and explain how to use motion and stereo to construct depth, or how to carve the visual world into objects and actions. Indeed, most parents don't know how they do this themselves. And yet it appears that each normal child comes to construct visual depth, shape, colors, objects, and actions pretty much the same way as any other normal child. Each normal child, without being taught, reinvents the visual world; and all do it much the same way. This is remarkable, because in so doing each child overcomes the fundamental problem of vision. . . . The image at the eye has countless possible interpretations.

6. Markman (1994).
7. Locke, J. (1690).
8. Chomsky (1959).
9. Meanwhile, the ethology work of Konrad Lorenz and Nikko Tinbergen, which studied the natural and instinctive behaviors of organisms and came from a European tradition that was relatively free of behaviorism, was making its way to the United States.
10. Breland & Breland (1961).
11. Other scientists responsible for the so-called cognitive revolution include the psychologists George Miller and Jerome Bruner, the linguist Alvin Liberman, the neurobiologist Eric Lenneberg, and the computer scientist Herbert Simon, among others. The historical development has been documented in many places, including Gardner (1987). A recent personal assessment can be found in Miller (2003).
12. James (1890), p. 462 of the 1981 reprinting.
13. Chomsky (1965, 1968, 1975, 1980), Piatelli-Palmarini (1980).
14. Fodor (1983).
15. Legate & Yang (2002). The most comprehensive counts show that there is probably somewhere around 1 in 3,000,000; MacWhinney (2004).
16. Crain & Nakayama (1987).
17. Smith, Tsimpli, & Ouhala (1993), Smith & Tsimpli (1995).
18. Dummett (1986).
19. Gopnik (1990), Gopnik & Crago (1991).
20. Watkins, Dronkers, & Vargha-Khadem (2002).
21. Vargha-Khadem, Watkins, Alcock, Fletcher, & Passingham (1995).
22. Bellugi, Marks, Bihrle, & Sabo (1988), Clahsen & Almazan (1998), Clahsen & Temple (2003), Morris & Mervic (1999), Zukowski (2001).
23. Fisher, Vargha-Khadem, Watkins, Monaco, & Pembrey (1998).
24. Enard et al. (2002).
25. Shu et al. (2005).
26. Cited in *Toronto Globe and Mail*, June 27, 2003.
27. Yang (1998, 2002).

## Chapter 3: Silent Rehearsals

1. For a summary of infant speech perception research, see the classic Jusczyk (1997).
2. Mehler, Jusczyk, Lambertz, Halsted, Bertocini, & Amiel-Tison (1988), Nazzi, Bertocini, & Mehler (1998).
3. Jilka (2000).
4. Patel & Daniele (2003).
5. Eimas, Siqueland, Jusczyk, & Vigorito (1971).
6. Caramazza, Chialant, Capasso, & Miceli (2000).
7. Delattre, Liberman, & Cooper (1955).
8. Liberman, Delattre, & Cooper (1952).
9. Stevens (1989).
10. The reader is strongly encouraged to listen to an audio clip at http://yale.edu/linguist/paba.wav, where the 80 ms to 0 ms range is divided into nine sections, each separated by 10 ms of voicing delay.
11. Liberman, Harris, Kinney, & Lane (1961).
12. Peterson & Barney (1952).
13. Liberman, Cooper, Shankweiler, & Studdert-Kennedy (1967), Liberman & Mattingly (1985). Liberman & Mattingly (1989).
14. The details of this process are not always spelled out; see Klatt (1989).
15. Eimas & Miller (1980).
16. Streeter (1976).
17. Trehub (1976).
18. Miyawaki, Strange, Verbrugge, Liberman, Jenkins, & Fujimura (1975).
19. Eimas (1975).
20. Kuhl & Miller (1975), Kuhl & Padden (1982), Kluender, Diehl, & Killeen (1987).
21. Cutting & Rosner (1974), Pisoni (1977), Jusczyk, Pisoni, Walley & Murray (1980).
22. Wyttenbach, May, & Hoy (1996).
23. This is by no means a consensus opinion—there is none—though it has been expressed by other researchers. See Petitto (1997), Hauser, Chomsky, & Fitch (2002). More directly to speech perception and especially sign language, see Baker, Idsardi, Golinkoff, & Petitto (2005).
24. Campbell, Woll, Benson, & Wallace (1999), Emmorey, McCullough, & Brentari (2003).
25. Kegl, Senghas, & Coppola (1999). For similar work, see Feldman, Goldin-Meadow, & Gleitman (1978), Goldin-Meadow (2003), Singleton & Newport (2004), Sandler, Meir, Padden, & Aronoff (2005).
26. "No words to describe monkeys' play." http://news.bbc.co.uk/1/3013959.stm
27. Pepperberg (1999), Anderson (2004).
28. Stager & Werker (1997). Note that the contrast can be learned as long as it is used in complementary distributions, for which minimal pair words is a naturally occurring example; see Maye, Werker, & Gerken (2002).
29. Cutler, Mehler, Norris, & Segui (1989).

30. Werker & Tees (1984a).
31. Greenough, Black, & Wallace (1987), Kolb (1989).
32. Bruer (1999).
33. Werker & Tees (1984a, 1984 b), Best, McRoberts, & Sithole (1988).
34. Bradlow, Pisoni, Yamada, & Tohkura (1997).
35. Polka & Werker (1994).
36. The learning of the vowels in the native language follows essentially the same universalist-to-specialist route, though the specialization is a bit quicker, perhaps because children have "more" experience with vowels than consonants; see Kuhl (1983), Kuhl, Williams, Lacerda, Stevens, & Lindblom (1992).
37. Newport (1990), Elman (1993).

Chapter 4: Wuckoo

1. Jusczyk & Aslin (1995), Saffran, Aslin, & Newport (1996), Jusczyk (1999), Yang (2004).
2. Brent & Siskind (2001).
3. Bertocini & Mehler (1981), Bijeljac-Babic, Bertocini, & Mehler (1993), Eimas (1999).
4. The matters are more complicated than what's portrayed here; see Gambell & Yang (2005). It is not clear how infants distinguish heavy syllables from unstressed ones; see Hayes (1995), Sluijter, van Heuven, & Pacily (1996).
5. Jusczyk, Cutler, & Redanz (1993), Jusczyk, Houston, & Newsome (1999).
6. Examples of spoonerisms are taken from Vicky Fromkin's entry "Slips of the tongue: Windows to the mind" for the Linguistic Society of America (www.lsadc.org).
7. Halle (1978). Children's knowledge of rhyming: Dollaghan (1994).
8. Jusczyk (1999), Chambers, Onishi, & Fisher (2003).
9. Fodor (1975, 1998), Pinker (1989), Levin (1993), Pustejovsky (1995), Hale & Keyser (2002), Murphy (2002).
10. For general discussion of how children learn the meaning of words, see Gleitman (1990), Baldwin (1993), Markman (1994b), Pinker (1994), Bloom (2001), Hall & Waxman (2004).
11. Jusczyk & Hohne (1997).
12. Peters (1983), Pinker (1984), Yang (2004).
13. The proper experiment has been done by professional psychologists. Bortfeld, Morgan, Golinkoff, & Rathbun (2005).
14. Cited in Halle (1978).
15. Phillips, Pellathy, Marantz, Yellin, Wexler, Poeppel, McGinnis, & Roberts (2000).
16. Jakobson, Fant, & Halle (1962), Halle (1983).
17. Flanagan (1972), Schroeder (1993), Bell (1922).
18. See the summary of the "Talking Heads" project maintained by Philip Rubin at the Haskins Laboratory. (http://www.haskins.yale.edu/haskins/HEADS/contents.html).

19. Kuhl & Meltzoff (1982).
20. Lieberman, Crelin, & Klatt (1972).
21. Locke (1993).
22. MacNeilage & Davis (1993).
23. Oller & Eilers (1988).
24. Petitto & Marentette (1991), Petitto (2000), Petitto, Holowka, Sergio, & Ostry (2001).
25. Boysson-Bardies & Vihman (1991).
26. Boysson-Bardies, Hallé, Sagart, & Durand (1989), Boysson-Bardies, Vihman, Roug-Hellichius, Durand, Landberg, & Arao (1992).
27. Boysson-Bardies (1993).
28. Berko & Brown (1960).
29. Smith (1973)
30. Ferguson & Farwell (1975), Vihman (1996).
31. Studdert-Kennedy (2002), Studdert-Kennedy & Goldstein (2003).
32. Kahn (1976).
33. Kehoe & Stoel-Gammon (1997), Klein (1981), Carter & Gerken (2004).
34. Menn (2000).
35. The *New York Times* columnist and language pundit William Safire has another explanation (March 20, 2005)—which is wrong; see the University of Pennsylvania linguist Mark Liberman's blog at http://itre.cis.upenn.edu/~myl/languagelog/archives/001999.html. The Stanford linguist Geoffrey Nunberg has another explanation, which is offered in Nunberg (2004).

## Chapter 5: Word Factory

1. Martin (1986), Pullum (1991).
2. Woodbury (1991).
3. Miller (1996).
4. *Guinness World Records* (1992).
5. Kiparsky (1982).
6. Chomsky (1951).
7. Zue & Lafferriere (1979).
8. Menn & Stoel-Gammon (2001).
9. We put aside the case where a short vowel is inserted between the verb and past-tense suffix *d*, as in *pat–patted* and *pad–padded*. In the later discussion of noun plurals, we put aside the case such as *kiss–kisses, buzz–buzzes,* where a short vowel (*e* in *es*) is inserted between the root and the plural suffix *s*. In both cases, however, the insertion of a vowel is eminently reasonable: two *d/t*'s and two *s/z*'s in a row are just too hard to say.
10. Anderson (1974), Halle (1990).
11. Chomsky (1995), p. 380.
12. Anderson (1981).
13. Without beating around the bush, we give the flapping rule in its full glory: if *t/d* is between two vowels (*betting/bedding,* but not *hit/hid*), and the second vowel is not stressed (*atom/Adam,* but not *atomic/ordain*), then flap!

14. Bromberger & Halle (1989).
15. Seidl & Buckley (2005).
16. Grinstead (1994), Phillips (1995), Guasti (2002).
17. Pinker (1984), Slobin (1985).
18. Allen (1996).
19. Figure extracted with the text-processing tool of Brill (1995) on the basis of child-directed speech (MacWhinney 1995). See also Theakston, Lieven, & Tomasello (2003), Legate & Yang (2006). The use of auxiliary verbs (*is* and *does*) does not fall under the general rule of adding -*s* and does not contribute to the learning of the rule; see Lasnik (1999), Becker (2004), Wilson (2003).
20. But it is *not* the stem. Halle & Marantz (1993); cf. Anderson (1992).
21. Halle (1962), Idsardi (2005), Ristad (1994).
22. Savage-Rumbaugh & Lewin (1994), Kaminski, Call, & Fischer (2004); see Bloom (2004), Markman & Abelev (2004). After the spectacular failure of ape language projects in the 1960s and 1970s, at least no one is claiming the existence of grammar in other species; see Terrace et al. (1979), Seidenberg & Petitto (1979), Anderson (2004).
23. For a useful attempt, see Marcus, Pinker, Ullman, Hollander, Rosen, & Xu (1992).
24. Pine (1992), Tomasello & Mervis (1994).
25. Clark (1993).
26. Sapir (1928).
27. Which is indeed one of the most studied problems in language acquisition. For three distinct perspectives, see Rumelhart & McClelland (1986), Pinker (1999), Yang (2002); cf. Halle & Mohanan (1985). For general assessment, see Yang (2000a).
28. Bloch (1947).
29. Marcus et al. (1992), Pinker (1999), Clahsen (1999). On plausible computational models of rule learning, see Mooney & Califf (1995), Sussman & Yip (1997), Molnar (2001), Yang (2005).
30. Marcus et al. (1992), Xu & Pinker (1995).
31. Halle & Mohanan (1985), Yang (2002).
32. Sometimes they do leave the verb unmarked when past tense should be used. This is due to independent factors that would take us too far afield. See Wexler (1994), Rizzi (1994), Hyams (1996), Legate & Yang (2006).
33. Berko (1958).
34. Snow (1977), Fernald (1985).
35. See a recent science program, *The Secret Life of the Brain*, WNET, New York. (www.pbs.org/wnet/brain/episode2/babytalk/index.html)
36. An excellent survey of language learning in indigenous languages, with special attention to the cross-cultural differences, can be found in O'Neil & Honda (2004).
37. Newport, Gleitman, & Gleitman (1977).
38. Cazden (1972).

## Chapter 6: Colorless Green Ideas

1. Chomsky (1957, 1955/1975).
2. As of October 24, 2005.
3. Including one entitled "Coiled Alizarine" by the Sterling Professor of English emeritus John Hollander at Yale University:

   Curiously deep, the slumber of crimson thoughts:
   While breathless, in stodgy viridian
   Colorless green ideas sleep furiously

4. Osterhout et al. (2002), Neville et al. (1991).
5. Brown (1973).
6. Braine (1963), Tomasello (1992), Pinker (1984), Macnamara (1982), Crain (1991), Poeppel & Wexler (1993), Wexler (1998), Carey (1995), de Villiers (2002), Yang (2002).
7. Shipley, Smith, & Gleitman (1969).
8. Golinkoff et al. (1987).
9. Avrutin & Brun (2001).
10. Quoted in Fromkin, Rodman, & Hyams (2002).
11. Hauser, Chomsky, & Fitch (2002).
12. Miller & Chomsky (1963).
13. Officially, it's called the theta criterion; Gruber (1965), Chomsky (1981).
14. Gleitman (1990), Lasnik (1990).
15. Pinker (1989), Levin (1993), Hale & Keyser (2002).
16. Naigles (1990, 1996), Fisher et al. (1994), Gillette et al. (1999).
17. Braine (1971), Baker & McCarthy (1981), Bowerman (1983), Marcus (1993).
18. Gold (1967), Angluin (1980), Valiant (1984), Blumer et al. (1989), Vapnik (1995). For applications in language learning, see Wexler & Culicover (1980), Berwick (1985), Nowak, Komarova, & Niyogi (2002).
19. Since the demise of behaviorism in the 1950s, no one has taken the tabula rasa view of human nature seriously and, consequently, no one seriously doubts that humans are uniquely prepared with insider information to acquire language. On this account, everyone believes in innate knowledge. Some debates still linger on the nature of such knowledge, which is ultimately an empirical question, rather than a logical one. The universal grammar perspective advocated here holds that at least a significant part of this knowledge applies specifically to language and is not reducible to the properties of other components of human cognition.
20. Those who have a taste for exotic languages and extreme sport may do well to consult the linguist Mark Baker's book *Atoms of language* (2001).
21. Searle (1969), Rizzi (1997).
22. The notion of transformations was introduced by Zellig Harris (1951), Chomsky's teacher at the University of Pennsylvania, though Chomsky made innovative use of it (and made it famous).

23. "Free word order" languages like Warlpiri, and to a less extent, German, Japanese, Turkish, and others, were once thought to be qualitatively different from languages such as English where the word order is more rigid. This turns out not to be the case, but to show that, a lot of work has been done on these languages, analyzing sentence structures in excruciating detail; see Hale (1983), Legate (2002).

24. Originally called the A-over-A principle, this is one of the first general constraints on transformations that linguists ever discussed. What I present here is a simplification of a vast literature on such phenomena, much of which is still under investigation. Chomsky (1961), Ross (1967).

25. Kathleen Rhem, Associated Press, August 6, 2003.

26. Otsu (1981), de Villiers, Roeper, & Vainikka (1990).

27. Pullum (1999).

28. Examples from Giannakidou (2002).

29. Mencken (1921).

30. Author's own notes and data from transcripts for American children (MacWhinney 1995) (http://childes.psy.cmu.edu).

31. For example, the author Ian Bruton-Simmonds, of The Queen's English Society, delivered the 2003 Christmas lecture at The Churchill Society entitled "A criticism of modern linguistics, with suggestions for improvement of English through the BBC." Mr. Bruton-Simmonds's publications include *Mend your English: Or, What we should have been taught at primary school* (1992).

32. Its official name is Condition C of the "Binding Theory"; there is a Condition A and B as well. Chomsky (1981). This is a very complicated research area, and I have glossed some details.

33. Crain & McKee (1985). Adapted from Colin Phillips's lecture notes, University of Maryland, College Park.

34. Chomsky (1995, 2005), Hauser, Chomsky, & Fitch (2002).

## Chapter 7: Twenty Questions

1. Chomsky (1981, 1986, 1995), Rizzi (1990), Kayne (1994), Chomsky & Lasnik (1993). Though the parameter theory is most closely identified with Chomsky and his colleagues' work, it broadly includes other grammatical frameworks; see Bresnan (2001), Sag & Wasow (1999), Frank (2002), Steedman (2000).

2. These dual tasks have been the focus of modern linguistics theories from the beginning; see Chomsky (1955/1975). They are better known as "descriptive adequacy" and "explanatory adequacy," respectively; see Chomsky (1965).

3. Unless otherwise noted, the data (Edo, Navajo, Japanese, and Welsh) used in the description of linguistic parameters is taken from Baker (2001).

4. Japanese uses case markers on nouns: think of them as suffixes. For instance, -*ga* marks the nominative case, typically associated with the subject, -*o* marks the accusative case, typically associated with the object.

5. Hawkins (1983), Kayne (1994). For those who are familiar with the statistical technique known as principal component analysis, parameters can be

viewed as Nature's solution for reducing the dimensionality of linguistic expressions.

6. There are exceptions. Harmony is a tendency, not an absolute constraint on language: for instance, a language may have a majority of phrases with heads initially, and a handful others that have heads finally. It may be speculated that more harmonious grammars are easier on the child learner and are more stable than less harmonious ones over the course of history—and hence its prevalence observed in the world's languages.

7. Examples taken from *Wycliffe Sermons, Love: Lyf of Jesus Christ* (1400–1450), Chaucer's *Parson's Tale* and *Merchant's Tale*, respectively. See Kroch & Santorini (forthcoming).

8. The precise height of verbs in Japanese is not entirely clear.

9. Hyams (1986), Hyams & Wexler (1993).

10. Dryer (1992), Hawkins (1994).

11. Kayne (1994).

12. This is known broadly as the Sapir-Whorf hypothesis, after two leading linguists from the first half of the twentieth century. It holds, in a variety of forms, that the properties of the linguistic system and those of the cognitive/conceptual system ("thought") of a cultural or ethnic group are causally related. But this hypothesis, at least in its stronger forms, has received no empirical support and has in fact led to absurdity: the Eskimo snow vocabulary myth is likely a direct consequence. Somehow the Sapir-Whorf manages to retain its popularity, presumably because it is seemingly so plausible. For critical discussion, see Berlin & Kay (1969), Pinker (1994a).

13. Nisbett (2003).

14. Xinran, quoted in *The Guardian*, October 23, 2005.

15. Baker (2001).

16. Gibson & Wexler (1994), Fodor (1998), Dresher (1999), Lightfoot (1999), Yang (2005)

17. It is of course possible that *some* child may strike it lucky and hop on the right grammar with relatively few tries. But the theory needs to be stronger: it must ensure that the success of grammar learning cannot be dependent on luck. See Berwick & Niyogi (1996).

18. Hyams (1986), Valian (1991), Wang, Lillo-Martin, Best, & Levitt (1992).

19. Huang (1984), Rizzi (1968), Legate (2002).

20. There are many languages such as Pashto (spoken in Afghanistan) that allow the omission of the object because these languages have mostly unambiguous agreement morphology between the verb and the object; see Huang (1984), Rizzi (1986).

21. Pinker (1984), Valian (1991), Bloom (1993), Gerken (1991), Rizzi (1994), Hyams (1996), Wexler (1998).

22. Wang et al. (1992).

23. Allen (1996).

24. Hyams & Wexler (1993), Roeper & Rohrbarcher (1994), Bromberg & Wexler (1995).

25. Mayr (1942). This is a theme that Mayr returned to throughout his long and prolific career (Mayr 1963, 1982, 1991, 1999).

26. Wood (2003).
27. Gelman (2003).
28. Mayr (1991), p. 40.
29. Lewontin (1983), pp. 65–66. Italics original.
30. Lewontin (1974), p. 5.
31. See Bush & Mosteller (1951), Atkinson, Bower, & Crothers (1965), Herrn-stein & Loveland (1975), Yang (1999, 2002), Yang & Gutman (1999). A concrete probability-learning model can be applied to grammar as follows:

Given an input sentence $s$, the learner selects a grammar $G_i$ with probability $p_i$:

a. if $G_i \rightarrow s$ then $\begin{cases} p'_i = p_i + \gamma(1 - p_i) \\ p'_j = (1 - \gamma)p_j & \text{if } j \neq i \end{cases}$

b. if $G_i \nrightarrow s$ then $\begin{cases} p'_i = (1 - \gamma)p_i \\ p'_j = \frac{\gamma}{N-1} + (1 - \gamma)p_j & \text{if } j \neq i \end{cases}$

The "fitness" of a grammar can be defined as the probability with which it fails to analyze a sentence in a linguistic environment (e.g., how often a Japanese grammar fails in an English-speaking environment such as Boston). Let this value be $c_i$ for grammar $G_i$. It follows that

$$\lim_{t \to \infty} P_1(t) = \frac{c_2}{c_1 + c_2}$$

$$\lim_{t \to \infty} P_2(t) = \frac{c_1}{c_1 + c_2}$$

Obviously, the target grammar that is actually used in the environment never fails (i.e., its $c$ value is zero), while all other grammars have nonzero probabilities of being punished (i.e., their $c$ values are greater than zero). It thus follows that the target will necessarily eliminate all the other competitors. In a bilingual or multilingual environment, these grammars will form a stable combination when learning stops: this has important consequences for the study of language change in Chapter 8.

For details, see Yang (2002).

32. Hubel & Wiesel (1962).
33. Changeux (1986), Edelman (1987). See also Dawkins (1971), Young (1965).
34. Brown (1973).
35. Roeper & Rohrbarcher (1994).
36. Chomsky (1977), Lasnik & Saito (1992)
37. Chinese adults are of course monolingual users of the Chinese grammar. American children, though, are in an interesting stage of mixes. They still have access to the Chinese grammar, though decreasing propensity while the Chinese grammar is gradually eliminated. It's simpler to draw up an equation:

Child English = $p^*$Adult Chinese + $(1-p)^*$Adult English

That is, with probability $p$, a toddler in New York is momentarily a monolingual speaker of Chinese, with the option of dropping subjects and objects should the context permit; the rest of the time she speaks English. We don't know what the precise value of $p$ is; moreover, it is a variable whose value changes over time and eventually goes down to zero when the Chinese grammar is wiped out. But that hardly matters. The *relative* proportion of missing objects and missing subjects ought to be the same for children in New York and adults in Beijing: in both populations, it is exactly the same grammar at work. This prediction is strongly confirmed by the linguist Qi Wang and her colleagues' data, where the speech of two-year-olds in Connecticut and Mandarin speakers from Beijing were recorded and compared. Wang et al. (1992).

38. Roeper (2000), Crain & Thornton (1998), Crain & Pietroski (2002), Piatelli-Palmarini (1989), Lightfoot (1991), van Kampen (1997), Chiechia, Guasti, & Gualmini (1999), Kroch (2001), Kupisch (2004), Rizzi (2005), Becker (2005, 2006). Arguably, the root of these ideas goes back to Roman Jakobson's landmark work, where the parallels between child language as potential adult languages were observed; see Jakobson (1941/1968).
39. Chien & Wexler (1990), Wexler & Thornton (1999).
40. Old English data taken from Keenan (2002).
41. Burzio (1991), Reuland (2001), Elbourne (2005).
42. Crain & Thornton (1998), Thornton (1990), McDaniel (1989).
43. Robertson & Reeve (1952).
44. van der Lely & Battell (2003), Legate & Yang (2006).
45. These include the DELV-ST (Diagnostic Evaluation of Language Variation) test (2003. San Antonio, TX: The Psychological Corporation) courtesy of Harry Seymour, Tom Roeper at the University of Massachusetts, and Jill de Villiers at Smith College, and the Rice/Wexler test (American Psychological Society), courtesy of Mable Rice at the University of Kansas and Ken Wexler at MIT.

## Chapter 8: The Superiority of the German Language

1. Darwin (1996/1859), p. 342.
2. Campbell (1997).
3. Chomsky & Halle (1968).
4. Aitchison (2001), p. 20.
5. Examples from Crystal (1997). While the variations mean the same thing, they put somewhat different emphasis on the information structure of speech.
6. Darwin (1871). Quotation from 1882 edition, p. 19.
7. Cited in Aitchison (2001).
8. Harrington, Palethorpe, & Watson (2000).
9. Pinker (1994a).
10. The examples about Latin and its descendants are taken from University of Pennsylvania linguistics professor Eugene Buckley's teaching materials.
11. Sapir (1921), p. 124.

12. Mayr (1982).
13. Address to the Asiatic Society in Calcutta on February 2, 1786.
14. Anderson & Lightfoot (2002).
15. Hungarian, Estonian, and Finnish are other possible non-Indo-European languages spoken in Europe.
16. Cavalli-Sforza (2001).
17. Renfrew (1987).
18. Greenberg (1966, 1987).
19. Swadesh (1952).
20. Ringe (1992). Ringe and colleagues have also published a series of works using computer models to reconstruct linguistic phylogeny using the data that are available; see Nakleh, Ringe, & Warnow (2005).
21. Hockett (1958).
22. Labov (1962).
23. Called a *schwa*.
24. Cited in Aitchison (2001), p. 63.
25. Labov (1966).
26. Examples adapted from Hughes (2000), pp. 365–67.
27. Gould (1989).
28. Conway Morris (1998).
29. Andersen (1973), Battye & Roberts (1995),
30. Pinker (1999). It's more complicated than that; see Yang (2002).
31. Ellegard (1953), Kroch (1989, 2001).
32. Sun (1996).
33. Pintzuk (1999), Santorini (1992), Kroch & Taylor (1997), Kroch (2001).
34. Weinreich, Labov, & Herzog (1968)
35. Gallistel (1990), Labov (1994).
36. Krebs (1978).
37. Twain (1880).
38. Marcus et al. (1995), Pinker (1999), Clahsen (1999).
39. *Nearly* perfect. There are very few words that permit the verb to be in a position that is not second. And we are restricting our discussion to declarative sentences, rather than imperatives or embedded clauses.
40. Lightfoot (1997).
41. Old English appeared not to have the German-like rigid V2 word order; see Kroch & Taylor (1997).
42. Let the two competing grammars be $G_1$ and $G_2$. In the case of English vs. German, the advantage of English over German lies in the V≠2 sentences, and that of German over English lies in the sentences whose subject follows the verb. Let $\alpha$ be the frequency of advantage for $G_1$ over $G_2$, and let $\beta$ be that of advantage for $G_2$ over $G_1$.

Let the probabilities of $G_1$ and $G_2$ be $p$ and $q$ in generation $n$ respectively where p + q = 1. Learners in generation n + 1 will hear the amount of $\alpha p$ that is compatible with $G_1$ but not with $G_2$, and the amount of $\beta q$ that is compatible with $G_2$ but not with $G_1$. Under the model of learning established in Chapter 7, it follows that the probabilities of $G_1$ and $G_2$, or p and q, are as follows:

$$p' = (\alpha p)/(\alpha p + \beta q)$$
$$q' = (\beta q)/(\alpha p + \beta q)$$

The stable points of this dynamical systems are easy to find. This leads to what I have audaciously called the fundamental theorem of language change:

$$G_2 \text{ eliminates } G_1 \text{ if and only if } \beta > \alpha$$

See Yang (2000b, 2002) for details. For similar approaches, see Niyogi & Berwick (1995), Briscoe (2002), Cucker, Smale, & Zhou (2004), Pearl (2005).

It ought to be clear to those familiar with mathematical theories of genetic evolution that the methods employed here have explicitly followed the classic models of selection; see, e.g., Lewontin (1974), Roughgarden (1979).

43. We will not discuss how English lost its V2. The situation was far more complicated than the space allowed here, and language contact was likely involved; see Kroch, Taylor, & Ringe (2000), Yang (2000b).
44. Roberts (1993), Vance (1997).
45. Kiparsky (1994).
46. Niyogi & Berwick (1995), Nowak, Komarova, & Niyogi (2001), Briscoe (2002).


Epilogue: The Infinite Gift

1. Cited in Wang (1991).

# Glossary

**accusative:** the case marking that is typically used on the object. See **case.**

**adjective:** a major category of words that typically describe properties or states: "hot," "happy."

**agreement:** the marking of person, number, gender, etc. on the verb, including the auxiliary: "I do" versus "he does." Some languages such as Italian and Spanish have rich and distinctive agreement patterns, while others, such as Mandarin Chinese, have no agreement at all.

**antecedent:** the entity that a pronoun refers to. In general, an antecedent can be established in the context, or in the sentence that contains the pronoun.

**argument:** the participants in an event or the bearers of a state. "*Russell* likes *pizza*," "*Bunnies* are nice." Certain verbs have a fixed number of arguments that must be filled by noun phrases in a grammatical sentence. See **intransitive, transitive,** and **ditransitive verb.**

**article:** a major category of words that are usually combined with nouns for referential purposes: "*a* dog" vs. "*the* dog."

**articulatory features:** the specification of vocal tract movement and coordination in speech production.

**auxiliary verb:** a class of verbs that mark tense, person, agreement, etc. but do not contribute additional meanings themselves. For example, "Rabbits *are* fast," "Yale *will* <u>beat</u> Harvard," "*Did* John <u>read</u> the news?": note the differences from the underlined main verbs.

**babbling:** infants' spontaneous vocalization that consists of rhythmic consonant-vowel sequences such as "baba" and "mama," which are unfortunately not words. Typically takes place at the sixth month.

**back formation:** a new word formed from an existing word (e.g, by removing a suffix) as if the existing word were a derivative of the new word: e.g., "edit" from "editor."

**behaviorism:** the doctrine that dominated American psychology and social sciences in the first half of the twentieth century. It denied the validity of the study of mental phenomena and aimed to explain animal and human behaviors by exclusively appealing to external stimulus in the environment. A tabula rasa predisposition of the organism is often asserted.

**case:** a form of words that express the roles of participants in an event or in a state of affairs. English makes three case distinctions on the pronoun: e.g., "I" (subject/nominative), "me" (object/accusative), and "my/mine" (possessor). See **nominative, accusative.**

**categorical perception:** the ability to perceive discrete categories or units of information in stimuli that vary along a continuous scale.

**co-articulation:** the phenomenon where sequences of speech sounds (e.g., consonants and vowels) are overlapping and inseparable.

**coda:** the consonant or consonant sequence that follows the vowel, such as *ng* in "strong." The coda is combined with the vowel to form the rime. Codas are language specific, and must be learned by children. See **rime.**

**cognate:** words in distinct languages that have the same linguistic origins but may have diverged over time due to language change.

**comparative method:** a technique used by linguists to compare cognates and deduce the historical relations among languages. See **cognate.**

**complementizer:** a major category of words that mark the beginning of a sentence or a clause.

**consonant:** an element of speech that is produced with a blockage or constriction of the vocal tract.

**ditransitive verb:** a verb that takes three arguments, "Russell *gave* Zelda a book."

**double negative:** in English, a much derided grammatical feature consisting of two negative elements (e.g., "I *don't* want *no* milk"). It is used in numerous languages across the world, many of which are considered socially prestigious.

**essentialism:** a philosophical and scientific perspective that attributes a set of essential and idealized properties to the object under observation, and views specific instances of the object as imperfect realizations of the essence.

**expletive:** a placeholder that must occupy the position of the subject even though it does not contribute to the meaning of the sentence, such as "there" and "it" in English.

**feature spreading:** a very common phonological process whereby neighboring sounds become more similar by sharing articulatory features.

**free word order language:** a language in which the word order is more flexible than English though not entirely unrestricted.

**fricative consonant:** a consonant that is produced with the airflow partially blocked in the vocal tract, often resulting in a hissing sound: *f, s, v, z.*

**grammar:** the mental rules of sentence formation that are generally a form of unconscious knowledge. It is to be distinguished from *prescriptive grammar,* which gives explicit instruction on how to use language.

**head:** the word around which a phrase is built and from which it derives its meaning.

**head-directionality:** a parameter that specifies whether the **head** generally precedes (or follows) the rest of the phrase that it defines.

**high amplitude sucking (HAS):** a popular experimental technique that assesses an infant's attention shifts by measuring the frequency of sucking on a pacifier.

**Indo-European:** The collection of language families that include most languages in Europe, India, and southwest Asia. See **Proto-Indo-European.**

**intransitive verb:** a verb that takes only one argument, e.g., "Russell *laughs.*"

**language gene:** the FOXP2 gene, which is involved in the normal learning of language but also involved in the development of body parts and other cognitive functions.

**larynx:** the voice box, a muscular organ that forms the air passage to the lungs and holds the vocal cords. For newborns, the larynx is located in a high position in the vocal tract, making articulate speech impossible. The larynx starts to become lower by the third or fourth month as a matter of physiological maturation.

**modularity:** a dominant idea in modern cognitive science that views the mind as a collection of functionally—though not necessarily physiologically—separate compartments or modules, each of which is responsible for a specific aspect of cognition.

**morphemes:** the smallest units that contribute meaning to words, such as *un-real-iz-abil-ity.*

**morphology:** the process of word formation, or the subfield of linguistics that studies word formation. Morphology can generate an infinite number of potential words. See **prefix, suffix, root.**

**motherese:** also known as **parentese.** A specific kind of speech and grammatical patterns that some adults in Western societies often adopt in speaking to infants and children. Not a universal mode of speech to children.

**movement:** see **transformation.**

**nasal consonant:** a consonant that is produced with the airflow through the nose: *m, n, ng.*

**nominative:** the marking of case that is typically used on the subject. See **case.**

**noun:** a major category of words that typically denote things, persons, events, and abstract entities: "stone," "firefighters," "war," "terror."

**onset:** a consonant or consonant sequence that precedes the vowel, for example, *str* in "strong." The onset is combined with the rime to form the syllable. Onsets are language specific (e.g., *tsr* is not a valid onset of English) and thus must be learned by children.

**parameters:** a technical term from the principles and parameters theory, referring to the fairly narrow ways in which human language grammars may differ. These include variations in word order, transformation, and other aspects of grammar; the specific values of the parameters for a given language must be learned by children during language acquisition.

**phonology:** the sound patterns of words that are characterized by the rules and regulations of pronunciation.

**phrase:** a sequence of words that behaves as a unit: noun phrase (NP), verb phrase (VP), prepositional phrase (PP). See **head.**

**polysynthetic:** a type of language (e.g., Eskimo) that is characterized by very long "words," which are composed of the equivalent of separate words and phrases in a language like English.

**postposition:** a **preposition** that follows the noun phrase; used in languages such as Japanese and Navajo.

**prefix:** a morpheme that goes before the **root,** such as *mis-* in "*mis*-understand." See **morpheme.**

**preposition:** a major category of words that usually denote temporal or spatial relations: "*in* the car," "*for* a while."

**principles:** a technical term from the principles and parameters theory, referring to the rules and constraints found in the grammars of all human languages. The principles are believed—and have been shown, in many cases—to be innately available to children.

**pronoun:** a word that can stand in place of a whole noun phrase, as long as the identity is clear from the context. In English, these include *I, we, me, us, my, our, mine, ours, you, your, yours, he, him, his, she, her, hers, it, its, they, them, their, theirs,* etc.

**pronoun drop:** a parameter that specifies whether the subject pronoun can be omitted when the **agreement** patterns on the verb are sufficiently unambiguous.

**prosody:** a set of complex features of speech including volume, pitch, intonation, rhythm, and melody of sentences.

**Proto-Indo-European:** the language thought to be the ancestor of Indo-European languages and, according to a popular account, spoken by a prehistorical people in what is now Turkey.

**recursion:** the ability to apply a procedure repeatedly to form ever larger linguistic units. Arguably the defining feature of human language, and the source of its infinity. Although recursion is most closely identified with grammar—there are an infinite number of sentences—it also shows up in morphology, as one can always add morphemes to form ever longer words.

**rime:** the sub-syllable unit that consists of the **vowel** and the **coda,** such as *ong* in "strong." The rime is combined with the **onset** to form the **syllable.**

***r*-less speech:** also known as non-rhotic speech. Omission of the consonant *r* in coda. Distinctive of the dialects of Boston, New York, and England.

**root:** also known as **stem.** The part of a word from which the central meaning of the whole is derived, and to which **prefixes** and **suffixes** can be added. For example, the root of "un-read-able" is "read."

**Scandal of Induction:** the fallibility of experience as the foundation of knowledge. More specifically, the difficulty of acquiring knowledge when there are a potentially infinite number of hypotheses consistent with learning experience.

**sensitive period:** the first few years of life during which normally developing children will use linguistic experience from adults to learn languages. In the rare cases where children are deprived of such experience during this period, no language learning is possible.

**sign language:** the manual languages used by deaf communities. Sign languages are usually invented and refined by the communities of users, and are as rich and complex as spoken languages. Although the specific properties of sign languages are in general unrelated to those of the spoken languages in the environment, the general structures of sign languages and spoken languages are remarkably similar.

**spoonerism:** a particular speech error that switches onsets and rimes across words. Named after the Reverend William Spooner, an Oxford don in the nineteenth century. Rather than expressing suppressed thoughts, as Freud once supposed, this type of speech error reveals the structure of syllables in speech.

**stop consonant:** a consonant that is produced with the airflow completely blocked momentarily in the vocal tract: *p, t, k, b, d, g.*

**stress:** the syllable(s) in a word that are more accentuated in pronunciation, as in "*baby language.*"

**structure dependence:** a principle of **universal grammar** that defines grammatical relations—such as the movement of **auxiliary verbs**—in terms of hierarchically arranged phrases rather than linearly arranged words.

**subject drop:** a phenomenon exhibited in children learning English, characterized by the systematic omission of subjects. One of the many empirical findings suggesting that language learning is not simply the imitation of adults, who do not generally omit subjects.

**suffix:** a morpheme that follows the root, such as *-ing* in "understand-*ing*"

**syllable:** a vowel with consonants preceding or following it. Syllable function together as a unit to form words, such as "mon-key," "a-bout," "Ein-stein." See also **onset, rime, coda.**

**telegraphic speech:** children's earliest combinations of words that resemble telegram messages truncated out of full sentences.

**tense:** the temporal reference of the event in a sentence, e.g. past ("He *walked*"), present ("He *walks*"), future ("He *will* walk"). Other languages may make more or fewer distinctions. In a sentence, there is a designated position that hosts the tense information, which may be combined with verbs.

**topic drop:** a parameter that specifies whether a noun phrase can be omitted if its identity is sufficiently clear from the context.

**transformation:** also known as **movement.** It refers to the process by which a sentence is changed into another word by rearrangement of words or phrases in order to achieve certain expressive functions. See **structure dependence.**

**transitive verb:** a verb that takes two arguments, "Russell *pushes* Zelda."

**universal grammar:** the general principles and constraints that govern the properties of all human languages, including phonology, morphology, grammar, meanings, etc. Introduced by Noam Chomsky.

**verb:** a major category of words that typically describe events, actions, but also abstract activities and mental processes: "fight," "cut," 'think," "intimidate."

**verb second:** a grammatical property most commonly associated with modern Germanic languages (except English) that places the tensed verb in the second position in a declarative sentence, preceded by a phrase (of any kind) that serves as the topic or focus of the sentence.

**verb-tense:** a parameter that specifies, whether the verb raises to the tense node or the tense node lowers to the verb. See **tense.**

**verb to complementizer:** a parameter that specifies, for a given language, whether the verb moves all the way to the complementizer position.

**visible speech:** A. Melville and Alexander Graham Bell's theory of speech that views the production of speech as the composite actions of a number of distinct articulators. See **articulatory features.**

**voiced consonant:** a consonant that is produced with vibration of the vocal cord: e.g., *b, d, g, v, z, m, n, ng.*

**voiceless consonant:** a consonant that is produced without vibration of the vocal cord: e.g, *p, t, k, f, s.*

**vowel:** an element of speech produced without constriction of the vocal tract.

**wh-movement:** a parameter that specifies whether wh-words (e.g., "how," "why," "who," etc.) move to form questions.

# Bibliography

Aitchison, J. (2001). *Language change: Progress or decay.* Cambridge: Cambridge University Press.

Allen, S. (1996). *Aspects of argument structure acquisition in Inuktitut.* Amsterdam: John Benjamins.

Andersen, H. (1973). Abductive and deductive change. *Language,* 49:765–93.

Anderson, S. (1974). *The organization of phonology.* New York: Academic Press.

———. (1981). Why phonology isn't "natural." *Linguistic Inquiry,* 12:493–539.

———. (1992). *A-morphous morphology.* Cambridge: Cambridge University Press.

———. (2004). *Doctor Dolittle's delusion: Animals and the uniqueness of human languages.* New Haven, CT: Yale University Press.

Anderson, S., & Lightfoot, D. (2002). *The language organ.* Cambridge: Cambridge University Press.

Angluin, D. (1980). Inductive inference of formal languages from positive data. *Information and Control,* 45:117–35.

Atkinson, R., Bower, G., & Crothers, E. (1965). *An introduction to mathematical learning theory.* New York: Wiley.

Avrutin, S., & Brun, D. (2001). The expression of specificity in a language without determiners: Evidence from child Russian. In Do, A., Dominguez, L., & Johansen, A. (eds.). *Proceedings of BUCLD 25.* Somerville, MA: Cascadilla Press. 70–81.

Baker, C., & McCarthy, J. (eds.). (1981). *The logical problem of language acquisition.* Cambridge, MA: MIT Press.

Baker, M. (2001). *Atoms of language.* New York: Basic Books.

Baker, S., Idsardi, W., Golinkoff, R., & Petitto, L. (2005). The perception of handshapes in America Sign Language. *Memory and Cognition,* 33:887–904.

Baldwin, D. (1993). Infants' ability to consult the speaker for clues to word reference. *Journal of Child Language,* 20:395–418.

Bates, R., & Jackson, J. (1980). *Glossary of geology.* Falls Church, VA: American Geological Institute.

Battye, A., & Roberts, I. (1995). Introduction. In Battye, A., & Roberts, I. (eds.). *Clause structure and language change.* Oxford: Oxford University Press. 1–30.

Becker, M. (2004). Copula omission is a grammatical reflex. *Language Acquisition,* 12:157–67.

————. (2006). There begins to be a learnability puzzle. *Linguistic Inquiry* (in press).

Bell, A. G. (1922). Prehistoric telephone days. *National Geographic*, 41:223–42.

Bellugi, U., Marks, S., Bihrle, A., & Sabo, H. (1988). Dissociation between language and cognitive functions in Williams syndrome. In Bishop, D., & Mogford, K. (eds.). *Language development in exceptional circumstances.* Hillsdale, NJ: Lawrence Erlbaum. 177–89.

Berko, J. (1958). The child's learning of English morphology. *Word*, 14:150–77.

Berko, J., & Brown, R. (1960). Psycholinguistic research methods. In Mussen, P. (ed.). *Handbook of research methods in child development.* New York: Wiley. 517–57.

Berlin, B., & Kay, P. (1969). *Basic color terms.* Berkeley: University of California Press.

Bertocini, J., & Mehler, J. (1981). Syllables as units in infant speech perception. *Infant Behavior and Development*, 4:247–60.

Berwick, R. (1985). *The acquisition of syntactic knowledge.* Cambridge, MA: MIT Press.

Berwick, R., & Niyogi, P. (1996). Learning from triggers. *Linguistic Inquiry*, 27:605–22.

Best, C., McRobert, G., & Sithole, N. (1988). The phonological basis of perceptual loss for non-native contrasts: Maintenance of discrimination among Zulu clicks by English-speaking adults and infants. *Journal of Experimental Psychology: Human Perception and Performance*, 14:345–60.

Bijeljac-Babic, R., Bertocini, J., & Mehler, J. (1993). How do 4-day-old infants categorize multisyllabic utterances? *Developmental Psychology*, 29:711–21.

Bloch, B. (1947). English verb inflection. *Language*, 23:399–418.

Bloom, P. (1993). Grammatical continuity in language development: The case of subjectless sentences. *Linguistic Inquiry*, 24:721–34.

————. (2001). *How children learn the meanings of words.* Cambridge, MA: MIT Press.

————. (2004). Can a dog learn a word? *Science*, 304:1605.

Blumer, A., Ehrenfeucht, A., Haussler, D., & Warmuth, M. (1989). Learnability and the Vapnik-Chervonenkis dimension. *Journal of ACM*, 36:929–65.

Bortfeld, H., Morgan, J., Golinkoff, R., & Rathbun, K. (2005). Mommy and me: Familiar names help launch babies into speech stream segmentation. *Psychological Science*, 16, 298–304.

Bowerman, M. (1983). The "no negative evidence" problem: How do children avoid constructing an overly general grammar? In Hawkins, J. (ed.). *Explaining language universals.* Oxford: Blackwell. 73–101.

Boysson-Bardies, B. (1993). Ontogeny of language-specific phonetic and lexical production. In Boysson-Bardies B., de Schonen, S., Jusczyk P., MacNeilage, P., & Morton, J. (Eds). *Changes in speech and face processing in the first year of life.* Kluwer: Dordrecht. 353–63.

Boysson-Bardies, B., Hallé, P., Sagart, L., & Durand, C. (1989). A cross-linguistic investigation of vowel formants in babbling. *Journal of Child Language*, 16:1–17.

Boysson-Bardies, B., & Vihman, M. (1991). Adaptation to language: Evidence from babbling and first words in four languages. *Language*, 67:297–319.

Boysson-Bardies, B., Vihman, M., Roug-Hellichius, L., Durand, C., Landberg, I., & Arao, F. (1992). Maternal evidence for infant selection from the target language: A cross-linguistic phonetic study. In Ferguson, C., Menn, L., & Stoel-Gammon, M. (eds.). *Phonological development*. Parkton, MD: York Press. 369–91.

Bradlow, A., Pisoni, D., Yamada, R., & Tohkura, Y. (1997). Training Japanese listeners to identify English /r/ and /l/: IV. Some effects of perceptual learning on speech production. *Journal of the Acoustical Society of America*, 101:2299–2310.

Braine, M. (1963). The ontogeny of English phrase structure: The first phase. *Language*, 39:1–13.

———. (1971). On two types of models of the internalization of grammars. In Slobin, D. (ed.). *The ontogenesis of grammar: A theoretical symposium*. New York: Academic Press. 153–181.

Breland, K., & Breland, M. (1961). The misbehavior of organisms. *American Psychologist*, 16:681–84.

Brent, M., & Siskind, J. (2001). The role of exposure to isolated words in early vocabulary development. *Cognition*, 81:B33–B44.

Bresnan, J. (2001). *Lexical-functional syntax*. Oxford: Blackwell.

Brill, E. (1995). Transformation-based error-driven learning and natural language processing: A case study in part of speech tagging. *Computational Linguistics*, 21:543–65.

Briscoe, E. (2002). Evolutionary perspectives on diachronic syntax. In Pintzuk, S., Tsoulas, G., & Warner, A. (eds.). *Diachronic syntax: Models and mechanisms*. Oxford: Oxford University Press. 255–300.

Bromberg, H., & Wexler, K. (1995). Null subjects in child wh-questions. In *MIT Working Papers in Linguistics*, 26:221–47.

Bromberger, S., & Halle, M. (1989). Why phonology is different. *Linguistic Inquiry*, 20:51–70.

Brown, R. (1973). *A first language*. Cambridge, MA: Harvard University Press.

Bruer, J. (1999). *The myth of the first three years: A new understanding of early brain development and lifelong learning*. New York: Free Press.

Bruton-Simmonds, I. (1992). *Mend your English: Or, What we should have been taught at primary school*. London: Ivy Publications.

Burzio, L. (1991). The morphological basis of anaphora. *Journal of Linguistics*, 27:81–105.

Bush, R., & Mosteller, F. (1951). A mathematical model for simple learning. *Psychological Review*, 68:313–23.

Campbell, L. (1997). *Historical linguistics*. Cambridge, MA: MIT Press.

Campbell, R., Woll, B., Benson, P., & Wallace, S. (1999). Categorical perception of face actions: The role in sign language and in communicative facial display. *Quarterly Journal of Experimental Psychology*, 1:67–95.

Caramazza, A., Chialant, D., Capasso, R., & Miceli, G. (2000). Separable processing of consonants and vowels. *Nature*, 403:428–30.

Carey, S. (1995). Continuity and discontinuity in cognitive development. In Osherson, D. (ed.). *An invitation to cognitive science*. Vol 3. Cambridge, MA: MIT Press. 101–29.

Carey, S., & Bartlett, E. (1978). Acquiring a single new word. *Papers and Reports on Child Language Development*. Stanford, CA: Stanford University. Vol. 15:17–29.

Carter, A., & Gerken, L. (2004). Do children's omissions have traces? *Journal of Child Language*, 31:561–86.

Cavalli-Sforza, L. (2001). *Genes, peoples, and language*. Berkeley: University of California Press.

Cazden, C. (1972). *Child language and education*. New York: Holt, Reinhart, and Winston.

Chambers, K., Onishi, K., & Fisher, C. (2003). Infants learn phonotactic regularities from brief auditory experience. *Cognition*, 87:B69–B77.

Changeux, J.-P. (1986). *The neuronal man*. Oxford: Oxford University Press.

Chien, Y.-C., & Wexler, K. (1990). Children's knowledge of locality conditions in binding as evidence for the modularity of syntax and pragmatics. *Language Acquisition*, 1:225–95.

Chierchia, G., Guasti, M., & Gualmini, A. (1999). Nouns and articles in child grammar and the syntax/semantic gap. Paper presented at GALA, Potsdam, Germany.

Chimpanzee sequencing and analysis consortium. (2005). *Nature*, 437:69–98.

Chomsky, N. (1951). Morphophonemics of Modern Hebrew. Master's thesis, University of Pennsylvania.

———. (1955/1975). *The logical structure of linguistic theory*. Portions published by Plenum (New York).

———. (1957). *Syntactic structures*. The Hague: Mouton.

———. (1959). Review of B. F. Skinner's *Verbal behavior*. *Language*, 35:26–58.

———. (1964). A review of B. F. Skinner's *Verbal behavior*. In Fodor, J. A., & Katz, J. (ed.). *The structure of language: Readings in the philosophy of language*. Englewood Cliffs, NJ: Prentice-Hall. 547–78.

———. (1965). *Aspects of theory of syntax*. Cambridge, MA: MIT Press.

———. (1968) *Language and mind*. New York: Harcourt Brace. Expanded edition in 1972.

———. (1975). *Reflections on language*. New York: Pantheon.

———. (1977). On wh-movement. In Culicover, P., Wasow, T., & Akmajian, A. (eds.). *Formal syntax*. New York: Academic Press. 71–132.

———. (1980). *Rules and representations*. New York: Columbia University Press.

———. (1981). *Lectures on government and binding*. Dordrecht: Foris.

———. (1986). *Knowledge of language*. New York: Praeger.

———. (1995). *The minimalist program*. Cambridge, MA: MIT Press.

———. (2005). Three factors in language design. *Linguistic Inquiry*, 36:1–22.

Chomsky, N., & Halle, M. (1968). *The sound pattern of English*. New York: Harper & Row.

Chomsky, N., & Lasnik, H. (1993). The theory of principles and parameters. In Jacobs, J. et al. (eds.). *Syntax: An international handbook of contemporary research*. Berlin: Walter de Gruyter. Vol. 1:506–69.

Clahsen, H. (1999). Lexical entries and rules of language. *Behavioral and Brain Sciences*, 22:991–1013.

Clahsen, H. (ed.). *Generative Perspectives on Language Acquisition*. Amsterdam: John Benjamins. 91–128.

Clahsen, H., & Almazan, M. (1998). Syntax and morphology in Williams syndrome. *Cognition*, 68:167–98.

Clahsen, H., & Temple, C. (2003). Words and rules in children with Williams syndrome. In Levy, Y., & Schaeffer, J. (eds.). *Language competence across populations*. Hillsdale, NJ: Erlbaum. 323–52.

Clark, E. (1993). *Lexicon in acquisition*. Cambridge: Cambridge University Press.

Conway Morris, S. (1998). *The crucible of creation: The Burgess Shale and the rise of animals*. Oxford: Oxford University Press.

Crain, S. (1991). Language acquisition in the absence of experience. *Behavioral and Brain Sciences*, 14:597–650.

Crain, S., & McKee, C. (1985). The acquisition of structural restrictions on anaphora. In Berman, S., Choe, J.-W., & McDonough, J. (eds.). *Proceedings of NELS*. Amherst, MA: GLSA. Vol. 15:94–110.

Crain, S., & Nakayama, M. (1987). Structure dependency in grammar formation. *Language*, 63:522–43.

Crain, S., & Pietroski, P. (2002). Why language acquisition is a snap. *Linguistic Review*, 19:163–83.

Crain, S., & Thornton, R. (1998). *Investigations in universal grammar: A guide to experiments in the acquisition of syntax and semantics*. Cambridge, MA: MIT Press.

Crystal, D. (1997). *The Cambridge encyclopedia of the English language*. Cambridge: Cambridge University Press.

Cucker, F., Smale, S., & Zhou, D.-X. (2004). Modeling language evolution. *Foundations of Computational Mathematics*, 315–43.

Curtiss, S. (1977). *"Genie": A psycholinguistic study of a modern day "wild child."* New York: Academic Press.

Cutler, A., Mehler, J., Norris, D., & Segui, J. (1989). Limits on bilingualism. *Nature*, 340:229–30.

Cutting, J., & Rosner, B. (1974). Categories and boundaries in speech and music. *Perception and Psychophysics*, 16:564–70.

Darwin, C. (1871). *Descent of man and selection in relation to sex*. London: Murray. 1882.

———. (1996/1859). *The origin of species*. Oxford: Oxford University Press.

Dawkins, R. (1971). Selective neurone death as a possible memory mechanism. *Nature*, 229, 118–119.

de Villiers, J. (2002). Continuity and modularity in language acquisition and research. In Wijnen, F., Verrips, M., & Santelmann, L. (eds.). *Annual Review of Language Acquisition*, 1, 1–64.

de Villiers, J., Roeper, T., & Vainikka, A. (1990). The acquisition of long-distance rules. In Frazier, L., & de Villiers, J. (eds.). *Language processing and language acquisition*. Dordrecht: Kluwer. 257–97.

de Waal, F. (1989). *Peacemaking among primates*. Cambridge, MA: Harvard University Press.

Delattre, P., Liberman, A., & Cooper, F. (1955). Acoustic loci and transitional cues for consonants. *Journal of the Acoustical Society of America*, 27:769–73.

Descartes, R. (1662/1969). *Discours de la méthode*. Part 5. In *The essential Descartes*. (1969). New York: Penguin.

Dollaghan, C. (1994). Children's phonological neighborhoods: Half empty or half full? *Journal of Child Language*, 21:257–71.

Dresher, E. (1999). Charting the learning path: Cues to parameter setting. *Linguistic Inquiry*, 30:27–67.

Dryer, M. (1992). The Greenbergian word order correlations. *Language*, 68:81–138.

Dummett, M. (1986). A nice derangement of epitaphs: some comments on Davidson and Hacking. In Lepore, E. (ed.). *Truth and interpretation*. Oxford: Blackwell. 459–76.

Edelman, G. (1987). *Natural Darwinism: The theory of neuronal group selection*. New York: Basic Books.

Eimas, P. (1975). Auditory and phonetic coding of the cues for speech: Discrimination of the [r-l] distinction in young infants. *Perception and Psychophysics*, 18:341–47.

———. (1999). Segmental and syllabic representations in the perception of speech by young infants. *Journal of the Acoustical Society of America*, 105, 1901–11.

Eimas, P., & Miller, J. (1980). Discrimination of the information for manner of articulation. *Infant Behavior and Development*, 3:367–75.

Eimas, P., Siqueland, E., Jusczyk, P., & Vigorito, J. (1971). Speech perception in infants. *Science*, 171:303–6.

Elbourne, P. (2005). On the acquisition of Principle B. *Linguistic Inquiry*, 36:333–65.

Ellegard, A. (1953). *The auxiliary do: The establishment and regulation of its use in English*. Stockholm: Almqvist & Wiksell.

Elman, J. (1993). Learning and development in neural networks: The importance of starting small. *Cognition*, 48:71–99.

Emmorey, K., McCullough, S., & Brentari, D. (2003). Categorical perception in American Sign Language. *Language and Cognitive Processes*, 18:21–45.

Enard, W., Przeworski, M., Fisher, S., Lai, C., Wiebe, V., Kitano, T., Monaco, A., & Pääbo, S. (2002). Molecular evolution of *FOXP2*, a gene involved in speech and language. *Nature*, 418:869–72.

Feldman, H., Goldin-Meadow, S., & Gleitman, L. (1978). Beyond Herodotus: The creation of language by linguistically deprived deaf children. In Lock, A. (ed.). *Action, symbol, and gesture: The emergence of language*. New York: Academic Press. 351–414.

Ferguson, C., & Farwell, C. (1975). Words and sounds in early language acquisition. *Language*, 51:419–39.

Fernald, A. (1985). Four-month-old infants prefer to listen to motherese. *Infant Behavior and Development*, 8:181–95.

Fisher, C., Hall, S., Rakowitz, L., & Gleitman, L. (1994). When it is better to receive than to give: Syntactic and conceptual constraints on vocabulary growth. *Lingua*, 92:333–75.

Fisher, S., Vargha-Khadem, F., Watkins, K., Monaco, A., & Pembrey, M. (1998). Localisation of a gene implicated in a severe speech and language disorder. *Nature Genetics*, 18:168–70.

Flanagan, J. (1972). Voices of men and machines. *Journal of the Acoustical Society of America*, 51:1375–87.

Fodor, J. A. (1975). *The language of thought.* Cambridge, MA: Harvard University Press.

———. (1983). *Modularity of the mind.* Cambridge, MA: MIT Press.

———. (1998). *Concepts: Where cognitive science went wrong.* New York: Oxford University Press.

Fodor, J. D. (1998). Unambiguous triggers. *Linguistic Inquiry*, 29:1–36.

Frank, R. (2002). *Phrase structure composition and syntactic dependencies.* Cambridge, MA: MIT Press.

Fromkin, V., Rodman, R., & Hyams, N. (2002). *An introduction to language.* Seventh edition. Stamford, CT: Heinle.

Gallistel, R. (1990). *The organization of learning.* Cambridge, MA: MIT Press.

Gambell, T., & Yang, C. (2005). Mechanisms and constraints in word segmentation. Unpublished manuscript, Yale University.

Gardner, H. (1987). *The mind's new science.* New York: Basic Books.

Gelman, S. (2003). *The essentialist child: Origins of essentialism in everyday thought.* New York: Oxford University Press.

Gerken, L. (1991). The metrical basis for children's subjectless sentences. *Journal of Memory and Language.* 30:431–51.

Gesell, A. (1941). *Wolf child and human child.* New York: Harper.

Giannakidou, A. (2002). N-words and negative concord. Unpublished manuscript, University of Chicago.

Gibson, E., & Wexler, K. (1994). Triggers. *Linguistic Inquiry*, 25, 355–407.

Gillette, J., Gleitman, L., Gleitman, H., & Lederer, A. (1999). Human simulations of lexical acquisition. *Cognition*, 73(2):135–76.

Gleitman, L. (1990). The structural sources of verb meanings. *Language Acquisition*, 1:1–55.

Gold, E. (1967). Language identification in the limit. *Information and Control.* 10:447–74.

Goldin-Meadow, S. (2003). *The resilience of language.* New York: Psychology Press.

Golinkoff, R., Hirsh-Pasek, K., Cauley, K., & Gordon, L. (1987). The eyes have it: Lexical and syntactic comprehension in a new paradigm. *Journal of Child Language*, 14:23–45.

Goodall, J. (1986). *The chimpanzees of Gombe: Patterns of behavior.* Cambridge, MA: Harvard University Press.

Goodman, N. (1955). *Fact, fiction, and forecast.* Cambridge, MA: Harvard University Press.

Gopnik, M. (1990). Feature-blind grammar and dysphasia. *Nature*, 344:715.

Gopnik, M., & Crago, M. (1991). Familial aggregation of a developmental language disorder. *Cognition*, 39:1–50.

Gould, J., & Marler, P. (1987). Learning by instinct. *Scientific American*, 256:74–85.

Gould, S. J. (1989). *Wonderful life.* New York: Norton.

Greenberg, J. (1966). *The languages of Africa.* Bloomington: Indiana University Press.

——. (1987). *Languages in the Americas.* Stanford, CA: Stanford University Press.

Greenough, W., Black, J., & Wallace, C. (1987). Experience and brain development. *Child Development,* 58:539–59.

Grinstead, J. (1994). Consequences of the maturation of number morphology in Spanish and Catalan. M.A. thesis, UCLA.

Gruber, J. (1965). Studies in lexical relations. Doctoral dissertation, MIT.

Guasti, M. (2002). *Language development: The growth of grammar.* Cambridge, MA: MIT Press.

Hale, K. (1983). Warlpiri and the grammar of non-configurational languages. *Natural Language and Linguistic Theory* 1:5–47.

Hale, K., & Keyser, J. (2002). *Prolegomenon to a theory of argument structure.* Cambridge, MA: MIT Press.

Hall, D., & Waxman, S. (2004). *Weaving a lexicon.* Cambridge, MA: MIT Press.

Halle, M. (1962). Phonology in generative grammar. *Word,* 18:54–72.

——. (1978). Knowledge unlearned and untaught: What speakers know about the sounds of their language. In Halle, M., Bresnan, J., & Miller, G. (eds.). *Linguistic Theory and Psychological Reality.* Cambridge, MA: MIT Press. 294–303.

——. (1983). On distinctive features and their articulatory implementations. *Natural Language and Linguistic Theory,* 8:149–76.

——. (1990). Phonology. In Osherson, D., & Lasnik, H. (eds.). *An invitation to cognitive science.* Cambridge, MA: MIT Press. Vol. 1:53–68.

Halle, M., & Marantz, A. (1993). Distributed morphology and the pieces of inflection. In Hale, K., & Kerser, J. (eds.). *The view from building 20.* Cambridge, MA: MIT Press. 111–76.

Halle, M., & Mohanan, K.-P. (1985) Segmental phonology of Modern English. *Linguistic Inquiry,* 16:57–116.

Harrington, J., Palethorpe, S., & Watson, C. (2000). Does the Queen speak the Queen's English? *Nature,* 407:215–29.

Harris, Z. (1951). *Methods in structural linguistics.* Chicago: University of Chicago Press.

Hauser, M. (2000). *Wild minds.* New York: Henry Holt.

Hauser, M., Chomsky, N., & Fitch, T. (2002). The faculty of language: What is it, who has it, and how did it evolve? *Science,* 298:1569–79.

Hawkins, J. (1983). *Word order universals.* New York: Academic Press.

——. (1994). *A performance theory of order and constituency.* Cambridge: Cambridge University Press.

Hayes, B. (1995). *Metrical stress theory.* Chicago: University of Chicago Press.

Herrnstein, R., & Loveland D. (1975). Maximizing and matching on concurrent ratio schedules. *Journal of the Experimental Analysis of Behavior,* 24:107–16.

Hockett, C. (1958). *A course in modern linguistics.* New York: Macmillan.

Hoffman, D. (1998). *Visual intelligence.* New York: Norton.

Huang, J. (1984). On the distribution and reference of empty pronouns. *Linguistic Inquiry,* 15:531–74.

Hubel, D., & Wiesel, T. (1962). Receptive fields, binocular interaction and functional architecture in the cat's visual cortex. *Journal of Physiology,* 160: 106–54.

Hughes, G. (2000). *A history of English words.* Oxford: Blackwell.

Hyams, N. (1986). *Language acquisition and the theory of parameters.* Dordrecht: Kluwer.

———. (1996). The underspecification of functional categories in early grammar. In Clahsen, H. (ed.). *Generative perspectives on language acquisition.* Amsterdam: John Benjamins. 91–128.

Hyams, N., & Wexler, K. (1993). On the grammatical basis of null subjects in child language. *Linguistic Inquiry,* 24:421–59.

Idsardi, W. (2005). Poverty of stimulus arguments in phonology. Manuscript, University of Maryland.

Jacob, F. (1977). Evolution as tinkering. *Science,* 196:1161–66.

Jakobson, R. (1941/1968). *Child language, aphasia, and phonological universals.* The Hague: Mouton.

Jakobson, R., Fant, G., & Halle, M. (1962). *Preliminaries to speech analysis: The distinctive features and their correlates.* Cambridge, MA: MIT Press.

James, W. (1890). *The principles of psychology.* Cambridge, MA: Harvard University Press. Reprinted in 1981.

Jilka, M. (2000). The contribution of intonation to the perception of foreign accent. Doctoral dissertation, University of Stuttgart, Germany.

Jusczyk, P. (1997). *The discovery of spoken language.* Cambridge, MA: MIT Press.

———. (1999). How infants begin to extract words from speech. *Trends in Cognitive Sciences,* 3:323–28.

Jusczyk, P., & Aslin, R. (1995). Infants' detection of the sound patterns of words in fluent speech. *Cognitive Psychology,* 46:65–97.

Jusczyk, P., Cutler, A., & Redanz, N. (1993). Preference for the predominant stress patterns of English words. *Child Development,* 64:675–97.

Jusczyk, P., & Hohne, E. (1997). Infants' memory for spoken words. *Science,* 277:1984–86.

Jusczyk, P., Houston, D., & Newsome, M. (1999). The beginnings of word segmentation in English-learning infants. *Cognitive Psychology,* 39:159–207.

Jusczyk, P., Pisoni, D., Walley, A., & Murry, J. (1980). Discrimination of the relative onset of two-component tones by infants. *Journal of the Acoustical Society of America,* 222:175–77.

Kahn, D. (1976). Syllable-based generalizations in English phonology. Ph.D. dissertation, MIT. Published in 1980 by Garland Press, New York.

Kaminski, J., Call, J., & Fischer, J. (2004). Word learning in a domestic dog: Evidence for "fast mapping." *Science,* 304:1682.

Kayne, R. (1994). *The antisymmetry of syntax.* Cambridge, MA: MIT Press.

Keenan, E. (2002). Explaining the creation of reflexive pronouns in English. In Minkova, D., & Stockwell, R. (eds.). *Studies in the history of English: A millenial perspective.* Berlin: Mouton de Gruyter. 325–55.

Kegl, J., Senghas, A., & Coppola, M. (1999). Creation through contact: Sign language emergence and sign language change in Nicaragua. In De Graff, M.

(ed.). *Language creation and language change.* Cambridge, MA: MIT Press. 179–237.

Kehoe, M., & Stoel-Gammon, C. (1997). The acquisition of prosodic structure: An investigation of current accounts of children's prosodic development. *Language,* 73:3–44.

Kiparsky, P. (1982). From cyclic phonology to lexical phonology. In v. d. Hulst, H., & Smith, N. (eds.). *The structure of phonological representations.* Dordrecht: Foris. 131–75.

———. (1994). Indo-European origins of Germanic syntax. In Roberts, I., & Battye, A. (eds.). *Clause structure and language change.* Oxford: Oxford University Press. 140–67.

Klatt, D. (1989). Review of selected models of speech perception. In Marslen-Wilson, W. (ed.). *Lexical representation and processes.* Cambridge, MA: MIT Press. 169–226.

Klein, H. (1981). Production strategies for the pronunciation of early polysyllabic lexical items. *Journal of Speech and Hearing Research,* 24:389–405.

Kluender, K., Diehl, R., & Killeen, P. (1987). Japanese quail can learn phonetic categories. *Science,* 237:1195–97.

Kolb, B. (1989). Brain development, plasticity, and behavior. *American Psychologist,* 44:1203–12.

Krebs, J. (1978). Optimal foraging: Decision rules for predators. In Krebs, J., & Davies, N. (eds.). *Behavioral ecology.* Oxford: Blackwell. 23–63.

Kroch, A. (1989). Reflexes of grammar in patterns of language change. *Language Variation and Change,* 1:199–244.

———. (2001). Syntactic change. In Collins, C., & Baltin, M. (eds.). *Handbook of contemporary syntactic theory.* Oxford: Blackwell. 699–729.

Kroch, A., & Santorini, B. (forthcoming). *An introduction to transformational syntax.* New York: Harcourt Brace.

Kroch, A., & Taylor, A. (1997). Verb movement in Old and Middle English: Dialect variation and language contact. In van Kemenade, A., & Vincent, N. (eds.). *Parameters of morphosyntactic change.* Cambridge: Cambridge University Press. 297–325.

Kroch, A., Taylor, A., & Ringe, D. (2000). The Middle English verb-second constraint: A case study in language contact. In Herring, S. (ed.). *Textual parameters in older languages.* Philadelphia: Benjamins. 353–91.

Kuhl, P. (1983). Perception of auditory equivalence classes for speech in early infancy. *Infant Behavior and Development,* 6:263–85.

Kuhl, P., & Meltzoff, A. (1982). The bimodal perception of speech in infancy. *Science,* 218:1138–41.

Kuhl, P., & Miller, J. (1975). Speech perception by the chinchilla: Voiced-voiceless distinction in alveolar plosive consonants. *Science,* 190:69–72.

Kuhl, P., & Padden, D. (1982). Enhanced discriminability at the phonetic boundaries for the voicing feature in macaques. *Perception and Psychophysics,* 32:542–50.

Kuhl, P., Williams, K., Lacerda, F., Stevens, K., & Lindblom, B. (1992). Linguistic experiences alter phonetic perception in infants by 6 months of age. *Science,* 255:606–8.

Labov, W. (1962). The social history of a sound change on the island of Martha's Vineyard, Massachusetts. Master's thesis, Columbia University.

———. (1966). *The social stratification of English in New York City.* Washington, DC: Center for Applied Linguistics.

———. (1994). *Principles of linguistic change. Vol. I: Internal factors.* Oxford: Blackwell.

Lane, H. (1979). *Wild boy of Aveyron.* Cambridge, MA: Harvard University Press.

Lasnik, H. (1990). *Essays on restrictiveness and learnability.* Boston: Kluwer.

———. (1999). *Minimalist analysis.* Malden, MA: Blackwell.

Lasnik, H., & Saito, M. (1992). *Move alpha.* Cambridge, MA: MIT Press.

Legate, J. A. (2002). Warlpiri: Theoretical implications. Doctoral dissertation. MIT.

Legate, J. A., & Yang, C. (2002). Empirical reassessments of poverty stimulus arguments. *Linguistic Review,* 151–62.

———. (2006). Morphosyntactic learning and the development of tense. *Language Acquisition.* (In press.)

Levin, B. (1993). *English verb classes and alternations: A preliminary investigation.* Chicago: University of Chicago Press.

Lewontin, R. (1974). *The genetic basis of evolutionary change.* New York: Columbia University Press.

———. (1983). The organism as the subject and object of evolution. *Scientia,* 118:65–82.

Liberman, A., Cooper, F., Shankweiler, D., & Studdert-Kennedy, M. (1967). Perception of the speech code. *Psychological Review,* 74:431–61.

Liberman, A., Delattre, P., & Cooper, F. (1952). The role of selected stimulus variables in the perception of unvoiced stop consonants. *American Journal of Psychology,* 65:497–516.

Liberman, A., Harris, K., Kinney, J., & Lane, H. (1961). The discrimination of relative-onset time of the components of certain speech and non-speech patterns. *Journal of Experimental Psychology,* 61:379–88.

Liberman, A., & Mattingly, I. (1985). The motor theory of speech perception revised. *Cognition,* 21:1–36.

———. (1989). A specialization for speech perception. *Science,* 243:489–94.

Lieberman, P., Crelin, E., & Klatt, D. (1972). Phonetic ability and related anatomy of newborn and adult humans, Neanderthal man, and the chimpanzee. *American Anthropologist,* 74:287–307.

Lightfoot, D. (1991). *How to set parameters.* Cambridge, MA: MIT Press.

———. (1997). Shifting triggers and diachronic reanalysis. In van Kemenada, A., & Vincent, N. (eds.). *Parameters of morphosyntactic changes.* Cambridge: Cambridge University Press. 253–72.

———. (1999). *The development of language: Acquisition, change, and evolution.* Oxford: Blackwell.

Locke, J. (1690). An essay concerning human understanding. Woozley, A. D. (ed.). Cleveland: Meridian Books, 1965. Book 3.IX.9.

Locke, J. L. (1993). *The child's path to spoken language.* Cambridge, MA: Harvard University Press.

Macnamara, J. (1972). Cognitive basis of language learning in infants. *Psychological Review,* 79:1–13.

———. (1982). *Names for things: A case study of human language.* Cambridge, MA: MIT Press.

MacNeilage, P., & Davis, B. (1993). Motor explanations of babbling and early speech patterns. In Boysson-Bardies, B., de Schonen, S., Jusczyk P., Mac-Neilage, P., & Morton, J. (Eds). *Changes in speech and face processing in the first year of life.* Kluwer: Dordrecht. 341–52.

MacWhinney, B. (2004). A multiple process solution to the logical problem of language acquisition. *Journal of Child Language,* 31:883–914.

———. (1995). *The CHILDES Project: Tools for analyzing talk.* Mahwah, NJ: Lawrence Erlbaum.

Marchman, V., & Bates, E. (1994). Continuity in lexical and morphological development: A test of the critical mass hypothesis. *Journal of Child Language,* 21:339–66.

Marcus, G. (1993). Negative evidence in language acquisition. *Cognition,* 46:53–85.

Marcus, G., Brinkman, U., Clahsen, H., Wiese, R., & Pinker, S. (1995). German inflection: The exception that proves the rule. *Cognitive Psychology,* 29:189–256.

Marcus, G., Pinker, S., Ullman, M., Hollander, M., Rosen, J., & Xu, F. (1992). *Overregularization in language acquisition.* Stanford, CA: Society for Research in Child Development.

Markman, E. (1994). Constraints on word meaning in early language. *Lingua,* 92:199–227.

Markman, E., & Abelev, M. (2004). Word learning in dogs? *Trends in Cognitive Sciences,* 8:479–81.

Markson, L., & Bloom, P. (1997). Evidence against a dedicated system of word learning in children. *Nature,* 385:813–15.

Marler, P. (1991). The instinct to learn. In Carey, S., & Gelman, R. (eds.). *The epigenesis of mind: Essays in biology and cognition.* Hillsdale, NJ: Erlbaum. 37–66.

Martin, L. (1986). Eskimo words for snow: A case study in the genesis and decay of an anthropological example. *American Anthropologist,* 88:418–23.

Maye, J., Werker, J., & Gerken, L. (2002). Infant sensitivity to distributional information can affect phonetic discrimination. *Cognition,* 82:B101–B111.

Maynard Smith, J., & Szathmary, E. (1997). *The major transitions in evolution.* New York: Oxford University Press.

Mayr, E. (1942). *Systematics and the origin of species.* New York: Columbia University Press.

———. (1963). *Animal species and evolution.* Cambridge, MA: Harvard University Press.

———. (1982). *The growth of biological thought.* Cambridge, MA: Harvard University Press.

———. (1991). *One long argument: Charles Darwin and the genesis of modern evolutionary thought.* Cambridge, MA: Harvard University Press.

———. (2001). *What evolution is.* New York: Basic Books.

McDaniel, D. (1989). Partial and multiple wh-movement. *Natural Language and Linguistic Theory,* 7:565–604.

Mehler, J., Jusczyk, P., Lambertz, G., Halsted, N., Bertocini, J., & Amiel-Tison, C. (1988). A precursor of language acquisition in young infants. *Cognition*, 29:144–78.

Mencken, H. L. (1921). *The American language.* New York: Knopf.

Menn, L. (2000). Phonological development. In Gleason, J. (ed.). *Language development.* Columbus, OH: Merrill. 69–121.

Menn, L., & Stoel-Gammon, C. (2001). Phonological development: Learning sounds and sound patterns. In Berko Gleason, J. (ed.). *The development of language.* Fifth edition. Needham Heights, MA: Allyn & Bacon. 70–124.

Miller, G. (1996). *The science of words.* New York: Freeman.

———. (2003). The cognitive revolution: A historical perspective. *Trends in Cognitive Sciences,* 7:141–44.

Miller, G., & Chomsky, N. (1963). Finitary models of language users. In Luce, R., Bush, R., & Galanter, E. (eds.). *Handbook of Mathematical Psychology.* Vol. 2. New York: Wiley. 419–91.

Miyawaki, K., Strange, W., Verbrugge, R., Liberman, A., Jenkins, J., & Fujimura, O. (1975). An effect of linguisitic experience: The discrimination of /r/ and /l/ by native speakers of Japanese and English. *Perception and Psychophysics,* 18:331–40.

Molnar, R. (2001). Generalize and sift in the learning of phonological rules. Master's thesis, Department of Electrical Engineering and Computer Science. MIT.

Mooney, R., & Califf, M. (1995). Induction of first-order decision lists: Results on learning the past tense of English verbs. *Journal of Artificial Intelligence Research,* 3:1–24.

Morris, C., & Mervic, C. (1999). Williams Syndrome. In Goldstein, S., & Reynolds, C. (eds.). *Handbook of neurodevelopmental and genetic disorders in children.* New York: Guilford Press.

Murphy, G. (2002). *The big book of concepts.* Cambridge, MA: MIT Press.

Naigles, L. (1990). Children use syntax to learn verb meanings, *Journal of Child Language.* 17:357–74.

———. (1996). The use of multiple frames in verb learning via syntactic bootstrapping. *Cognition,* 58:224–51.

Nakleh, L., Ringe, D., & Warnow, T. (2005). Perfect phylogenetic networks: A new methodology for reconstructing the evolutionary history of natural languages. *Language.* 382–420.

Nazzi, T., Bertocini, J., & Mehler, J. (1998). Language discrimination by newborns: Towards an understanding of the role of rhythm. *Journal of Experimental Psychology: Human Perception and Performance,* 24:756–66.

Neville, H., Nicol, J., Barss, A., Forster, K., & Garrett, M. (1991). Syntactically based sentence processing classes: Evidence from event-related brain potentials. *Journal of Cognitive Neuroscience,* 3:155–70.

Newport, E. (1990). Maturational constraints on language learning. *Cognitive Science,* 14:11–28.

Newport, E., Gleitman, H., & Gleitman, L. (1977). Mother, I'd rather do it myself: Some effects and noneffects of maternal speech style. In Snow, C., & Ferguson, C. (eds.). *Talking to children: Language input and acquisition.* Cambridge: Cambridge University Press. 109–150.

Nisbett, R. (2003). *The geography of thought: How Asians and Westerners think differently . . . and why.* New York: Free Press.

Niyogi, P., & Berwick, R. (1995). The logical problem of language change. MIT Artificial Intelligence Laboratory Memo No. 1516.

Nowak, M., Komarova, N., & Niyogi, P. (2001). The evolution of universal grammar. *Science.* 291:114–18.

———. (2002). Computational and evolutionary aspects of language. *Nature,* 417:611–17.

Nunberg, G. (2004). *Going nucular.* New York: Public Affairs.

O'Neil, W., & Honda, M. (2004). Awakening our language. Santa Fe, NM: Indigenous Language Institute.

Oller, D., & Eilers, R. (1988). The role of audition in infant babbling. *Child Development,* 59:441–49.

Osterhout, L., Allen, M., McLaughlin, J., & Inoue, K. (2002). Brain potentials elicited by prose-embedded linguistic anomalies. *Memory and Cognition,* 30:1304–12.

Otsu, Y. (1981). Universal grammar and syntactic development in children: Toward a theory of syntactic development. Ph.D. dissertation, MIT.

Patel, A., & Daniele, J. (2003). An empirical comparison of rhythm in language and music. *Cognition,* 87:B35–B45.

Pearl, L. (2005). Addressing acquisition from language change. University of Pennsylvania Working Papers in Linguistics. 11.1.

Pepperberg, I. (1999). *The Alex studies: Cognitive and communicative abilities of grey parrots.* Cambridge, MA: Harvard University Press.

Peters, A. (1983). *The units of language acquisition.* Cambridge: Cambridge University Press.

Peterson, G., & Barney, H. (1952). Control methods used in a study of vowels. *Journal of the Acoustical Society of America,* 24:175–84.

Petitto, L. A. (2000). On the biological foundations of human language. In Emmorey, K., & Lane, H. (eds.). *The signs of language revisited: An anthology in honor of Ursula Bellugi and Edward Klima.* Mahwah, NJ: Lawrence Erlbaum. 447–71.

Petitto, L.A., & Marentette, P. (1991). Babbling in the manual mode: Evidence for the ontogeny of language. *Science,* 251:1483–96.

Petitto, L. A., Holowka, S., Sergio, L., & Ostry, D. (2001). Language rhythms in baby hand movement. *Nature,* 413:35–36.

Phillips, C. (1995). Syntax at age 2: Cross-linguistic differences. In *MIT Working Papers In Linguistics.* Cambridge, MA. 26:325–82.

Phillips, C., Pellathy, T., Marantz, A., Yellin, E., Wexler, K., Poeppel, D., McGinnis, M., & Roberts, T. (2000). Auditory cortex access phonological categories: A MEG study. *Journal of Cognitive Neuroscience.* 12:1038–55.

Piatelli-Palmarini, M. (1989). Evolution, selection, and cognition: From "learning" to parameter setting in biology and the study of language. *Cognition,* 31:1–44.

Piatelli-Palmarini, M. (ed.). (1980). *Language and learning: The debate between Jean Piaget and Noam Chomsky.* London: Routledge & Kegan Paul.

Pine, J. (1992). How referential are "referential" children? Relationships between maternal-report and observational measures of vocabulary composition and usage. *Journal of Child Language*, 23:573–89.

Pinker, S. (1984). *Language learnability and language development*. Cambridge, MA: Harvard University Press.

———. (1989). *Language learnability and cognition*. Cambridge, MA: MIT Press.

———. (1994a). *The language instinct*. New York: Morrow.

Pinker, S. (1994b). How could a child use verb syntax to learn verb semantics? *Lingua*, 92:377–410.

———. (1999). *Words and rules*. New York: Basic Books.

Pintzuk, S. (1999). *Phrase structure in competition: Variation and change in Old English word order*. New York: Garland.

Pisoni, D. (1977). Identification and discrimination of the relative onset of two component tones: Implications for a voicing perception in stops. *Journal of the Acoustical Society of America*, 61:1352–61.

Poeppel, D., & Wexler, K. (1993). The full competence hypothesis. *Language*, 69:1–33.

Polka, L., & Werker, J. (1994). Developmental changes in perception of nonnative vowel contrasts. *Journal of Experimental Psychology: Human Perception and Performance*, 20:421–35.

Pullum, G. (1991) *The great Eskimo vocabulary hoax*. Chicago: University of Chicago Press.

———. (1999). African American Vernacular English is not Standard English with mistakes. In Wheeler, R. (ed.). *The workings of language: From prescriptions to perspectives*. New York: Praeger. 39–58.

Pustejovsky, J. (1995). *The generative lexicon*. Cambridge, MA: MIT Press.

Quine, W. V. O. (1960). *Words and objects*. Cambridge, MA: MIT Press.

Renfrew, C. (1987). *Archaeology and language: The puzzle of Indo-European origins*. London: Pimlico.

Reuland, E. (2001). Primitives of binding. *Linguistic Inquiry*, 32:439–92.

Ringe, D. (1992). *On calculating the factor of chance in language comparison*. Philadelphia: American Philosophical Society.

Ristad, E. (1994). The complexity of morpheme acquisition. In Ristad, E. (ed.). *Language computations*. Providence, RI: American Mathematical Society.

Rizzi, L. (1986). Null objects in Italian and the theory of PRO. *Linguistic Inquiry*, 17:501–557.

———. (1990). *Relativized minimality*. Cambridge, MA: MIT Press.

———. (1994). Some notes on linguistic theory and language development: The case of root infinitives. *Language Acquisition*, 3:371–93.

———. (1997) The fine structure of the left periphery. In Haegeman, L. (ed.). *Elements of grammar*. Dordrecht: Kluwer. 281–338.

———. (2005). Grammatically based target-inconsistencies in child language. Manuscript, University of Siena.

Roberts, I. (1993). *Verbs and diachronic syntax: A comparative history of English and French*. Dordrecht: Kluwer.

Robertson, F., & Reeve, E. (1952). Studies in quantitative inheritance: I. The effects of selection of wing and thorax length in *Drosophila melanogaster*. *Journal of Genetics*, 50:414–48.

Roeper, T. (2000). Universal bilingualism. *Bilingualism: Language and Cognition*, 2:169–85.

Roeper, T., & Rohrbarcher, B. (1994). Null subjects in early child English and the theory of economy of projection. Technical report 94-12. The Institute for Research in Cognitive Science. University of Pennsylvania.

Ross, J. (1967). Constraints on variables in syntax. Doctoral dissertation, MIT.

Roughgarden, J. (1979). *Theory of population genetics and evolutionary ecology*. New York: Macmillan.

Rumelhart, D., & McClelland, J. (1986). On learning the past tense of English verbs: Implicit rules or parallel distributed processing? In McClelland, J., Rumelhart, D., & the PDP Research Group (eds.). *Parallel Distributed Processing: Explorations in the microstructure of cognition*. Cambridge, MA: MIT Press. 216–71.

Saffran, J., Aslin, R., & Newport, E. (1996). Statistical learning by 8-month-olds. *Science*, 274:1926–28.

Sag, I., & Wasow, T. (1999). *Syntactic theory*. Stanford: CSLI Publications.

Sandler, W., Meir, I., Padden, C., & Aronoff, M. (2005). The emergence of grammar: Systematic structure in a new language. *Proceedings of National Academy of Sciences*. 102:2661–665.

Santorini, B. (1992). Variation and change in Yiddish subordinate clause word orders. *Natural Language and Linguistic Theory*, 10:595–640.

Sapir, E. (1921). *Language: An introduction to the study of speech*. New York: Harcourt Brace.

———. (1928). *Language: An introduction to the study of language*. New York: Harcourt Brace.

Savage-Rumbaugh, S., & Lewin, R. (1994). *Kanzi: The ape at the brink of the human mind*. New York: Wiley & Sons.

Schroeder, M. (1993). A brief history of synthetic speech. *Speech Communication*, 13:231–37.

Searle, J. (1969). *Speech acts: An essay in the philosophy of language*. Cambridge: Cambridge University Press.

Seidenberg, M., & Petitto, L. (1979). Signing behavior in apes: A critical review. *Cognition*, 7:177–215.

Seidl, A., & Buckley, E. (2005). On the learning of arbitrary phonological rules. *Language Learning and Development*, 1:289–316.

Shipley, E., Smith, C., & Gleitman, L. (1969). A study in the acquisition of language: Free responses to command. *Language*, 45:322–42.

Shu, W. et al. (2005). Altered ultrasonic vocalization in mice with a disruption in the *FOXP2* gene. *Proceedings of the National Academy of Science*, 102:9643–48.

Singleton, J., & Newport, E. (2004). When learners surpass their models: The acquisition of American Sign Language from inconsistent input. *Cognitive Psychology*, 49:370–407.

Slobin, D. (1985). *The crosslinguistic study of language acquisition*. Hillsdale, NJ: Erlbaum.

Sluijter, A., van Heuven, V., & Pacily, J. (1996). Spectral balance as an acoustic correlate of linguistic stress. *Journal of the Acoustical Society of America,* 100:2471–85.

Smith, N. (1973). *The acquisition of phonology.* Cambridge: Cambridge University Press.

Smith, N., & Tsimpli, I. (1995). *The mind of a savant: Language learning and modularity.* Oxford: Blackwell.

Smith, N., Tsimpli, I., & Ouhala, J. (1993). Learning the impossible: The acquisition of possible and impossible languages by a polyglot savant. *Lingua,* 91:279–347.

Snow, C. (1977). The development of conversation between mothers and babies. *Journal of Child Language,* 4:1–22.

Stager, C., & Werker, J. (1997). Infants listen to more phonetic detail in speech perception than in word-learning tasks. *Nature,* 338:381–82.

Steedman, M. (2000). *The syntactic process.* Cambridge, MA: MIT Press.

Stevens, K. (1989). On the quantal nature of speech. *Journal of Phonetics,* 17:3–45.

Streeter, L. (1976). Language perception of 2-month-old infants shows effects of both innate mechanisms and experience. *Nature,* 259:39–41.

Studdert-Kennedy, M. (2002). Mirror neurons, vocal imitation, and the evolution of particulate speech. In Stamenov, M., & Gallese, V. (eds.). *Mirror neurons and the evolution of the brain and language.* Amsterdam: John Benjamins. 207–27.

Studdert-Kennedy, M., & Goldstein, L. (2003). Launching language: The gestural origin of discrete infinity. In Christiansen, M., & Kirby, S. (eds.). *Language evolution: The states of the art.* Oxford: Oxford University Press.

Sun, C. (1996). *Word order change and grammaticalization in the history of Chinese.* Stanford, CA: Stanford University Press.

Sussman, G., & Yip, K. (1997). A computational model for the acquisition and use of phonological knowledge. MIT Artificial Intelligence Laboratory, Memo 1575.

Swadesh, M. (1952). Lexicostatistic dating of prehistoric ethnic contacts. *Proceedings of American Philosophical Society,* 96:452–63.

Terrace, H., Petitto, L., Sanders, R., & Bever, T. (1979). Can an ape create a sentence? *Science,* 206:891–902.

Theakston, A., Lieven, E., & Tomasello, M. (2003). The role of the input in the acquisition of third person singular verbs in English. *Journal of Speech, Language, and Hearing Research,* 46:863–77.

Thornton, R. (1990). Adventures in long-distance moving: The acquisition of complex wh-questions. Ph.D. dissertation, University of Connecticut.

Tomasello, M. (1992). *First verbs: A case study of early grammatical development.* Cambridge: Cambridge University Press.

Tomasello, M., & Mervis, C. (1994). The instrument is great, but measuring comprehension is still a problem. *Monographs of the Society for Research in Child Language,* 59:174–79.

Trehub, S. (1976). The discrimination of foreign speech contrasts by infants and adults. *Child Development,* 47:466–72.

Twain, M. (1880). *A tramp abroad.* London: Chatto & Windus.

Valian, V. (1991). Syntactic subjects in early speech of American and Italian children. *Cognition*, 40:21–82.

Valiant, L. (1984). A theory of the learnable. *Communication of the ACM*, 27:1134–42.

Vance, B. (1997). *Syntactic change in medieval French: Verb-second and null subjects*. Dordrecht: Kluwer.

van der Lely, H., & Battell, J. (2003). Wh-movement in children with grammatical SLI: a test of the RDDR hypothesis. *Language*, 79:153–81.

van Kampen, J. (1997). *First steps in wh-movement*. Delft: Eburon.

Vapnik, V. (1995). *The nature of statistical learning theory*. Berlin: Springer.

Vargha-Khadem, F., Watkins, K., Alcock, K., Fletcher, P., & Passingham, R. (1995). Praxic and nonverbal cognitive deficits in a large family with a genetically transmitted speech and language disorder. *Proceedings of the National Academy of Science*, 92:930–33.

Vihman, M. (1996). *Phonological development: The origins of language in the child*. Oxford: Blackwell.

Wang, Q., Lillo-Martin, D., Best, C., & Levitt, A. (1992). Null subject vs. null object: Some evidence from the acquisition of Chinese and English. *Language Acquisition*, 2:221–54.

Wang, W. S.-Y. (1991). Introduction. In Wang, W. S.-Y. (ed.). *The emergence of language: Development and evolution*. San Francisco: W. H. Freeman.

Watkins, K., Dronkers, N., & Vargha-Khadem, F. (2002). Behavioral analysis of an inherited speech and language disorder: Comparison with acquired aphasia. *Brain*, 125, 452–464.

Weinreich, U., Labov, W., & Herzog, M. (1968). Empirical foundations for a theory of language change. In Lehman, W., & Malkiel, Y. (eds.). *Directions for historical linguistics: A symposium*. Austin: University of Texas Press. 95–188.

Werker, J., & Tees, R. (1984a). Cross-language speech perception: Evidence for perceptual reorganization during the first year of life. *Infant Behavior and Development*, 7:49–63.

———. (1984b). Phonemic and phonetic factors in adult cross-language speech perception. *Journal of the Acoustical Society of America*, 75:1866–78.

Wexler, K. (1994). Optional Infinitives, head movement, and the economy of derivation in child language. In Lightfoot, D., & Hornstein, N (eds.). *Verb Movement*. Cambridge: Cambridge University Press, 305–350.

———. (1998). Very early parameter setting and the unique checking constraint: A new explanation of the optional infinitive stage. *Lingua*, 57:23–79.

Wexler, K., & Culicover, P. (1980). *Formal principles of language acquisition*. Cambridge, MA: MIT Press.

Wexler, K., & Thornton, R. (1999). *Principle B, VP ellipsis, and interpretation in child grammar*. Cambridge, MA: MIT Press.

Wilson, S. (2003). Lexically specific constructions in the acquisition of inflection in English. *Journal of Child Language*, 30:75–115.

Wood, G. (2003). Uncle Ben. *New York Review of Books*, vol. 50, no. 19: December 4.

Woodbury, A. (1991). Counting Eskimo words for snow: A citizen's guide. Manuscript, University of Texas at Austin.

Wyttenbach, R., May, M., & Hoy, R. (1996). Categorical perception of sound frequencies by crickets. *Science*, 273:1542–44.

Xu, F., & Pinker, F. (1995). Weird past tense errors. *Journal of Child Language*, 22:531–56.

Yang, C. (1998). Toward a variational theory of language acquisition. Memo, Artificial Intelligence Laboratory, MIT.

———. (1999). A selectionist theory of language development. In *Proceedings of the 37th Meeting of the Association for Computational Linguistics*. Stroudsburg, PA: Association for Computational Linguistics. 431–55.

———. (2000a). Dig-dug, think-thunk. *The London Review of Books*, 22:10.

———. (2000b). Internal and external forces in language change. *Language Variation and Change*, 12:231–50.

———. (2002). *Knowledge and learning in natural language*. New York: Oxford University Press.

———. (2004). Universal grammar, statistics, or both. *Trends in Cognitive Sciences*, 8:451–56.

———. (2005) Grammar acquisition as parameter setting. In Bates, E., Li, P., & Tzeng, O. (eds.). *Handbook of East Asian Psycholinguistics*. Cambridge: Cambridge University Press. 136–147.

———. (2006). On productivity. In Pica, P., & Rooryck, J. (eds.). *Language variation yearbook*. 330–77.

Yang, C., & Gutmann, S. (1999). Language learning via Martingales. The Sixth Conference of the Mathematics of Language. July 24, 1999. Orlando, FL.

Young, J. (1965). The nervous pathways for poisoning, eating, and learning in octopus. *Journal of Experimental Biology*, 43:581–93.

Zue, V., Daly, N., Glass, J., Goodine, D., Leung, H., Phillips, M., Polifroni, J., Seneff, S., & Soclof, M. (1989). The collection of preliminary analysis of a spontaneous speech database. Speech and Natural Language, workshop held at Cape Cod, Massachusetts. October 15–18, 1989.

Zue, V., & Lafferriere, M. (1979). Acoustical study of medial /t/, /d/ in American English. *Journal of the Acoustical Society of America*, 66:1039–50.

Zukowski, A. (2001). Uncovering grammatical competence in children with Williams syndrome. Unpublished doctoral dissertation, Boston University.

# Acknowledgments

If only writing a book on how children learn language were as easy as children's learning language. I thank many people who shepherded this book through the past two years.

Julie Anne Legate read everything I wrote and made sure I was coherent; I thank her for her intelligence, patience, and support. Russell Cheng Legate-Yang was three when I started writing, and had turned five by the time I was done; I thank him for being a willing (and sometimes unwilling) research subject and a great son.

Many friends and colleagues have contributed to the final product in various ways. These include Steve Anderson, Bob Berwick, Ann Bradlow, Noam Chomsky, Stephen Crain, John Frampton, Tim Gambell, Jean Berko Gleason, Lila Gleitman, Louis Goldstein, Sam Gutmann, the late Stephen Jay Gould, John Halle, Morris Halle, Norbert Hornstein, Bill Idsardi, Edith Kaan, Tony Kroch, Dick Lewontin, the late Ernst Mayr, Andrew Nevins, Colin Phillips, Massimo Piatelli-Parlmarini, Tom Roeper, Jill de Villiers, Bill Wang, and Ken Wexler. Above all, I am indebted to the numerous researchers in linguistics and psychology whose work has elucidated the mystery of language learning by children. Although the study of language and mind has no shortage of controversies, I trust that the synthesis presented in this book pays tribute to all sides.

I thank my family members Kira Hensley, Donalyn Legate, and Tianen Yang for detailed comments on the manuscript. They are the ideal readers for such a book—curious, intelligent, nonlinguists—and made sure that it was actually written in English. My students at Yale University, where portions of the material were used for teaching, also provided useful feedback. Part of the writing was done under the auspices of a Morse Faculty Fellowship at Yale University, which I gratefully acknowledge.

This book would not have been possible without help and support from the publishing world. Ravi Mirchandani suggested that this book may be worth reading, and Gillian Blake believed that it may be worth writing; I thank them both. Rachel Sussman, Sarah Knight, and in particular Karen Thompson provided invaluable editorial assistance. Most important, I thank Colin Harrison, my editor, and Susan Rabiner, my agent. Colin is the editor of editors: he showed me the craft of writing far beyond the scope of this book. Susan believed in this project from the start and helped nurture it to the finish.

Hockessin, Delaware
December 2005

# Index

# About the Author

CHARLES YANG teaches linguistics and psychology at Yale University. Trained as a computer scientist at MIT's Artifical Intelligence Laboratory, he has written extensively on children and language and contributes articles to *The London Review of Books,* among other literary publications. He lives in Delaware with his wife, a frequent research collaborator, and young son, a frequent research subject.